On Believing

On Believing

Being Right in a World of Possibilities

DAVID HUNTER

Great Clarendon Street, Oxford, OX2 6DP,
United Kingdom

Oxford University Press is a department of the University of Oxford.
It furthers the University's objective of excellence in research, scholarship,
and education by publishing worldwide. Oxford is a registered trade mark of
Oxford University Press in the UK and in certain other countries

© David Hunter 2022

The moral rights of the author have been asserted

First Edition published in 2022

Impression: 1

All rights reserved. No part of this publication may be reproduced, stored in
a retrieval system, or transmitted, in any form or by any means, without the
prior permission in writing of Oxford University Press, or as expressly permitted
by law, by licence or under terms agreed with the appropriate reprographics
rights organization. Enquiries concerning reproduction outside the scope of the
above should be sent to the Rights Department, Oxford University Press, at the
address above

You must not circulate this work in any other form
and you must impose this same condition on any acquirer

Published in the United States of America by Oxford University Press
198 Madison Avenue, New York, NY 10016, United States of America

British Library Cataloguing in Publication Data

Data available

Library of Congress Control Number: 2021948591

ISBN 978–0–19–285954–9

DOI: 10.1093/oso/9780192859549.001.0001

Printed and bound in the UK by
TJ Books Limited

Links to third party websites are provided by Oxford in good faith and
for information only. Oxford disclaims any responsibility for the materials
contained in any third party website referenced in this work.

To my unbelievable daughters

Contents

Acknowledgments	ix
Introduction	1
1. On the Nature of Believing	7
1.1 A Deliberative Position	8
1.2 Possibilities, Facts, and Reasons	11
1.3 Acting in the Light of a Possibility	14
1.4 Effects, Manifestations, and Exercises	18
1.5 Belief States Are Not Causes	19
1.6 Belief Properties Are Not Causal Qualities	27
1.7 Non-Human Belief and Naturalism	33
2. The Ontology of Believing	36
2.1 Propositions, Possibilities, Belief States, and Belief Properties	37
2.2 Belief Properties, Sortals, and Qualities	39
2.3 Belief States and Realizers	44
2.4 Believing Is Not an Action or Activity	46
2.5 Believing Is Not a Relation	52
2.6 Believing and Understanding	60
3. The Objects of Believing	64
3.1 Individuating Belief Properties	65
3.2 Pure Cases and the Modal View of Belief	68
3.3 Certainty, Probability, and Agnosticism	75
3.4 Speech Acts and Aboutness	81
3.5 Knowledge, Inquiry, and Action	83
3.6 Making the Propositional View Fit	85
3.7 A History of Neglect	89
3.8 Representation without Propositions	93
4. Believing without Representing	96
4.1 Believing and Truth	96
4.2 Belief Properties and States Are Neither True Nor False	100
4.3 Tokens, Types, and Confusing Nominals	101
4.4 Beliefs and Realizers	104
4.5 Derivative Truth	105
4.6 On Wanting	108

viii CONTENTS

5. Objectivity and Credal Illusions	111
5.1 Objectivity and Credal Illusions	113
5.2 Unbelievable Possibilities	116
5.3 Future Possibilities	119
5.4 Mere Possibilities	122
5.5 Denying Objectivity	125
5.6 Objectivity and the Inevitability of Credal Illusions	128
6. Subjectivity and Credal Necessities	131
6.1 The BB Principle	132
6.2 BB and the Center of a Conception	137
6.3 Being in Position	141
6.4 Credal Necessities and Transparency	147
6.5 Subjectivity, Force, and Content	150
6.6 Subjective Uncertainty	153
6.7 Rational Action	155
7. Credal Agency	160
7.1 Inference as a Mental Act	160
7.2 Inference Is Not an Onset of Believing	164
7.3 Inference Is Acting on Oneself	168
7.4 The Ontology of Inference	171
7.5 Inferring in Light of a Possibility	174
7.6 Inference Is Not Intentional	177
7.7 Inference Is Voluntary	180
7.8 Inference and Deduction	185
7.9 Unwilling Inference	191
8. Credal Norms	193
8.1 Believing and Attributive Goodness	194
8.2 Truth and Epistemic Value	196
8.3 Credal Credit	200
8.4 Belief Directives and Knowledge	202
8.5 Belief Directives and Evidence	207
8.6 Credal Blame	214
Appendix	221
Bibliography	227
Index	235

Acknowledgments

I can't believe how long it took me to write this book. The various false starts, delays, and detours are my fault, but in all honesty many were provoked by years of generous conversation with lots of people. Any good ideas I have were made good by these conversations.

My deepest philosophical debts are to my teachers, Charles Travis and Robert Stalnaker. Charles was my undergraduate supervisor at McGill, and Bob supervised my PhD at MIT. Not only did they spark my interest in the topics of this book, but they demonstrated how to think clearly about them, how to separate philosophical puzzles from problems, and the benefits of doing philosophy slowly. They have very different styles, but the same remarkable amount of philosophical imagination and honesty. And while their background interests and preoccupations differ, they share a Wittgensteinian inheritance that makes their views on belief and representation closer than one might think. Indeed, my central ideas are ones I first found (or think I found) in both their works. Every page bears a debt to them.

I have only recently realized how deep my debt is to Judith Jarvis Thomson. I never took a course with her at MIT, which I now regret. But I was her teaching assistant in an introduction to ethics course, and I learned from her classroom example the twin virtues of philosophical rigor and intellectual modesty. Since then I have learned an enormous amount from her published work. Her views on rationality, action, and normativity have been hugely influential for me, and that influence pervades the final chapters of this book. But I have also learned from her method. No one is better, it seems to me, at arranging a philosophical topic by carefully teasing apart claims and problems that had seemed tightly connected, and then patiently setting some aside in order to make progress on others. I have tried hard to emulate her method.

My personal debts to Sergio Tenenbaum and Mark McCullagh are enormous and wide-ranging. I have discussed with them all the topics in this book, and they have been incredibly patient and constructive as I struggled to work out my ideas. Mark, in particular, helped me find the courage to unbury the lede. He also suggested the title. Without their friendship and support I would never have finished the book.

Early versions of the book were the topic of two wonderful workshops, one in Erlangen organized by Gerhard Ernst and one in Montreal organized by Christine Tappolet. I benefited enormously from their generous and thoughtful comments and from those by Aude Bandini, Ulf Hlobil, David Horst, Liz Jackson, Stephanie

X ACKNOWLEDGMENTS

Leary, Berislav Marušic, Erasmus Mayr, Miriam McCormick, Verena Wagner, and the others who attended the events. Karl Schafer sent me very helpful comments on a complete draft of the book, and Gurpreet Rattan gave me very helpful ones on an early draft of the middle chapters.

Over the years, I have benefited from conversations on the topics of this book with many people, including Maria Alvarez, Matt Boyle, David Braun, Michael Brent, Lucy Campbell, Herman Cappelen, Naomi Eilan, Luca Ferrero, Anton Ford, Olav Gjelsvik, Matthias Haase, Adrian Haddock, Peter Hanks, Pamela Hieronymi, Jennifer Hornsby, John Hyman, Guy Longworth, Eric Marcus, Conor McHugh, Al Mele, Sasha Newton, Lilian O'Brien, Lucy O'Brien, Sarah Paul, Johannes Roessler, Will Small, Sebastian Rödl, Jonathan Schwenkler, Nishi Shah, Sarah Stroud, Michael Thompson, Rachael Wiseman, Jonathan Way, and Daniel Whiting. Many of my colleagues at Ryerson have also discussed these topics with me, and I am especially indebted to Julien Beillard, David Checkland, David Ciavatta, Boris Hennig, Andrew Hunter, Klaas Kraay, Thomas Land, Kym Maclaren, and Rohan Sud. I know I am forgetting people who helped me. I apologize.

A special thanks goes to Peter Momtchiloff, at Oxford University Press, whose patient support and wise editorial advice over many years have been invaluable. I am also extremely grateful to the anonymous reviewers whose constructive, generous, and encouraging reports helped me enormously. Lisa Fedorak prepared the index.

I am extremely grateful to my friend Lee Robinsong for permission to use his painting for my cover. Lee is a Quebec-based painter whose signature Circulist style emerged from his interface with the natural landscapes of Manitoba and British Columbia's Desolation Sound. Influenced by the Cubist perspectives of Picasso and Braque, and the Cree teachings of the Medicine Wheel, Circulism ties together the belief that you can view an object from every direction simultaneously and that everyone views the same object differently. Lee's Circulist paintings offer the viewer a subjective, holistic view of the natural world. "Maple Tree" uses the physical form of the torus to give a simultaneously concave and convex circular perspective, with the exterior landscape mirrored on the interior. I wish I could put things into words as clearly and beautifully as he can paint them.

Parts of Chapters 5 and 6 develop material that appeared in (Hunter 2008) and (Hunter 2017); bits of Chapters 2 and 7 appeared in (Hunter 2018a); and parts of Chapter 8 appeared in (Hunter 2018c). I thank the publishers for permitting me to include the material here. Ryerson University and the Social Sciences and Humanities Research Council of Canada have generously provided research leave and financial support that helped make this book actual. I thank Mary Gormally for permission to use the quote from G.E.M. Anscombe as an epigraph for my introduction.

I wrote this book in Toronto, which is in the Dish With One Spoon Territory. The Dish With One Spoon is a treaty between the Anishinaabe, Mississaugas, and

Haudenosaunee that bound them to share the territory and protect the land. Subsequent Indigenous Nations and peoples, Europeans, and all newcomers have been invited into this treaty in the spirit of peace, friendship, and respect. I am grateful for their invitation and I publish this book with that spirit in my heart.

I have left the most important debts to the end. They are to Jane, Miranda, and Emily. But it is hard to put into words what I owe them. Their love and support are beyond belief.

Introduction

Belief is the most difficult topic because it is so difficult to hold in view and correctly combine the psychological and the logical aspects.

(Anscombe 1995, 26)

This book is about believing, about having a perspective on things. The leading idea is familiar enough: to believe something is to be right or wrong, correct or incorrect, depending on how things are. But to fill out this idea, to say how believing differs from other mental states, to see how it matters for what people do and how they react, to appreciate the limits of belief, and to understand why there are things a person ought to believe, we need to combine the logical and psychological aspects that Anscombe alludes to with normative ones she does not. In this introduction, I will sketch in very broad strokes the combination I will develop in this book. To keep this presentation as clean as possible, I won't mention here the many philosophers whose important work I am developing or responding to.

Here is the whole picture in brief. To believe something is to be in position to do, think, and feel things in light of a possibility whose obtaining would make one right. The logical aspect is that whether one is right or wrong in believing something depends only on whether that possibility obtains, on whether its obtaining is a fact. The psychological aspect is that what one does, thinks, and feels can be rationalized or explained by that possibility. But while our beliefs make a difference to what we might do, they don't make a difference to what we *can* do. They don't add to our abilities or our causal powers. Rather, they make a difference to the (potential) reasons we have to exercise and manifest the capacities and dispositions we already have or will acquire, and since we are reasonable, this can make a difference to what we are likely to do. In believing something we are either right or wrong, but believing is not a sort of representing. The objects of belief are ways things are or could have been, not representations of such ways, and belief states are not themselves true or false. There are limits to what a person can believe, and these are set by who she is and by what is possible. The limits give rise to credal illusions and ground the essential subjectivity of belief. Through voluntary acts of inference a person can make up her own mind and so become responsible for believing what she does. Whether it is reasonable for her to believe something may depend on what else she believes, but whether believing it is to her credit or discredit depends on whether it shows her to be good in some way.

On Believing: Being Right in a World of Possibilities. David Hunter, Oxford University Press. © David Hunter 2022.
DOI: 10.1093/oso/9780192859549.003.0001

2 INTRODUCTION

Whether she ought to believe it depends on whether she ought to know it, and this in turn depends on what she ought to do, think, feel, and be. These credal norms are thus not evidential matters. Rather, they concern where a person ought to be positioned in a world of possibilities. The chapters to follow will develop and defend these views in detail, but it will be helpful to expand on them a bit more in the rest of this introduction.

On my view, to believe something is to be in a certain rational position. What do I mean by *a position*? The primary contrast I have in mind is with capacities and dispositions. In gaining knowledge or belief a person does not gain an ability to do, think, or feel anything. The change, rather, is in the reasons or potential reasons she has to exercise the capacities and to manifest the dispositions she already has or will acquire. And this makes a difference to what she is likely to do because she is reasonable, not because knowing and believing are themselves capacities. A believer is able to act in light of how she takes things to be, but states of belief are not themselves capacities, and nor are they causes or causal properties. When a person deliberates, she attends to ways things are and need to be, or anyway to the ways she takes them to be and to need to be. She attends to what reasons she thinks she has to do, think, and feel things. She sees herself as set—as *in position*—to respond to those reasons. It is up to her whether, how, and when to respond. That is what I mean when I say that believing is a matter of being in a certain position. It is in some ways like being in a spatial position, and I'll draw on this analogy in what follows.

My account rests on a view about the ontology of belief. I take it that to believe something is to have a belief property, but there are different kinds of properties and the differences matter. I will argue that belief properties are qualities and not sortals. The contrast is between properties (like being rich or being heavy) that are instantiated *in* objects or substances and those (like being human or being gold) whose instantiations *are* objects or substances. This is of fundamental importance. Seeing it will help us keep our focus on the believer and avoid the temptation to hypostasize belief states, treating them as if they were objects. This temptation is encouraged by the familiar ambiguity in "belief" between the state of believing and the object believed. And it encourages thinking that belief states have semantic, causal, and normative features, and that deliberation involves reflecting on our belief states. As I see it, belief states have no such features and this picture of deliberation is misleading. To properly understand the semantic, explanatory, agential, and normative aspects of believing, it helps to see that belief properties are qualities. It helps by putting the believer, rather than her belief states, at the heart of an account of believing. In developing these points I'll rely on a different analogy, this time between believing and owning.

A second ontological matter concerns the individuation of belief properties. I take it that belief properties are individuated by their objects. On my view, these are possibilities—ways things are, were, might yet be, or could have been. This contrast between what is actual and what is possible, between the reasons there are and those there could have been, is at the heart of believing. It is at the heart of knowing too, since the objects of knowing are facts. In knowing something, a person is set to do, think, and feel things in light of a way things are, in light of the obtaining of some possibility. On my view, believing is like knowing in this respect. In believing that some possibility obtains, a person takes herself to be set to respond to the world's being that way. She sees herself as set to do, think, and feel things in light of what she takes to be a fact. If she is right, then that possibility does obtain, though if she merely believes it then she does not know it. If she is wrong, then she has anyway got a grip on a way that things could have been. The objects of belief are possibilities because, as I see it, the objects of belief are (potential) reasons.

The view that possibilities are the objects of belief is, to put it mildly, controversial. It entails that when people differ in their beliefs, or when a person changes her mind, this always involves a difference or change in which contingent possibilities they take to obtain. This is a traditional view about the individuation of belief, though it has always been a minority one. Most theorists take certain familiar stories to be straightforward counter-examples to it. The stories involve people who are confused or mistaken about which thing is which, or what stuff is what, or about who, where, or when they are. I don't think these stories really are counterexamples to that view. I'll argue that they always involve a difference over which contingent possibilities obtain. This means the stories are not counterexamples to the traditional idea, but I don't deny that they are puzzling. Nor do I deny that they are instructive. What I deny is that they teach us that there are more belief properties than there are possibilities.

The stories are puzzling because it is hard to understand what the characters in them believe, how they take things to be. It is an open question, I think, how an account of belief ought to respond to such puzzles. For more than a century, theorists have sought to individuate belief properties finely enough to resolve the puzzles, to show that there is nothing puzzling in what the characters believe. The fact that no consensus has emerged suggests to me that this was the wrong way to respond to the puzzling cases. As I see it, an account of belief can shed light on them without resolving them, just as an account can shed light on visual illusions without showing them not to be illusions. It can do this by showing how they arise, why they persist, and what they reveal about more ordinary non-puzzling cases. Taking the objects of belief to be possibilities can do this. It helps us to see that these puzzling cases will arise on *any* account that takes it to be an objective matter what there is to believe. Indeed, while my view might be wrong about what there is to believe, about the *limits* of belief, any view will face cases where someone seems to believe beyond the limits. As I see it, these puzzle cases are a price we pay for the objectivity of belief.

4 INTRODUCTION

The view that the objects of belief are possibilities is controversial for a second reason. It conflicts with the idea that the objects of belief are representations, things that by their very nature are true or false. On my view, this idea gets the connection between believing and truth wrong. Believing is not a form of representing and its objects are not representations. A person who believes something is right or wrong depending on whether the possibility that is the object of her belief obtains. But her believing is not true or false and it has no semantic or aboutness properties. The temptation to hypostasize believing can lead us astray here, suggesting that beliefs are mental representations. So can the idea that believing is like inner assertion or like picturing. In believing something, a person does not represent the world, at least not in the way she would if she asserted or drew a picture of what she believes. Asserting and picturing are intentional actions that presuppose believing and so cannot explain it. The image of believing as like being in a position is meant to suggest an alternative to this representational idea.

I said that the puzzling stories are instructive. This is because they help us to think about the limits of belief and to identify their sources. Some limits are objective or impersonal while others are subjective or personal. The objective ones apply to all believers. Most fundamentally, what anyone can believe depends on the facts—on which possibilities obtain—and on their relations to those facts. These credal limits make believing an objective matter, but this objectivity comes at the cost of credal illusions, where a person thinks she has got hold in belief of a way that things could have been when in fact she has not. These are the illusions I mentioned above. They are starkest as one reflects on the limits of possibility itself. My view of belief faces these puzzles most directly, because it takes the objects of belief to be possibilities. But that is not the source of the puzzle and we cannot avoid the illusions by rejecting it. The risk of credal illusion arises because believing distinguishes how things are from how they could have been. Without this distinction, and so without the risk of such illusion, there can be no believing.

In addition to objective or impersonal limits to belief, there are also subjective or personal ones. There are things that a person cannot help but believe. Some of these are about herself, and they mark her perspective on the world as essentially hers. This subjectivity is not a matter of *what* she believes, since others can believe those things too. The subjectivity, rather, is that for her those possibilities are credal necessities, things that she—but only she—must believe if she is to believe anything. One central credal necessity, I will argue, is that a believer must believe that the world contains herself believing the things she does. These objective and subjective limits belong on the logical side of Anscombe's contrast. They are inevitable if a person is to be right or wrong about how things are. They are the price of belief itself.

Within these limits a person is responsible for believing what she does. Through reasoning she can change or maintain the reasons she has, or thinks she has. She cannot infer at will, since inference is always a response to how things are from her point of view. But inference is voluntary, since different responses will be equally reasonable and how and when she responds will be up to her. Focusing on cases of deductive inference can obscure this voluntariness. It is hard to see how a person could believe the premises of a valid bit of reasoning without believing the conclusion. My focus will be on cases where the reasoning is strong but not valid, where the person has good but not conclusive evidence for the conclusion she draws. It is then up to her whether and when to draw the conclusion. And she knows, as she draws the inference, the reasons she has and the conclusion she draws. Inference thus involves the sort of self-knowledge present when a person acts voluntarily. It is by exercising this ability to make up our own minds through inference that we become responsible for believing what we do.

I end the book by discussing some normative aspects of believing. Here again I put the believer at the heart of the story, and the distinction between qualities and sortals plays a central role. I consider three normative matters. I first argue that belief properties are not goodness-fixing properties. What I mean is that no instance of believing is a better or worse instance of believing than any other. In particular, the fact that a person is right or reasonable in believing something does not make their believing a better believing. This normative point follows, I argue, from the fact that belief properties are qualities and that no qualities are goodness-fixing properties. This means that norms of belief cannot be grounded in the nature of believing itself. Rather, I argue, they are grounded in facts about the believers themselves.

Believing something can be to a person's credit or discredit. It is to her credit when it is evidence that she is good in some way. This depends on the sortals she falls under and, more specifically, on the goodness-fixing ones. Some sortal properties are goodness-fixing but not all are. Being a parent is, since some parents are better parents than others. Likewise for being a streetcar driver, being a teacher, and, of course, being a person. But there is no such thing as being a good object, a good living thing, or even a good believer. I will suggest that believing something is to a person's credit when it is evidence that she is good with respect to some goodness-fixing sortal she falls under. For example, Jones believes that the streetcar she drives stops at Garden Avenue and believing that is to her credit as a streetcar driver since it does stop there and a good streetcar driver knows her route. Credal credit depends in this way on the believer's goodness-fixing sortals.

There are also things a person ought to believe and this too depends on the sortals she falls under, but here the story is more complicated. For a person can fall under a goodness-fixing sortal that she ought not to. She might then believe something that she ought not to believe even though believing it is to her credit. A spy might believe something she shouldn't even if she is a good spy for believing it. What someone ought to believe, I will argue, depends on what she needs to know to be good with respect to her permitted goodness-fixing sortals. There are things Jones needs to know, and so needs to believe, because knowing them is required for her to be a good parent, streetcar driver, or person. These credal requirements have little to do with what else she believes or knows. Credal credits and requirements turn on a believer's sortal properties and are not an epistemic or evidential matter. Rather, they are a matter of the position she does or ought to occupy among the ways things are.

I'll end by indulging in a different set of images. I said that knowing and believing fundamentally concern a contrast between ways things are and ways they could have been, between actuality and possibility, but I also said that knowing and believing are not ways of representing that contrast. Instead, and here is the new image, they are ways of being more or less at home among the ways things are. Knowing is being set to do, think, and feel in light of the actual. Mere believing is being set to do, think, and feel in light of the possible. To say what a person believes is to identify those possibilities that can explain what she might knowingly do, think, and feel. The main task of inquiry is to settle ourselves among the facts, to find our home among them, so that we are positioned to do, think, and feel as we should in light of the ways things are. The goal is to be as good as we can in the world we are in. Since we are limited and fallible we will never fully be at home, but even in merely believing we are settled in among a world of possibilities, and the light they cast is still that of reason, since possibilities are potential reasons. In the light of ways things could have been we can be reasonable even if not fully right or perfectly good.

The aim of this book is to develop and defend these views.

1
On the Nature of Believing

On my view, to believe something is to be in position to do, think, and feel things in light of a possibility whose obtaining would make one right. These first four chapters develop and defend the ontological aspects of this view. In Chapter 2, I will argue that belief properties are qualities and not sortals. This point is fundamental to my view. Seeing it helps us avoid treating belief states as if they were objects that could have semantic, causal, normative, and other properties, and helps us put the believer at the heart of our account of believing. I will also argue in Chapter 2 that believing is neither a relation nor an action. In Chapter 3, I will argue that belief states are individuated by possibilities, by ways things are, were, might yet be, or could have been. This contrasts with the standard idea that they are individuated by propositions, by objects that are by their very nature representational. And it entails that a difference in belief is always a difference over which contingent possibilities obtain. This may be the most controversial aspect of my view, but I will argue that the familiar alleged counter-examples do not show that there are more belief properties than there are possibilities and that my view helps us see what these examples actually reveal about the nature of belief. In Chapter 4, I will argue that believing is not a matter of representing the world. Beliefs are not mental representations. Here again, we need to put the believer at the heart of the story. A believer is right or wrong when she believes something, but believing is not a form of representing, and belief states are neither true nor false. The logical heart of believing is that whether one is right depends only on whether some possibility obtains. This is what distinguishes believing from other mental states. The psychological heart is that what a person believes makes a difference to what can rationalize her actions, thoughts, and feelings, and because believers are reasonable, this can also make a difference to what she is likely to do. That is the topic of this first chapter.

I will start by filling in the details of my view and then I will argue against its main alternatives. The first three sections flesh out the images at the center of my account. In Section 1.1, I will clarify what I mean when I say that believing is being in a certain sort of position. The position is that of an agent when it is up to her how to respond to the reasons she takes there to be. In developing this image, I'll sketch an account of agency and action that informs my view. In Section 1.2, I will clarify what I mean by a possibility and say a bit about the nature of reasons. In Section 1.3, I will develop my account of how believing that a possibility obtains can shed light on an action, thought, or feeling. Here the core idea is that any

On Believing: Being Right in a World of Possibilities. David Hunter, Oxford University Press. © David Hunter 2022.
DOI: 10.1093/oso/9780192859549.003.0002

8 ON THE NATURE OF BELIEVING

response that would be reasonable when an agent knows that some possibility obtains can be just as reasonable when she merely believes that it does. On my view, a deliberating agent attends to the reasons as she takes them to be. She sees herself as set—as *in position*—to exercise and manifest her capacities and dispositions in light of the facts, as she sees them to be. In these sections, I will also identify what I am taking for granted about believers and what this book aims to make sense of.

My view contrasts with standard ones on which a person's beliefs rationalize by generating or bringing about her actions, thoughts, and feelings. In Section 1.4, I'll distinguish three forms of this view. One takes belief states to be causes; a second views belief properties as dispositions; and a third treats them as capacities. I will argue that these alternatives get the ontology of belief states and properties wrong and misunderstand the way believing explains action. In Section 1.5, I will argue that belief states do not cause an agent's actions, thoughts, and feelings. Belief states have no causal powers of their own. My argument relies on a distinction among properties between sortals and qualities, a distinction I will develop at length in Chapter 2. In Section 1.6, I will argue that belief properties are not causal qualities. What I mean is that believing something does not add to an agent's capacities or dispositions. Here a distinction between what a thing can do and what it is likely to do will be important. In Section 1.7, I will summarize my view, discuss how it applies to non-humans like cats and dogs, and explain why my account is naturalistic, even though it denies that believing is a cause, a capacity, or a disposition.

1.1 A Deliberative Position

On my view, to believe something is to be in a certain position to exercise one's capacities and manifest one's dispositions. I want to clarify what I mean by being *in a position*. I will make two connected points. One is that believing something is not itself a capacity or disposition. (I will argue for this in Section 1.5.) In gaining a new belief, a person does not gain a power to bring about change or a liability to undergo a change. What alters, rather, is what reasons she has (or takes herself to have) to exercise and manifest her capacities and dispositions. The connected point concerns deliberation. Believers can attend to the reasons they have and it is sometimes up to them whether, when, and how to respond. They are set—or positioned—to respond to the facts as they take them to be. Indeed, they believe themselves to be so positioned. The image of being in a position is meant to capture these two connected points.

I will work up to this image in stages. I'll first discuss agency and the differences between capacities and dispositions. I'll then distinguish actions that are responses from those that are not, and then responses that are up to an agent from those that are not. But this is not a book about agency and action. What I say follows a familiar approach to these topics.[1] But I don't mind if what I say is read as terminological stipulation. Saying it will still help me clarify what I mean when I say that believing is being in a certain sort of position. And it will let me be transparent about what I am assuming about agency and action, and what I see my account of believing as aiming to clarify. In Section 1.2, I will say what I am assuming about the nature of reasons and in Section 1.3 I'll explain how possibilities can cast a rationalizing light.

I take it that all believers are agents. And I take it that to be an agent is to have a capacity to cause things to happen or change. I take an action to be an exercise of such a capacity. Crushing a can is exercising a capacity to crush. Walking is exercising a capacity to walk. Driving a streetcar is exercising, among others, a capacity to drive. Believers are not alone in being agents. All living things are agents and so are many non-living things. (Abstract objects like numbers are not agents.) My plants send their roots out in search of water, climb the fence, and turn with the sun. Hurricanes push over trees and large boulders crush cars. All of these, I will take it, are exercises of agency, where a thing causes something to happen or to change. That is, as I see it, what being an agent amounts to. Different agents can have the same causal powers. Boulders, trees, and people can crush things. And different agents can have different causal powers. People can walk but trees and boulders can't. Birds can fly, but people can't, at least not without help. People have far more causal powers than most other things and some of these are very impressive. We can write stories and poems, get married, make nuclear weapons, and so on. But being an agent, I will take it, is just a matter of having causal powers.

I also take it that all agents are liable to change. By a disposition I mean a liability to undergo change. Again, believers are not alone in being liable to change. Almost everything is. (Again, abstract objects are an exception.) Rocks and plants can be cut. Rose bushes and cats can become sick and die. Dogs have emotional lives like people, and can enjoy or suffer various feelings and pains. Different sorts of agents are liable to different sorts of changes. Manifesting a liability or a disposition is just a matter of undergoing or suffering a change that one is liable to.

The believers we are familiar with are all living things. I'm not sure this is necessary. Maybe we'll make robots that believe and know things but are not alive. This depends on what it is to be alive, and I won't take a stand on that here. But with living things we get a distinction between an action that is a response and one that is not. Plants and animals are able to exercise certain of their powers in response to changes in their circumstances. A plant responds to drought by

---

[1] For more on the idea that an action is a causing, and that agents are causers, see Thomson (1977), Bach (1980), Strawson (1992), Alvarez & Hyman (1998), and Hyman (2015). I'll return to this in Chapter 7 when I discuss inference.

sending its roots deeper into the soil. Pine trees send a sort of antifreeze into their needles as the temperature drops. Cats grow a thicker coat as winter approaches. Non-living agents, like rocks and hurricanes, do not exercise their powers in response to changes in their surroundings. When a boulder crushes a car, that action is not the boulder's response to a change in its environment. But in producing antifreeze, a pine tree is responding to environmental changes.

I won't offer an analysis of when an action is a response. Some things seem clear. A response may be preceded by a change inside the agent. The drought affected the plant's roots, whereas nothing changed inside the rock in the moments before it crushed the car. And plants have a complex internal system that is sensitive to droughts, whereas none of the boulder's internal complexity or structure is relevant to its crushing the car. Such differences are surely part of why a boulder's crushing a car is not a response while a pine tree's producing antifreeze is. I don't know necessary and sufficient conditions for an action's being a response, but I don't think this matters much. I don't know necessary and sufficient conditions for something's being a pine tree or a boulder, though I am quite sure that there are pine trees and boulders. Likewise, I am quite sure that some causings are responses. I am just going to take this distinction for granted. That is fair, I think, since the distinction is needed to understand things that are not believers. Plants don't have beliefs but some of them anyway can exercise their powers in response to their environment, just as believers can.

To understand believers we need a further distinction, one among responses. It is between those that are up to the agent and those that are not. I take it that it is not up to the plant whether to respond to the drought by sending its roots deeper. Likewise, it is not up to my cat whether to grow a thicker coat as the seasons change, and it is not up to me whether to dilate my pupils when the lights go on. These actions are responses to changes in the environment, but they are not responses that are up to the agent. By contrast, it is sometimes up to my cat whether to jump onto my lap when I call, and it is sometimes up to me whether to turn on the lights. I assume that nothing the plant does is up to it, in this sense, even when its action is a response. And of course nothing a boulder does is ever up to it.

I won't offer an account of when a response is one that is up to the agent. I won't try to say why some of my cat's responses, but none of my plant's responses, are up to it. I don't deny that there is a close tie between being a believer and being an agent whose responses are sometimes up to it. Plausibly, an agent is a believer only if some of her responses are up to her and any agent whose responses are sometimes up to her is a believer. But the tie here is not that of identity. An agent whose responses are sometimes up to her also has needs, wants, and plans, and these are different from knowing and believing. And the believers we are familiar with also have emotions. An account of believing is thus only one part of a full story of the sort of thing that believers are. This is important for understanding what I am hoping to achieve in this book. I am not aiming to offer an account of the nature of *believers*, of what makes believers the sort of agent they are. My aim is to get clear on what it is for an agent whose responses are sometimes up to her to believe something. I am going to take the idea of such an agent for granted.

The idea of a response's being up to the agent is tied to deliberation. When a response is up to an agent, the agent can deliberate about whether, how, and when to respond. When she does, her attention is on the facts (as she takes them to be) and she responds in light of them. Indeed, she sees herself as placed among those facts and as set to respond to them. An agent's response, when it is one that is up to her, is thus known to her. (I'll defend these claims about self-knowledge in Chapter 5.) But I don't want to over-intellectualize deliberation. As I see it, my cat is deliberating in the moments between hearing my call and jumping onto my lap. The facts she is attending to do not settle how, when or even whether she will respond. Her response is up to her, even if the reasons she attends to strongly favor one response over others.

I can now clarify what I mean when I say that to believe something is to be in a certain position. The position is that of an agent when it is up to her whether to exercise a capacity or manifest a disposition. In that position she attends to the facts as she takes them to be. How a person takes things to be is set by the possibilities she takes to obtain. Believing something doesn't add to an agent's capacities or dispositions. (I'll return to this in Section 1.5.) Rather, it adds to the set of reasons she has, or anyway to the ones she takes herself to have, and this makes a difference to which actions and reactions would be reasonable for her. Whether what she believes moves her to act depends on whether she attends to it and whether she takes it to heart.[2] When she believes that some possibility obtains, that possibility can then cast light on her responses, even when she is mistaken. Clarifying this is the aim of Section 1.3. But before I get to that I want to say something about facts, possibilities, and reasons.

1.2 Possibilities, Facts, and Reasons

The contrast between facts and possibilities is at the heart of my account of believing. Indeed, I take it to be at the heart of any account of believing, since on any account a believer can be mistaken. She can believe that things are a certain way even when they are not that way. She is then mistaken about whether some possibility obtains. Any account of the nature of belief has to accept the notion of a way that things could have been. The aim of this section is to make clear what I am assuming about the nature of possibility and about its links to reasons.

---

[2] I won't offer an account of the springs of action, though I return very briefly to the topic of acting on a belief in the appendix. My views are influenced by Falk (1963).

12   ON THE NATURE OF BELIEVING

By a possibility I mean a way that something is, was, might yet be, or could have been. I take it that anything actual is possible. If a thing is some way, then its being that way is a possibility for it. Since my table is brown, its being brown is a possibility for it. It is a possibility that *obtains*. But what is possible is not restricted to what is actual. A thing could have been some way that it is not. My table is not very clean, but it could have been. Had I been a little neater this morning, it would have been clean. So being clean is a possibility for my table, though it is one that does not obtain. Central to my view of belief is the idea that to believe something is to believe that some possibility obtains, to believe that it is a way that things are.

In addition to those possibilities that obtain and those that do not obtain, there are also possibilities that remain open. Perhaps my table will be clean tomorrow, in which case its being clean tomorrow remains a possibility for it. That possibility *exists*, we might say, even though it does not obtain. Whether a given possibility remains open depends on the facts. Those facts can make certain possibilities more or less likely to obtain and they can rule others out. I think it is very likely that my table will be clean tomorrow. But the fact that I am in Toronto now rules out the possibility of my being in New York one minute from now. If Determinism is true, of course, then the facts already settle or make certain which possibilities will obtain in the future. We can have beliefs about how likely some possibility is to obtain and I'll discuss this in Chapter 3. But at the heart of my account is the idea that to believe something is to believe that a certain possibility obtains.

Possibilities and facts are closely linked, though different views on that link are available. One might say that a fact is a species of possibility, namely one that obtains. On this view, the fact that the 504 streetcar stops at Garden Avenue is a fact because it—that very fact—is a possibility that obtains. By contrast, the possibility that the 504 stops at Fern is not a fact because, though it is a possibility, it is one that does not obtain. There is an elegance to this way of linking possibilities and facts, but one might instead say that a fact is the *obtaining* of a possibility.[3] A fact, then, would not be a species of possibility, but rather a modification of a possibility. Though somewhat less elegant, this way of linking facts and possibilities may better fit some of our ordinary ways of talking. I'll say more about these alternatives in Chapter 3. They don't differ about what facts or possibilities there are, but only over what it is to be a fact. I won't need to decide between them in order to develop my view of believing.

As my remarks suggest, I take possibilities to be properties of things. It is a property of my table that being clean is a possibility for it. I'll say more about the sort of property I have in mind in Chapter 3 when I distinguish qualities from sortals. But I won't offer an account of why a thing has the possibilities it does. I'm going to assume we have enough of a grip on what it possible. The idea that certain

---

[3] I take this idea from Hyman (2017), who argues that facts are the truth of a proposition.

POSSIBILITIES, FACTS, AND REASONS 13

things could have been different in more or less specifiable ways is not inherently puzzling or even controversial, it seems to me. A little observation and a little theory are usually enough to figure out what is possible for a thing and to explain how it could have been different. My dirty table can be clean but it cannot be alive and it cannot be a barn owl. I can be an author, but I cannot be square and I cannot be made of pure gold. I don't have a younger brother, but I would have if my parents had done certain things differently. There is milk in my fridge, but there would not have been had my kids drunk it all. The idea of this sort of contrast between how things are and how they could have been is needed for more than just an account of believing. And it seems to me as fundamental to our conception of things as the contrasts between objects and properties, states and events, and time and space. And like these contrasts, the one between how things are and how they could have been is not at heart an epistemic one. No doubt what possibilities we can know and talk about depends on our cognitive powers and our linguistic resources. But this is so for those other contrasts too. I will assume that the contrast between how things are and how they could have been is clear enough.

Let me turn, now, to what I will assume about reasons.[4] I take it that reasons are facts. Garden Avenue, the road itself, is not a reason to do, think, or feel anything, but the fact that the 504 Streetcar stops there is. It can be a reason to walk to Garden Avenue, for instance. It is a consideration in light of which it might well be reasonable for someone to do so. I won't try to say what makes some fact a reason for doing, thinking, or feeling something. I will also take it for granted that a fact can be a reason for one person to do, think, or feel something without being a reason for anyone else to do, think, or feel that thing. If Malik promised to help Sarah mow the lawn, then the fact that he made this promise can be a reason for him to help Sarah without being a reason for anyone else to help her. It might, though, be a reason for someone else to do, think, or feel something else. It might, for instance, be a reason for Sarah to expect Malik to help. I won't try to say how a fact gets to be a reason for one person to do one thing and someone else to do something else. Taking these facts about reasons for granted is fair, I think. My aim in this book is to get clear on what it is for an agent whose responses to reasons are sometimes up to her to believe something. Such an account should be consistent with a variety of views about the nature of reasons and about what makes some fact a reason to respond in one way rather than another.

I take it that a fact is among a *person's* reasons only if she knows the fact. An agent can have several reasons for doing something and do it for one reason but not another. The southern side of Garden Avenue is safer than the northern side and also more pleasant. Plausibly, these are reasons for walking along the southern side. Jones knows both facts, and so has these two reasons for walking along the southern

---

[4] What follows relies on the discussion of reasons in Thomson (2008).

14 ON THE NATURE OF BELIEVING

side. I take it that Jones might walk along the southern side both because it is safer and because it is more pleasant. She might act on both reasons. But I take it she might instead act on one and not the other. Perhaps Jones does not care much about safety and rarely pays much attention to facts about safety. (No doubt she should, but that is a separate matter.) In that case, she might walk along the southern side because it is more pleasant but not because it is safer, even though she knows it is safer (and appreciates that it is a reason to walk on the southern side).

I am not going to try to say what it is to care in this way about some reasons more than others. Nor will I try to say, more generally, what it is for an agent to do something for one reason but not another. (One familiar account holds that this is a matter of the causal role believing plays in generating a response. I will say in Section 1.5 why I reject this account.) One thing that seems clear is that agents know what reasons they are acting on, at least in paradigm cases. And relatedly, agents know what they are doing or trying to do when they act on reasons. Acting on reasons essentially involves self-knowledge in this way. But I won't try to offer a full account of this.

Nor am I going to try to explain why people typically do, think, and feel what it would be reasonable by their own lights for them to do, think, and feel. I am not sure just what needs to be explained about this. Someone who does something unreasonable may have some explaining to do, especially if they did it knowingly. But I am not sure why theorists of rational agency need to explain why rational agents typically act rationally. (A different question asks how there came to be rational agents, how they emerged through natural history. I also won't say anything about that here. But we can't answer that question until we know what rational agents are, and this book aims to understand what it is for a rational agent to believe something.) In any event, my more modest goal is to get clear on what it is for an agent, whose reasonable responses are sometimes up to her, to believe something. An account of believing can contribute to our understanding or explanation of how rational action is possible. But no account of believing can be the whole story.

1.3 Acting in the Light of a Possibility

On my view, when a person believes that some possibility obtains, that possibility can *cast light* on what she does, thinks, or feels. The aim of this section is to explain this image. My view adapts one about knowledge that says that a person knows some fact just in case she can do, think, and feel things in light of it.[5] That fact can

---

[5] This is a traditional idea with contemporary roots going back at least to Ryle (1949). But my take on it is influenced by Hornsby (2004), McDowell (2013), and Hyman (1999, 2015). Similar views are found in Stalnaker (1984, 1991). I develop a similar view about emotion in (2018b). I am indebted to Gerhard Ernst and to anonymous referees for helping me to think through the material that follows.

be her reason, or part of her reason, for doing, thinking, or feeling what she does. It can explain or rationalize it. This idea is sometimes put by saying that knowing is a capacity to guide one's actions in light of a fact, but I will argue in Section 1.6 that knowing and believing are not capacities. My aim in this section is to explain how knowing and believing can make a difference to what a person is likely to do without making a difference to what she *can* do.

This modal distinction I have in mind is a general one. Facts about what a thing is likely to do are independent of facts about what it can do. A thing can be more or less likely to do something that it is capable of doing. Jones is very likely to walk to Garden this afternoon and this is something that she already can do. The drop of acid is very likely to stain the rug, which is a power it already has. But the fact that a thing is likely to do something does not entail that it can do it. Jones cannot run 26 miles, though she is likely to run that far this summer once her training is done. The metal rod is very likely to burn the table, but it won't be able to until it has been sufficiently heated. How likely a thing is to do, at some future time, something that it cannot now do depends on, among other things, how likely it is that it will, at that future time, be able to do it. It is fairly likely that Jones *will* run 26 miles in the summer because it is very likely that she will then be *able* to run that far. So the likelihood of changes in a thing's abilities can affect the likelihood of its doing one thing or another. But the likelihood of a thing's doing something can also change without any change in its abilities or dispositions. Jones is more likely to answer our questions if we ask her nicely, but this doesn't make her more able to answer them. Putting the vase on top of the books makes it more likely to shatter, but doesn't make it more fragile, more disposed to shatter.

So the fact that a thing is likely to do something does not entail that it can do it. Likewise, the fact that a thing can do something does not entail that it is likely to do it. The sugar cube is soluble but it does not follow that the cube will or is at all likely to dissolve. The drop of acid can burn fabrics but it does not follow that it ever will. Whether a thing will or is likely to do something that it is able to do depends on its circumstances. The sugar cube will dissolve but only if it is in water, and whether it ever will be in water can be more or less likely. The drop of acid may never come into contact with fabric. To know whether a thing ever will do something that it can do we need to know about its circumstances. If it does do it, its circumstances will partly explain why it did. The fact that the sugar cube was in water is the reason why it dissolved, and the acid's touching the sofa is the reason why it burned the fabric. In this way, the facts about a thing's surroundings will explain why it exercises the capacities and manifests the dispositions it does.

This point about the explanatory role of surroundings is also true of things that people do intentionally. Jones walked up to Garden Avenue to get the 504 streetcar. She walked there because the 504 stops at Garden. That fact about her circumstance is part of why she walked there. It was among her reasons. That the 504 stops at Garden is a fairly stable fact about her circumstances, but more or less temporary

16 ON THE NATURE OF BELIEVING

facts can also explain a person's actions. Jones lifted her laptop to keep it dry when the coffee suddenly spilled. That sudden coffee spill is part of why she exercised her ability to lift the laptop. It was a reason to lift it. So just as with sugar cubes and drops of acid, the facts in a person's surroundings can sometimes explain what they do.

This brings us to the idea about knowledge that I mentioned in this section's opening paragraph. According to it, for a person to know some fact is for that fact to be among the reasons she has for doing, thinking, or feeling things. When a person does something on purpose, her doing it is explained by a given fact only if she knows that fact. For instance, the fact that the 504 stops at Garden Avenue can explain why Jones walked there only because she knows that it stops there. And when a person knows some fact, what she does, thinks, or feels can be explained by it. Because Jones knows that the 504 also stops at Grenadier, the fact that it does may be the reason why she walks to Grenadier. For a person to know some fact is for her to be positioned to have that fact cast light on what she does, thinks, and feels.

This is how knowing can make a difference to what a person is likely to do without making a difference to what she *can* do. To return to the image from the end of my introduction, knowing is like being at home in the world so that the facts can explain what one does, thinks, and feels. Being at home makes a difference to what one is likely to do by making a difference to the reasons one has for doing one thing or another, and it can make this difference even if it does not make a difference to what one can do. What one is likely to do is influenced by one's position among the facts, not because being in that position is itself a capacity or a disposition, but because those facts are reasons for doing, thinking, and feeling things.

I want to extend this view of knowing to believing. When a person knows something, she also believes it, so this view of knowing already covers the case where a person believes something in virtue of knowing it. But to get to a complete account of believing, we need to cover the two cases where a person merely believes. She may believe and be wrong; or she may be right, but fail to know. My proposed extension is straightforward, and rests on the idea that a possibility is a potential fact and so a potential reason. Any response that would be reasonable for a person who knows that some possibility obtains would generally also be reasonable if she instead merely believes that it does. Whether she is right depends on what reasons there are, and what reasons she has depends on what she knows, but any reasonable response for a person who knows is equally reasonable for one who merely believes. This reflects the fact that, from the inside, believing is just like knowing. In deliberating, a believer attends to the reasons she takes there to be, and these are the facts as she sees them. This is what I mean in saying that when a person believes that some possibility obtains, that possibility can shed light on what she does, thinks, and feels.

An immediate clarification is needed. Believing that some possibility obtains is not the same as believing that something is likely. Jones believes that the 504 stops at Garden, but Sarah is undecided. She does not believe that it does, but she thinks it might well. The fact that she thinks this can make a difference to the reasonableness of her actions, thoughts, and feelings. But believing that it might stop there cannot make the same difference as believing that it does. My account of believing is aimed to understand the difference that believing something makes, not the difference that believing *that something is likely* makes. But I'll say more about believing that something is likely in Chapters 3 and 7.

I'll consider the two cases of mere belief in more detail. Let's start with a mistaken belief. Sarah walked to Fern Avenue in the mistaken belief that the 504 stops there. That was not an unreasonable thing for her to do, given that belief. But did she have a reason? (To keep our focus on the role of belief, let's simplify by assuming that she had no other reason to walk to Fern and by ignoring the role that a person's other states, such as her hopes and needs, play in making their actions reasonable.) The fact that the 504 stops at Fern cannot have been her reason, since there is no such fact. What about the fact that she believed it. Could that have been her reason? This strikes me as somewhat implausible. From her point of view, Sarah is responding to what she considers to be a fact about the 504 streetcar, and not a fact about herself. I suggest we say that a person *has* a reason for doing something only if there *is* a reason for doing it, but then say that a person can act reasonably even if they have no reason for doing what they do. So I suggest we say (remembering our simplifying assumptions) that Sarah did not *have* a reason for walking to Fern, since the 504 does not stop there, but walking there in the belief that it does stop there was nonetheless reasonable. It was reasonable because: (i) she did what she did believing that the 504 stopped there; and (ii) had it stopped there, then that fact would have been a reason for walking there. (In addition, if Sarah had known that it stopped there, then that fact would have been *her* reason for walking there.) In sum: Sarah's walking there was reasonable because she believed a certain possibility obtained and, had it obtained, the fact of its obtaining would have been a reason for her to do what she did. That's what I mean when I say that that possibility cast light on what she did.

Consider now a case where a person is right, but does not know. Stephanie walks to Garden Avenue in the belief that the 504 stops at Garden, but she does not know that it does. The details of why she does not know won't matter. Because she does not know that the 504 stops at Garden, the fact that it does cannot have been Stephanie's reason for walking there. Still, what she did was reasonable, given her belief. What makes it so? I suggest we say this: what Stephanie did was reasonable because: (i) she did what she did believing that the 504 stops there; and (ii) it does in fact stop there, and the fact that it does is a reason to do what she did.

I've been explaining what I mean when I say that a possibility can shed light or rationalize. Once again, the idea is this. When a person believes that some possibility obtains, that possibility can cast light on what she does, thinks, or feels because either (i) it obtains and she knows that it does, in which case its

18 ON THE NATURE OF BELIEVING

obtaining is among her reasons; (ii) it obtains and she merely believes that it does, in which case that fact would have been among her reasons had she known it; (iii) it does not obtain but she believes it does, in which case had it obtained that fact would have been among her reasons had she known it. The key idea is just that in believing that some possibility obtains, one sees its obtaining as among one's reasons. That possibility can then cast light on what one does, thinks, or feels, even when it does not obtain. This is because, had one known it and not just believed it, its obtaining would have been among one's reasons.

1.4 Effects, Manifestations, and Exercises

My account of believing contrasts with three that are very common in the literature. All four agree that a person's beliefs make a difference to her actions, thoughts, and feelings. On my view, the beliefs make a difference to what reasons she takes herself to have, and this can make a difference to what she is likely to do, since people are likely to act on the reasons they take themselves to have. The three opposing views accept this, but add that beliefs make this difference by helping to generate or bring about those actions, thoughts, and feelings. The three views differ in their details. For simplicity, I will focus on the explanation of what people do, though what I will say applies equally to what they think and feel.

A *Causalist* proposal is that beliefs explain people's actions by causing them. When a person acts on something they believe, the action is an effect of that belief (or of it together with other contributing causes), and when this is so, the action is explained by the belief. For instance, when Jones walked to Garden Avenue in the belief that the 504 stops there, that belief caused (or was one thing that caused) her to walk there, or caused (or contributed to causing) the movements of her legs as she walked there. According to this Causal view, beliefs make a difference by having actions, thoughts, and feelings as effects.

On a *Dispositionalist* proposal, a person's beliefs explain their actions by being manifested in them. On this view, to believe something is to be disposed to do, or think or feel certain things in certain conditions. An analogy is often drawn with solubility, inflammability, and fragility. These are dispositions to change in certain ways in certain situations. The Dispositionalist idea is that when Jones walked to Garden Avenue in the belief that the 504 stops there, that action was a manifestation of that belief, in something like the way the vase's shattering when it hit the floor was a manifestation of its fragility. The belief played a role in generating the action, just as the fragility played a role in generating the shattering. According to this Dispositionalist view, beliefs make a difference by having actions, thoughts, and feeling as their manifestations.

Closely related is a *Capacities* proposal. It is more familiar as a view about knowledge. It says that when a person acts on their knowledge, the action is an exercise of that knowledge. On one version of this view, to know something is to have an ability to guide one's actions in certain ways. When Jones walked to Garden Avenue, knowing that the 504 stops there, she used or exercised her knowledge. As a view about belief, the idea is that to act on one's belief is, likewise, to exercise a capacity or ability to guide one's actions in light of a reason. On this Capacities view, beliefs make a difference by having actions, thoughts, and feelings as results of their exercises.

I will argue that we should reject these views. A person's actions are not an effect, a manifestation, or an exercise of her beliefs. As I see it, these proposals get the ontology of belief states and properties wrong and misunderstand the logical character of action explanation. In Section 1.5, I will argue that belief states are not causes. In Section 1.6, I will argue that belief properties are not causal properties and so do not make a difference to what a believer can do. Seeing all of this will clarify why I think that believing something is being positioned to do, think, or feel things in the light of certain reasons.

1.5 Belief States Are Not Causes

In this section, I will argue that when a person does, thinks, or feels something in light of something they believe their belief state does not cause them to do, think, or feel what they do. The argument will depend on fairly general claims about the nature of causation and about differences between agents, events, and states, but I think the claims are independently plausible.

Here is the argument in outline. Causes are either agents or events. A ball can break the window and so can the ball's hitting the window. But the states of a thing are not agents and they are not events. The ball's weighing 500 grams is not an agent or an event. So states are not causes. Belief states are like mass states in this respect. They are not causes. The aim of this section is to develop this argument. I'll end by suggesting that the causal idea also distorts the role that believing plays in deliberation. It treats believing as if it were a mental condition, such as addiction or kleptomania, that might push or pull a person against her will.

But I should note first that my argument will leave open that belief states might play a different causal role. A thing's states can make a difference to its causal powers, to what it can do, even if those states are not themselves causes. The ball's weighing 500 grams makes a difference to what the ball can break, and so it makes a difference to what the ball can cause. It makes that difference even though (as I will argue) the state of weighing 500 grams is not itself a cause. But as I see it, belief states are unlike mass states in this respect. What a person believes does not make a difference to what she can do, to her causal powers. This can be hard to see since her belief states do make a difference to what she is likely to do. In this

20 ON THE NATURE OF BELIEVING

respect, believing something is like being in a certain spatial location. I'll develop this line of thought in the next section.

In this section, I will first say something about causation and then explain why I am not persuaded by the standard reasons in favor of the causal view.[6] I will then argue that states are not causes because they are neither agents nor events. My argument will depend on an ontological claim about states that I will develop fully only in Chapter 2, but I'll sketch its outlines below.

To properly formulate the causal view we need to know what causation is, and I can't settle that here. But two widely held ideas about causation, together with three standard ideas about events, lead to a familiar worry with the causal view. The ideas about causation are that it is transitive and that a cause makes its effects inevitable. The three ideas about events are that every event has a cause, that only events are causes, and that a person's actions are events. Together, these ideas entail that events that occurred long before there were people made every one of our actions inevitable, and many see this as incompatible with freedom and responsibility. I will set this worry aside, but I will assume (for now) that these ideas about causation and events are right. I want to focus on whether a person's believing something is a cause, in this sense. More precisely, I want to focus on whether belief states have causal powers. I'll argue that they don't.

David Armstrong took it to be a conceptual truth that belief states are causes. Here is how he formulated the causal idea.

The concept of a mental state is the concept of something that is, characteristically, the cause of certain effects and the effect of certain causes. What sorts of effects and what sort of causes? The effects caused by the mental state will be certain patterns of behaviour of the person in that state. For instance, the desire for food is a state of a person or animal that characteristically brings about food-seeking and food-consuming behavior by that person or animal.

(Armstrong 1981, 23)

Armstrong offered his proposal as an analysis of the concept of belief, as an account of what we mean by the term "belief." It seems to me this is not very plausible. For Libertarians about action say that when a person acts freely, while she might well act *on* her beliefs, nothing causes her to act and nothing (aside from the agent herself) causes her body to move when she acts. Libertarians don't deny that a person's beliefs make a difference to what they do, think, and feel, and that the beliefs explain what they do. Here is how Thomas Reid put the point.

---

[6] My presentation here is influenced by the discussions in Steward (1997) and Floyd (2017). Arguments against a causalist view are given in, among other places, Frankfurt (1978), Bennett (1991), O'Connor (2000), Schueler (2003), Sehon (2005), Thompson (2008), Alvarez (2010), Steward (2014), and in several of the essays in Sandis (2009).What I say in this section and the next about the nature of mental states develops points made in Hunter (2001).

I grant that all rational beings are influenced, and ought to be influenced, by motives. But the influence of motives is of a very different nature from that of efficient causes. They are neither causes nor agents. They suppose an efficient cause, and can do nothing without it . . . Motives, therefore, may *influence* to action, but they do not act . . . motives suppose liberty in the agent, otherwise they have no influence at all.   (Reid 1991, 276–7)

More recently, Chisholm (1964) put the same idea this way: a person's beliefs and desires "incline without necessitating." Moreover, theorists who hold a Dispositionalist or Capacity view also deny that believing causes actions. The Dispositionalist thinks the link between believing and action is more like that between being soluble and dissolving, where there is a logical or conceptual link, not a causal one.[7] And the Capacities view says that the link is like that between being able to play piano and playing it. When Simon exercises that ability in playing the piano he is the agent, not his ability. These theorists can agree with the Causalist (and me) that what a person believes helps to rationalize what they do. And it might be that these theorists are mistaken, or even confused. But it seems implausible that their confusion is about the meaning of the word "belief," which is what Armstrong's view entails. As a claim about what we or philosophers have meant by "believing," then, the Causalist view seems to me not very plausible.

Donald Davidson (1984) offered Causalism, not as an analysis of the concept of believing, but as a theoretical hypothesis about how belief explains action. He had in mind cases where a person does something for one reason when they also had another. Jones walks along the southern side of Garden because it is more beautiful. She knows it is also safer, but she does not care about that. That's not why she walks along the southern side. Davidson's hypothesis was that when a person has multiple reasons for doing something and acts on one of them but not the other, this is because the one caused the action or caused it "in the right way." He did not so much support this proposal, or even spell out the "right" sort of causing, as challenge his opponents to offer a better alternative.

As I said in Section 1.1, I won't try to offer a better account of such cases. But it is not clear to me that such an account needs to say much about believing. For the cases concern what a person desires or cares about not what she believes. A person can have conflicting desires and she can care more about one thing than another. She might want to watch a TV show while also wanting to read her book, knowing she cannot do both at once. She might care about some things more than others, and she might know that doing something will bring her several things she wants or cares about at once. And she might even have desires she does not want to act on, and she might care about things she knows she shouldn't. She might want to

---

[7] The classic text is Melden (1961), but see also (Melden 1966).

eat the cookie, while wanting that desire not to move her. It often matters which of a person's desires they act on. Did the shopkeeper give the customer the right change because she cares about customer loyalty or because she cares about her reputation? Such questions matter because their answers reveal something about the person's character. Davidson's causal proposal was meant to help us answer this sort of question. If we know which desire or care caused the action, he thought, then we'd know which one she acted on.[8] But whether or not this proposal succeeds, the underlying complexity Davidson noted is absent in the case of believing. A person's beliefs cannot conflict in the way her desires or cares can. They don't compete with each other. Assessments of a person's character don't depend on which of her beliefs she acted on (though it does matter to a person's character what she believes; I return to this in the final chapter). So the question that Davidson said his Causalist proposal was designed to answer does not arise in the same way for belief.

Let me turn now to my arguments against Causalism. The first one is that it rests on what I think is a mistake about the ontology of belief states and of causation. (The second will be that it misconstrues belief's role in deliberation.) In the passage I quoted above, Reid says that motives are not agents. It is not just that motives do not cause a person to act or cause her actions. Motives are not agents at all. I think this is right, though I won't argue that what I am about to say is faithful to Reid. On my view, to believe something is to be in a certain mental state and a state is not the right sort of thing to be an agent, and so not the right sort of thing to have causal powers. It is only by hypostasizing states—treating them as if they were individuals—that one might think they are candidates for having causal powers.[9] Let me explain this.

This objection to the causal view rests on an ontological distinction between two kinds of properties: sortals and qualities. I'll develop the distinction in detail in Chapter 2, where I will argue that belief properties are qualities. Understanding this is, I think, essential to understanding the nature of believing. Here is the distinction in brief. Qualities are properties that are instantiated *in* individuals and substances, whereas the instantiation of a sortal *is* an individual. The property of being a rock is a sortal; the property of weighing 200 pounds is a quality. An instantiation of a quality belongs in a different ontological category from that of a sortal. One difference is that while the instantiations of sortals can have causal powers, the instantiations of qualities can't. The rock has causal powers, but its weighing 200 pounds, its being roughly spherical, and its being gray do not. The state of weighing 200 pounds is not the sort of thing that can have causal powers.

---

[8] Thanks to Erasmus Mayr for helping me think through this.
[9] For more on this critique of the Causal proposal, see Bennett (1991). Richard Floyd (2017) offers a plausible account of the origins of this hypostasizing and of its negative influence in the philosophy of mind, though he does not develop the distinction that follows in the text between sortals and qualities.

BELIEF STATES ARE NOT CAUSES   23

Likewise, a drop of acid has causal powers, but its state of being acidic does not. This does not mean that a thing's qualities make *no* difference to its causal powers. A 200-pound rock can do things, in virtue of weighing 200 pounds, that a tiny pebble can't. And because it is acidic, a drop of hydrochloric acid can melt things. So some qualities are causal qualities, in that they make a difference to a thing's causal powers. (I'll argue in the next section that belief properties are not causal qualities.) But this does not entail that the *instantiation* of a causal quality has causal powers. It is the rock that has the power to crush, not its weighing 200 pounds, even if its weighing 200 pounds is an instantiation of a causal quality. This distinction, and its relevance to agency and causality, is general and not restricted to mental qualities. It is not just that someone's believing that the 504 stops at Garden has no causal powers. No states do. In this way, the idea that belief states are causes misconstrues the ontology of believing.

Two things can obscure this ontological point in the case of believing. One is confusing believing something with thinking about or reflecting on what one believes. Believing is a state while thinking is an activity.[10] Suppose Jones falsely believes that Sarah has been spreading vile rumors about her. This might make Jones angry and hurt. But what exactly caused the hurt and anger? It is hard to see how it could be the believing itself, since Jones is in that belief state even when fast asleep and not feeling angry or hurt. More plausibly, the anger and hurt result from Jones' dwelling on or thinking about what (she thinks) Sarah did. The more Jones thinks about it, the angrier and more hurt she gets. An act of thinking about something can cause feelings, even if the state of believing itself cannot. Indeed, even imagining that Sarah spread these rumors might make Jones angry. In a way, even Davidson saw this. On his view, only events are causes and he acknowledged that mental states are not events. He thought he could get around this by taking the cause of a person's action to be, not the believing or desiring itself, but rather the onset or start of a believing or wanting. He took the onset of a state to be an event. This might save the causal story, but only by denying that belief states are causes. I won't pursue this idea here.

Another thing that obscures this ontological point about belief states is a familiar ambiguity in the word "belief." It is between what a person believes and their state of believing it. The first is often taken to be an object—standardly, a representation that has truth conditions essentially. (I'll challenge this in Chapter 3.) Representations are objects, and so they are instantiations of a sortal property. But a state of believing something is an instantiation of a quality and is not an object. (Again, I will argue for this in Chapter 2.) An analogy with owning can help see this distinction. When a person owns a book, the book they own is an object but their owning it is not. There is no ambiguity in "owning" as there is in

---

[10] I thank a reviewer for prompting me to make this point explicit. It is forcefully made in Falk (1963).

24   ON THE NATURE OF BELIEVING

"belief." We can speak of a person's possessions, but this is not ambiguous between what they own and their owning of it. But with "belief" we get precisely this ambiguity. Losing sight of it can lead one to treat belief states as if they were objects, and so as candidates for having causal powers. We can see this in a recent passage from José Luis Bermúdez. Bermúdez is explaining the view that "[i]ntentional realism treats beliefs and desires as the sorts of things that can cause behavior" (108). Making sense of this, he says,

> [m]eans taking into account the rational relations between beliefs and desires, on the one hand, and the behavior that they cause on the other....
>
> Yet, on the face of it, causation by content is deeply mysterious. It depends upon representations (stored information about the environment). *In one sense representations are simply objects like any other—they might be patterns of sound waves, populations of neurons, or pieces of paper.* Thought of in this way, it is no more difficult to understanding [sic]how representations can cause behavior than it is to understand how the doctor's hammer can make my leg move.
>
> But the representations we are interested in (*such as beliefs and desires*) are also things that bear a special semantic relation to the world...
>
> (Bermúdez 2020, 108; italics added)

A bit later, Bermúdez says that "almost all cognitive scientists and the vast majority of philosophers hold that brains and *the representations that they contain* are physical entities." (2020, 108–9; italics added). What I want to mark here is the slide from "belief," understood as a state of believing something, to "belief," understood as a representation believed. Once that slide is made, it is hard not to think that beliefs are the right sort of thing to have causal powers, that they are in relevant respects just like a doctor's hammer. Indeed, it would seem perverse to even question whether a belief *could* be a cause. But a rock's weighing 200 pounds is not an object like a doctor's hammer, and my owning a book is not an object I might use as, say, a paperweight. Likewise, a person's believing something is not an object like a doctor's hammer or a rock or a book. We can avoid this slide, and the resulting confusion, by keeping in mind the distinction between sortals and qualities.

I have argued that it is a mistake for the causal view to treat belief states as if they were things with causal powers. But what about treating them as like events? Events cause things to happen, and one might doubt that the distinction between events and states can be of much relevance. Perhaps the causal view should say that belief states are causes in something like the way that events are causes. I don't think this idea is very promising. To see why, it helps to note two points about the ontology of causation. One is that event causation and agent causation are interdependent. The other is that event causation always involves an agent exercising a specific causal power. The difficulty with modeling state causation on event causation is finding an appropriate agent with appropriate causal powers.

BELIEF STATES ARE NOT CAUSES   25

I'll first explain these two points about event causation and then explain why I think they make the idea of modeling state causation on event causation unpromising.[11]

The first point is that event causation and agent causation are interdependent. What I mean is that an event causes some outcome just in case some agent causes it. The event of the hammer's hitting the glass caused the glass to break if and only if the hammer caused the glass to break by hitting it. The hurricane caused the tree to fall just in case some volume of air that is part of the hurricane caused that tree to fall. Billy caused the scratch on the car if and only if some event Billy engaged in (such as his dragging the nail along the car's side) caused the scratch. The magnet caused the paper clips to move if and only its being placed close to them caused them to move. Events cause what they do by the actions of agents involved in them and agents cause what they do by exercising their causal powers. This interdependence of agent and event causation is the first point.

The second point is that agent causation always takes a specific form. What I mean is that an agent causes some outcome by exercising some specific causal power it has. The hammer caused the breaking of the glass by pushing it. The volume of air caused the tree to fall by bending it. Billy caused the scratch by dragging the nail over the car's surface. The magnet caused the paper clips to move by attracting them. Whenever an agent causes some outcome that causing took some specific form. Putting these two points together, we get that an event causes some outcome only if some agent involved in that event causes that outcome through an exercise of one of its causal powers.

Let's now return to the idea of modeling state causation on event causation. The idea would presumably be this. A state of some agent caused an outcome just in case that agent caused that outcome through an exercise of a causal power that it has in virtue of being in that state. We could say that the boulder's weighing 200 kilograms crushed the can because the boulder itself crushed the can by exercising a causal power it has in virtue of weighing 200 kilograms. It still sounds to me a little odd to say that the boulder's mass crushed the can, but I can see the appeal of this way of talking, and at least we have given a more or less clear sense to the idea of state causation.

But I don't think this proposal gives the causal view of belief what it needs. There are two difficulties. The causal view of belief says that a person's belief states can cause their actions. If Jones walked to Garden Avenue in the belief that the 504 stops there, then, according to the causal view, her belief caused her to walk there. But this is not what our proposal says. It says that a state of a thing can cause whatever outcomes that thing causes, but not that a state of a thing can cause it to cause those outcomes. So even if Jones' belief caused whatever she caused in

[11] What follows is indebted to discussion in Thomson (1987) and Hyman (2015).

26 ON THE NATURE OF BELIEVING

walking to Garden Avenue, what the causal view needs is that her belief caused *her* to cause those things. And our proposal does not yield this.

There is an even more serious difficulty, though defending it will have to wait until the next section. It concerns the second point I noted above, namely that whenever an agent causes some outcome that causing takes some specific form. According to the proposal, a state of a thing can be a cause when the state makes a difference to that thing's causal powers. The boulder's weighing 200 kilograms crushed the can, according to this proposal, because that mass property makes a difference to the boulder's causal powers. More specifically, it makes a difference to what the boulder can push. The difficulty is that belief properties do not make a difference to a person's causal powers. They don't make a difference to what she can do. My defense of this claim will have to wait until the next section.

I have argued that belief states are not causes. But none of this denies that entities inside Jones exercise causal powers when she walks to Garden Avenue. Muscles and nerves and tendons are all actively involved when she walks. What is being denied is just that any of those entities is involved in her believing that the 504 stops at Garden Avenue in the way the hammer is involved in the event of its hitting the glass or the magnet is involved in the event of its attracting the paper clips. Belief states are states a person is in. They are not states inside a person.

This first argument that the causal view gets wrong the ontology of belief states and of causation is not restricted to *psychological* states. I think it shows that no states are causes. (I'll turn in the next section to whether some states are causal states; that is, whether some qualities are causal qualities.) My second objection is that the causal view gets wrong the role believing plays in deliberation. The causal view dominates contemporary discussions within the philosophy of mind and cognitive psychology, but in moral psychology, where theorists have focused on deliberation and practical reasoning, the idea that beliefs and desires cause actions remains highly contested.[12] In these discussions, the position of the believer as she deliberates about what to do is put at the center of an account of rational action. To understand the dynamics involved in deliberation, we need to distinguish different sorts of influences. As a person deliberates, she attends to the facts as she takes them to be. These include facts about her environment, about what she and other people need, about the best available means to satisfy those needs, and so on. But she may also feel various inclinations or pulls, and these have a variety of sources. Sometimes the source is internal. When strong enough, they can move her against her will. This is true of strong emotions like jealousy or envy, and of psychological conditions like addiction and compulsion that have occurrent manifestations.[13] They can even move her without her knowledge. Getting clear on this is essential

---

[12] See for instance Wolf (1980), Dancy (2000), Scanlon (2014), and Thompson (2010).
[13] These examples are from Wolf (2015), who argues along similar lines that, at least according to our ordinary folk-psychological view, a person's character does not make them do things.

for understanding the position of agents as they deliberate. But agents are not pushed or pulled by their beliefs when they deliberate. As we saw earlier, *reflecting* on what we believe may move us, but merely believing it cannot. The influence of our believing something is very different from the feeling of being pushed or pulled by strong emotions, sudden urges, or standing physiological conditions. A fan of the causal view might agree but say that beliefs push and pull us in a different way. But the problem, it seems to me, is that beliefs don't pull or push us at all. The causal view misconstrues the role that believing something plays in deliberation. And it thereby misunderstands what it is to believe something.

At the start of this section, I mentioned two ideas about the nature of causation. One is that causation is transitive and the other is that a cause makes its effects inevitable. One could hold that mental states are causes and deny or modify those ideas. Al Mele, for instance, suggests that we deny that mental states make their effects inevitable (Mele 2017). Eric Marcus argues that beliefs are rational causes, where this is different from physical causation (Marcus 2012). Anscombe said that by "cause" we mean the origin or source of an event or state of affairs, and she denied that causes make their effects inevitable (Anscombe 1981b). While she denied that mental states are efficient causes of our actions, a fan of Causalism might say that our actions originate in our beliefs and, in this sense, are rationally caused by them without making them inevitable. I won't stop to consider such modified forms of the causal idea. My target has been the view we find in Armstrong, Davidson, and Bermúdez, on which belief states are things with causal powers. I think I have said enough to resist this view and to raise general difficulties with the idea that states are causes. I want to turn now to my claim that belief properties do not add to an agent's causal powers. Belief properties, I will now argue, are not causal qualities.

1.6 Belief Properties Are Not Causal Qualities

I have argued that belief states are not causes. Agents and events are causes but instantiations of qualities are not. Still, some qualities are *causal qualities*, in that their instantiation adds to a thing's causal powers. The properties of weighing 500 kilograms and of being an acid are causal qualities. In virtue of weighing that much, a rock can crush a tin can. In virtue of being an acid, vinegar can stain fabric. In this section, I will argue that belief properties are not causal qualities. Believing something does not add to an agent's causal powers or dispositions. There is no change that a person is able to bring about or undergo in virtue of believing something. In this respect, believing is like being in a spatial location. Believing makes a difference to the position from which a person deliberates by making a difference to the reasons she has or thinks she has, and this may make a difference to what she is likely to do. That is how beliefs explain.

28 ON THE NATURE OF BELIEVING

I'll first discuss two examples of causal qualities. I'll describe how causal dispositions are manifested and how causal capacities are exercised. Many take belief properties to be dispositions, and a common view holds that knowing is a capacity.[14] I will suggest that the main support for these views rests on not clearly distinguishing dispositions and capacities from opportunities and potentialities. Then I will argue that a person's action is neither a manifestation nor an exercise of their believing or knowing. These views, I will suggest, get the logic of action explanation wrong.

I'll start with an example of a causal disposition. Fragility is a causal disposition because it makes a difference to what changes a thing can undergo. The bridge was fragile and it collapsed during the earthquake. But its fragility did not cause the bridge to collapse. The collapsing of the bridge was a *manifestation* of the bridge's fragility, and dispositions do not cause their own manifestations. Rather, the earthquake caused that manifestation. It caused the collapse of the bridge. Still, the bridge's fragility was part of the causal story. For being fragile is a causal quality. It makes a difference to the changes a thing can undergo. So the bridge's fragility was causally relevant to the collapse, even though it was not itself a cause of the collapse.

Here is a second example, this time of a causal capacity. Being hot is a causal capacity because it makes a difference to what changes a thing can bring about. The metal rod was extremely hot and it burned the wooden table when it touched it. But its being so hot did not cause the burning or the burn. The burning was an *exercise* of the rod's capacity to cause burns, and capacities do not cause their own exercises. The contact with the table caused that exercise. It caused the rod to burn the wood. Still, even though the rod's temperature did not cause the burning or the burn, it was part of the causal story. For being that hot is a causal quality. It makes a difference to the changes a thing can bring about. So the rod's temperature was causally relevant to the burning, even though it was not itself a cause of the burning.

Is believing a causal disposition or a causal capacity? It is helpful to start by considering the familiar idea that knowing is a capacity. Here is how Anthony Kenny formulated it.

> . . . to know is to have the ability to modify one's behaviour in indefinite ways relevant to the pursuit of one's goals.   (Kenny 1989, 108–9)

Stalnaker offers a similar thought.

---

[14] This view has a long pedigree. It takes different forms and is supported in different ways in many places, including Ryle (1949), Price (1969), Stalnaker (1984), Kenny (1989), Schwitzgebel (2002), (Hunter 2009a), Hyman (2015), and Zimmerman (2018).

BELIEF PROPERTIES ARE NOT CAUSAL QUALITIES   29

I know whether P if I have the capacity to make my actions depend on whether P.   (Stalnaker 1991, 439)

Both Kenny and Stalnaker characterize knowledge as a capacity for action, but this restriction is not essential. John Hyman offers a less restrictive view. He says that knowing that P is a capacity to be guided by the fact that P, and he elaborates this in terms of reasons.

> How should the concept of being guided by a fact be understood? As I have said, to be guided by a certain fact is for this fact to be among one's reasons for doing or for not doing something; for believing or doubting or hoping or wanting something; or for not believing or doubting or hoping or wanting something; and so on. This list is not exhaustive. *Any verb can be added which can occur in a sentence of the form, 'A's reason for √ing was that P.'*
>
> (Hyman 2006, 902; italics added)

On the Capacities view, as I will understand it, knowing that P is the capacity to do, or feel or think something for the reason that P.

Part of the plausibility of the idea that knowing is a capacity stems, it seems to me, from two closely related ideas, neither of which I will deny. One is that a person who knows some fact is likely to guide her actions in light of it. (The other is that people have a capacity to know things. I'll consider this in a moment.) I think we should accept this first idea. Jones knows that the 504 stops at Garden, and because she knows it, she is likely to formulate and adjust her plans in light of that fact. But this does not show that knowing is a capacity. As we saw in Section 1.3, what a thing is likely to do depends not just on what it can do but also on its circumstances. We need to distinguish a thing's capacities from the opportunities or occasions it has to exercise them. In saying that an agent *can* do something, we may mean that she has a certain causal capacity. That is what we mean when we say that a person can walk, or that vinegar can stain fabric. But we may instead mean that the agent has an opportunity or occasion to exercise a capacity. In saying that Sonja can play "Happy Birthday" when she sits down at the piano, we don't mean that she acquires the capacity to play the song when she sits at the piano, or that she has it only when she is at a piano. She had the capacity to play it before she sat down. She has it when she is asleep. What she gained when she sat at the piano was an opportunity (or occasion) to exercise that capacity.

We thus need to distinguish the idea that knowing is a capacity from the idea, which I accept, that a person who knows some fact may guide her actions in light of it. Indeed, that idea informed the account of believing I developed in Section 1.3. I said that when a person believes that some possibility obtains, she may do, think, and feel things in light of that possibility. But on my view, in saying what someone believes we are describing, not her capacities or dispositions, but

30 ON THE NATURE OF BELIEVING

rather the rational position she is in and from which she will exercise and manifest the capacities and disposition she has. I find it helpful to think of an analogy with spatial locations. When Tamar visits London she may walk along Regent Street, and she is likely to ride the tube. This does not mean that in arriving in London she acquires a capacity she lacked when in Toronto. In walking along Regent Street she would exercise (among others) her capacity to walk, and she had that capacity in Toronto. What she gained, in arriving in London, is an opportunity or occasion to exercise that capacity on Regent Street. Likewise, it seems to me, in saying what a person believes we are characterizing the position she is in (or takes herself to be in) when she deliberates about how to respond to the reasons (as she takes them to be).

We also need to distinguish the idea that knowing is a capacity from a second idea. It is that people have a capacity to know things. Arguably, perception and inference are capacities or powers that people have and that when exercised can yield states of knowing. But it does not follow that states of knowledge are themselves capacities. We need to distinguish a capacity from both its exercise and from its results. Sonja has a capacity to play piano, but her exercise of that capacity—a particular playing by her of a piano—is not a capacity. It is an event. A drop of vinegar has the capacity to stain, but its exercise of the capacity (its staining the rug) is not a capacity, and neither is the result of that exercise (the stain). Likewise, even if perception is a capacity that produces knowledge, it would not follow that an instance of perceiving is a capacity nor that the result of the perception is a capacity. So to show that knowing is a capacity, we would need to show more than that people have a capacity to know.

But are perception and inference in fact capacities that people exercise and that yield states of knowledge? I don't need to settle this, but here is one consideration that suggests they are not. We need to distinguish a thing's capacities from its potentialities. A ball can roll down an incline. This does not mean that when a ball rolls down an incline it is exercising a capacity to roll. I don't think the ball is even manifesting a *disposition* to roll down an incline. Rather, rolling down an incline is a potential or a possibility for a ball. Similarly, a pine tree can live for sixty years. This does not mean that a pine tree has a capacity to live until sixty and that some pine trees exercise that capacity and others do not. It means, rather, that living for sixty years is a possibility or a potentiality for it. Here again, an analogy with spatial location is helpful. A person can be in London, but this does not mean that the people in London are exercising a capacity or manifesting a disposition to be in London. To say that some person can be in London is to say that being in London is a possibility or potentiality for them. Perhaps, then, when we say that Jones can know that Toronto is the capital of Ontario, we mean, not that she has a capacity whose exercise by her would result in her knowing that fact, but that knowing this fact is a possible state for her. As I said, I don't need to settle this issue. I will say more about inference in Chapter 6 and about whether it is a sort of

BELIEF PROPERTIES ARE NOT CAUSAL QUALITIES   31

action. But whatever the truth is about that, my present point is that even if people do have and exercise capacities to know, this would not entail that knowing is itself a capacity.

Indeed, there is good reason to doubt that knowing is a capacity. It concerns what manifests or reveals a person's knowledge when they act, and so the role believing plays in explaining action. When a person acts on something they know, they are exercising capacities they have, but their knowledge is manifested, not in the exercise of those capacities, but in the fact that they are exercising them *in light of the fact they know*.[15] When Sarah walks to Garden because the 504 stops there, she is exercising (among others) her capacity to walk. That is a capacity she has and can exercise whether or not she knows that the 504 stops at Garden. What manifests her knowledge is that she walked there *for the reason* that the 504 stops at Garden. Her knowing is made manifest, not in her walking, but in her walking for that reason.

This point about what manifests or reveals a person's belief is obscured in a famous passage where Ryle characterizes a person who believes that the ice is dangerously thin.

> ... to believe that the ice is dangerously thin is to be unhesitant in telling oneself and others that it is thin, in acquiescing in other people's assertions to that effect, in objecting to statements to the contrary, in drawing consequences from the original proposition, and so forth. But it is also to be prone to skate warily, to shudder, to dwell in imagination on possible disasters and to warn other skaters. *It is a propensity not only to make certain theoretical moves but also to make certain executive and imaginative moves, as well as to have certain feelings.*
>
> (Ryle 1949, 117–18; italics added)

This passage suggests that skating warily, asserting that the ice is thin, and, more generally, making certain "executive moves" manifest the skater's belief. But these are exercises of other capacities altogether: a capacity to skate and a capacity to assert. What manifests or expresses the skater's belief is the fact that she is doing those things *because (or so she thinks) the ice is thin*. By confusing the manifestation of knowledge and belief with the actions, feelings, and thoughts in which

---

[15] Peter Hacker (2013) argues that the phrase "can $\wp$ for the reason that P" does not name an ability, so even if it is true that for a person to know that P is for them to be able to do, think, and feel for the reason that P, it is wrong to call knowledge an ability. On his view, the phrase "can $\wp$" might name an ability, but there is no such ability as the ability to $\wp$ for some reason. My view is similar to Hacker's. Tim Williamson (2000) and Kieran Setiya (2013) have separately argued that knowing that P *explains* one's ability to be guided by the fact that P, and so cannot itself be that ability. On their view, that underlying state and the ability accompany one another as a matter of necessity but are nonetheless distinct. I agree with them that knowing that P is not an ability. But I don't think that guiding one's actions in light of a certain fact involves exercising an ability to do so. On my view, one can be *in position* to guide one's actions in light of a certain fact, but being in a position to exercise one's abilities is not itself an ability. For discussion of these criticisms of the ability view, see Hyman (2015).

32 ON THE NATURE OF BELIEVING

the knowledge or belief is exercised, Ryle needlessly opened himself to the charge that his view was reductionist and, worse, behaviorist.

This also explains why we should resist the idea that assertion is a privileged manifestation or expression of one's knowledge or belief. The point is not that one can assert something without knowing or believing it. Nor is the point that animals can know things without even being able to assert anything. Nor is it that knowing is expressed in what one feels and thinks and not just in what one does. Rather, the point is that assertion—that action—is not the right sort of thing to be a manifestation of one's knowledge or belief. For there is no thing that can be done, felt, or thought such that knowing that P is being able to do or feel or think that thing. When a person acts on a piece of knowledge, their knowledge is revealed, not in the action itself, but in the fact that they acted in light of the fact they know. Again, the analogy with spatial location is helpful. When Sonja walks along Regent Street, the fact that she is in London is manifested, not in her exercising her capacity to walk, but in the fact that she is exercising that capacity on Regent Street. Knowing (and believing) is a matter of being positioned in a space of reasons, and what a person knows (and believes) is manifested, not in her acts, thoughts, and feelings, but in (as she sees them) the reasons why she did, thought, and felt those things. In learning some new fact, we do not acquire a new capacity to do, think, or feel anything. Rather, we acquire a potential to do, think, or feel something in light of the learned fact.[16]

My focus so far has been on whether knowing is a capacity. Along the way I've indicated how what I have said extends to the idea that believing is a disposition. On my view, a person who merely believes that some possibility obtains can do, think, and feel things in light of that possibility. And she may have a capacity to believe things. But none of this entails that believing is a disposition to do, think, or feel anything. Rather, a person's believing something is revealed or made manifest in what rationalizes her actions, thoughts, and feelings. Believing, like knowing, is a matter of being in a certain position to exercise and manifest the capacities and dispositions one has.

Admittedly, my view may sound like a dispositionalist one. For I say that a person who believes that some possibility obtains is in position to exercise and manifest her capacities and dispositions in light of that possibility.[17] There is a sense of "disposition" on which it means being positioned in a certain way. The Oxford English Dictionary offers as a primary use "The plan shows the *disposition* of the rooms." This is a description, not of the rooms' powers or liabilities, but of their relative positions inside the building. I am happy to put my view in terms of

---

[16] For an application of this idea to emotions, see (Hunter 2018b).

[17] This was suggested to me once in conversation by Charles Travis. He suggested we think of believing as a disposition in the sense in which we might say that Napoleon's armies were in a certain disposition on the hillside.

this sort of disposition. What is more, I don't deny that people can typically be expected to act in ways that are reasonable, given the reasons they take themselves to have. Reasonable people take the steps they believe will lead to the outcomes they seek. Knowing what someone believes and knows is thus valuable in predicting their actions. But that is not because knowing and believing are capacities or dispositions like acidity and solubility. It is because people typically respond reasonably to the reasons they take themselves to have. That is why knowing and believing can make a difference to what a person is likely to do without making a difference to what she can do.

1.7 Non-Human Belief and Naturalism

The aim of this chapter has been to spell out my proposal that to believe something is to be in position to do, think, and feel things in light of a possibility whose obtaining would make one right. In Section 1.1, I developed the idea of a deliberative position. In Section 1.2, I clarified what I mean by possibilities and their links to reasons. In Section 1.3, I explained how a possibility can cast light. In Section 1.4, I identified three contrasting views about believing. One takes belief states to be causes, and the others take belief properties to be capacities or dispositions. In Sections 1.5 and 1.6, I explained why I think we should resist these views. In this final section, I want to restate my account, sketch how it extends to non-human animals, and explain why I consider my account to be naturalistic.

On my view, to believe something is to be in position to exercise and manifest one's capacities and dispositions in light of a possibility whose obtaining would make one right. Believers are agents some of whose responses are up to them. A believer sees herself as set—or as positioned—to respond to the facts, and so to the reasons, she takes there to be. Believing something does not add to the responses open to an agent in such a position. It does not add to her capacities or dispositions. Rather, it makes a difference to which responses would be reasonable for her. These are set by the possibilities she believes obtain. If she knows that one obtains, its obtaining is among her reasons. If she doesn't know it, then she is anyway attending to something that would have been among her reasons had she known it. Those possibilities *cast a light* by making a difference to what responses would be reasonable. This is the psychological aspect of believing. The logical one is that whether she is *right* in believing something depends only on what possibilities obtain.

My aim in this book is to explore how this account illuminates various aspects of believing. I will try to say what makes believing distinctive as a mental state. I will discuss its ontology. I will consider whether it is a form of representing. I will discuss how belief states are individuated. I will explore some of the objective and subjective limits of belief. I will consider when a person is responsible for believing something. And I will discuss how goodness fits into believing, when believing something is to a person's credit, and when she ought to believe something. But I am also going to take a lot for granted. I will take for granted the idea of an agent for whom it is sometimes up to her whether, how, and when to exercise her capacities and manifest her dispositions. I will also take for granted the notion of a reason and of some fact's being a reason for someone to do, think, or feel something. I see my account of belief as contributing to a systematic and complete story of what it is to be such an agent. But it is only one part of such a story.

How does this account extend to non-human animals like cats and dogs? As I suggested in Section 1.1, I consider cats and dogs to be agents, some of whose responses are up to them. It is up to my cat whether, how, and when to jump onto my lap when I call. Cats and dogs have a variety of capacities and have rich emotional states and dispositions. Some of these are the same as ours and some are different. I see no reason to think they do not know facts about their surroundings, even if it is sometimes hard for us to know just which facts they are responding to. When my cat hears the food drop into her bowl, she runs to the corner because that is where the food is. I see no reason to deny that she is running in light of a certain fact she knows. And so I see no reason to deny that she knows where her food is. Cats and dogs can communicate with each other, but they don't have our linguistic or reflective capacities. We can reflect on ourselves and our own nature in ways that they cannot. This makes a difference, not just because it extends the range of facts we can know, but because it allows us to imagine and then realize new ways for us to be. Self-reflection extends who and what we can be, and not just what we can know. I return to some of this in later chapters. My point here is that this is a difference in our reflective capacities, not a difference in whether we are agents who are able to do, think, and feel things in light of certain possibilities. It does not, it seems to me, show that cats and dogs are not believers.

I think of my view as naturalistic. This may be surprising, since I deny that belief states are causes and that belief properties are causal qualities. But nothing in these denials is incompatible with naturalism. My arguments turn on general ontological considerations that are not restricted to mental phenomena. I argued that belief states have no causal powers, but that the same is true of the rock's weighing 200 kilograms. I argued that belief properties are not causal qualities, but that the same is true of having a certain spatial location. Those claims about mass and spatial locations are not incompatible with naturalism. The distinctions I drew between capacities, dispositions, potentials, and opportunities can be accepted by everyone.

Moreover, none of the elements in my view pose an obstacle to a theorist aiming to *explain* how believers came to be. I have no objection to such an explanatory project. I too would like to better understand the natural emergence of beings who can be right or wrong about how things are. Such a project would need to explain the emergence of agents some of whose responses are sometimes up to them. Nothing in my view of believing is incompatible with the success of such a project. But no such project can succeed unless we understand clearly what it is for a person to be right or wrong. My work aims to contribute to an understanding of what that naturalizing theorist aims to naturalize.

While I view my account as naturalistic, I concede that my approach is philosophical. I'd like to think that it involves attending carefully to ordinary distinctions, following the logic only where it leads, treating distinct questions and topics separately, resisting the urge to overstate and exaggerate, and generally keeping an open mind. But no doubt I am the product of my training as much as anyone, and I am sure that I bring to this work biases that are both substantive and methodological. My views here are in response almost wholly to work by other philosophers. I say nothing about important work in many empirical sciences, including the cognitive sciences, developmental psychology, and comparative ethology.[18] My views and methods may disappoint someone with interests grounded in these more empirical disciplines. But I think my approach is recognizably philosophical and that it is a worthwhile way to go about trying to understand some of what makes human life distinctive and interesting.

---

[18] An excellent source for information on animal cognition is Andrews (2015).

2
The Ontology of Believing

In this chapter, I want to get clearer on the ontology of believing. On my view, to believe something is to be in a certain state and this, in turn, is to have a certain property. But there are different sorts of properties, and this matters to the ontology of belief. I will argue that belief properties are qualities, not sortals. That is, they are like the properties of being tall or of being rich and unlike those of being a chair or being human. Seeing this helps us avoid hypostasizing believing, treating a belief state as an object in its own right. Avoiding this is of fundamental importance, it seems to me. It matters to whether believing is representational, to whether belief states are causes, to the nature of inference, and to the ethics of belief. I will return to this fact about belief properties again and again in what follows. The main aim of this chapter is to develop this ontological point and to indicate its significance.

The tendency to hypostasize believing has different roots.[1] It is encouraged by ambiguities in our talk about our beliefs, and I will identify some of these below. But it also has deep roots in philosophical thinking about the mental. I have in mind a combination of ideas from the 17th and 18th centuries. One is a rationalist idea that our minds are better known than our bodies and surroundings, and the other is an empiricist idea that the "contents" of our minds are all items—ideas or impressions—in a stream of consciousness. Together these views encourage the thought that our beliefs are entities in the same ontological category as hearts and lungs only made out of consciousness. Even Russell was attracted to this, saying that each of us is immediately aware of the "events which happen in our minds," and this awareness is the "source of all of our knowledge of mental things" (Russell 1912, 27). This combination of views was a prime target of Ryle's *The Concept of Mind*, though his alternative was a dispositionalism that I argued in Chapter 1 we should resist. A better alternative, I suggest, is that believing is being positioned in a certain way among ways things are or could have been. It is a believer who is in such a position, not some part of her stream of consciousness or of her brain, and being in such a position is not an entity of any sort. In this sense, my view may be an extreme form of externalism about believing, at least when seen in contrast to that early-modern view.

---

[1] Richard Floyd (2017) contains an excellent discussion of these roots. I thank a reviewer for drawing my attention to Floyd's book.

On Believing: Being Right in a World of Possibilities. David Hunter, Oxford University Press. © David Hunter 2022.
DOI: 10.1093/oso/9780192859549.003.0003

PROPOSITIONS, POSSIBILITIES, BELIEF STATES   37

I will start, in Section 2.1, by distinguishing belief properties from propositions and possibilities and from belief states. In Section 2.2, I will argue that belief properties are qualities and not sortals and I'll develop an analogy between believing and owning. In Section 2.3, I will consider whether a person's believing something is realized by states of her brain or nervous system. I won't take a stand on this, but I'll argue that even if they are this would not entail that belief states are entities. My view that believing is a state contrasts with two others. One is that believing is an act or activity, and the other is that it is a relation. I'll consider those in Sections 2.4 and 2.5.

2.1 Propositions, Possibilities, Belief States, and Belief Properties

Let's start with a familiar quartet. Suppose that Jones believes that the 504 streetcar stops at Garden Avenue. We thus have the following.

1. The proposition that the 504 stops at Garden
2. The possibility that the 504 stops at Garden
3. Jones' believing that the 504 stops at Garden
4. The property of believing that the 504 stops at Garden

Eventually, I will add more items to this list. But these four will do for now.

The first item denoted on the list is a proposition.[2] I will assume that a proposition is an abstract entity that is true or false, or that anyway *can* be true or false, and that has truth conditions essentially. There are competing accounts of their nature.[3] Some hold that propositions exist independently of us while others claim that they come into existence through our thought and talk. Some take propositions to be sentence-like while others claim they are unstructured. And while most take propositions to be objects, some have recently argued that they are acts or act types.[4] These differences won't matter for my purposes. The key idea is that a proposition is something that is by its very nature true or false.

The second item on the list is a possibility. As I said in Chapter 1, I take possibilities to be properties of things. My table is not clean, but it could have been. Its being clean is a possibility for it. It is a possibility that does not obtain,

---

[2] To simplify my presentation I am going to ignore the fact that which proposition a sentence can be used to state varies depending on the context of its use. I have explored this in other work, in connection with belief attribution. On my view believing is not an essentially linguistic matter and does not require having a language. I don't think my criticisms of the propositional view depend on this simplification.

[3] For a recent sampling of views, see Rattan & Hunter (2013) and Moltmann &Textor (2017) and (King, Soames, & Speaks, 2014).

[4] This idea is defended by Soames (2010) and Hanks (2013).

38 THE ONTOLOGY OF BELIEVING

though it remains a possibility for it, since it may be clean tomorrow. I won't offer a general account of what makes something possible for a thing, and I will try to rely only on uncontroversial examples of what is possible. But I will say a little more in Chapter 3 about the ontology of possibilities, when I argue that possibilities are the objects of belief, and again in Chapter 5, where I consider some of the limits of belief. As it happens, the 504 streetcar does stop at Garden, so the second item on my list is a possibility that obtains. The 504 does not however stop at Wright Avenue, though it would have stopped there had city planners made a different decision. So that is a possibility that does not obtain, but could have. As I see it, possibilities and facts are close cousins. Borrowing something that J.L. Austin once said about facts, I take it that possibilities are "genuinely-in-the-world" (Austin 1979, 104). One can think of a fact as a possibility that obtains, or as the obtaining of a possibility. But what matters for now is that possibilities are not in any sense representations. They are not true or false, and they don't have semantic properties. As I see it, that is how possibilities and propositions differ.

I will call the third item on the list, Jones' believing that the 504 stops at Garden, a *belief state*. This is a terminological recommendation. As we will see in a moment, some use "belief state" to refer to what I will call belief properties. One might instead call this third item a *belief state of affairs*, but this is a mouthful. I would be happy to call it a *belief fact*, but some use "fact" as a word for a true proposition.[5] I don't think anything hangs on this terminology, so long as we don't confuse items like 1 and 3. The grounds for distinguishing them are clear. They belong in different ontological categories: 1 is an object but 3 is not. Moreover, the proposition that the 504 stops at Garden would have existed even if Jones had not believed it, and indeed, even if Jones had never been born. Perhaps propositions would not have existed if there had been no believers, but even so, someone other than Jones might have believed that the 504 stops at Garden, ensuring that proposition's existence. So, 3 has different existence conditions from 1 (and from 2) and this is grounds enough to distinguish them.

We also need to distinguish 3 from 4.

4. The property of believing that the 504 stops at Garden

I take it that 4 is a property that a person can have—that of believing that the 504 stops at Garden.[6] I'll call this a *belief property*. This, too, is a terminological proposal. One might instead call it a *belief state*.[7] This usage makes some sense,

---

[5] For discussion of these options, see Jonathan Bennett (1988).

[6] Irad Kimhi (2018) denies this. On his view, belief ascriptions do not ascribe properties. His reasoning is that while (i) the objects of belief are propositions, (ii) propositions are facts, and (iii) facts can't stand in relations. It seems to me, though, that Kimhi is assuming (iv) that belief ascriptions ascribe properties only if believing is a relation. In the final section of this chapter, I argue against (iv).

[7] See, for instance, Steward (1997).

since it is natural to say that many people can be in the state of believing that the 504 stops at Garden. But we can capture this equally well by saying that many people can have the property of believing that the 504 stops at Garden. And I want to reserve "state of belief" for a slightly different idea, which I explain below. So I will stick with calling 4 a belief property.

The grounds for distinguishing 4 from 3 are fairly clear. 4 is a certain property while 3 is a fact that consists in someone's having that property. It is the same difference as that between the property of being tall and the fact that Jones is tall. We should also distinguish 4 from 1. They belong to different ontological categories, since 1 is an object while 4 is a property. Many people can have or exemplify that property, but no one can have or exemplify that proposition.

As I said, I will eventually add some items to my list. But these are enough to help us settle two further questions about the ontology of believing. One concerns the sort of property that belief properties are. This is connected to whether belief states are the sorts of things that can be counted. The other question concerns their location.

2.2 Belief Properties, Sortals, and Qualities

To believe something, I take it, is to have a belief property. But there are different kinds of properties and these differences matter for an account of believing. Some properties are sortals and others are qualities. I will argue that belief properties are qualities.

Let's start by distinguishing sortals and qualities.[8] The property of being a chair is a sortal and that of being tall is a quality. On the traditional view, a thing's sortal properties differ from its qualities in three respects. First, its sortals contribute to its essence, making it the sort of thing it is. While it is (arguably) essential to a chair that it be a chair, it is not essential that it be tall, since we could shorten it. Second, a thing's sortal properties individuate it and distinguish it from other things. This is connected to both counting and to plurals. We can count the chairs in a room, and we can distinguish one chair from another, but we cannot count the talls in the room. We can count the tall chairs, or the tall cupboards, or the tall people, but this is done by counting the chairs, cupboards, and people who have the quality of being tall. To count, we need a sortal. As is often noted, we cannot

---

[8] The distinction between sortals and other kinds of properties rose to attention in discussion of identity, essence, and reference in Strawson (1959), Geach (1962), Quine (1960), and Wiggins (1967). For discussion of this history and of the relevance of the distinction between sortals and other properties, see Feldman (1973). Eric Marcus highlighted its relevance to the ontology of belief and other mental states, in Marcus (2006, 2009); views similarly opposed to the idea of a "token" belief are in Kenny (1989), Baker (1995), and Steward (1997). More recently, Richard Floyd (2017) has argued at length against the reification of belief, though his arguments do not start from a distinction between sortals and qualities.

40   THE ONTOLOGY OF BELIEVING

even count the tall *things* or tall *objects* since, on most views, the property of being a thing and that of being an object are not sortals, since there is no way to count the things or objects in, say, a room, and those properties don't determine existence conditions. What I mean is that (and this is the third difference between sortals and qualities), a thing's sortal properties determine what changes a thing of that sort can survive, and so how to re-identify it through changes. In knowing that a thing is a chair we know something about what it takes for it to continue in existence, what sorts of changes it can survive. But we know nothing about this merely in knowing that it is tall (or that it is an object). Again, we need a sortal—we need to know whether the thing is a tall person or a tall building. Likewise, we can sensibly ask whether some chair in the room now is the very same chair that was in the room earlier, but it makes little sense to ask whether the tallness of the chair now is the very same tallness it had earlier. A thing's size might change over time, and we can even imagine a chair's being tall in the morning, becoming short at lunch, and then becoming tall again in the afternoon. But it would make little sense to ask whether its morning tallness was the same or a different tallness from its afternoon tallness. As a slogan to capture these three respects in which sortals and qualities differ, we might say that while a quality is instantiated *in* a particular individual, the instantiation of a sortal *is* a particular individual.

The difference between sortals and other properties is reflected in language. We have seen that one linguistic clue to whether a property is a sortal is that the term for it takes a plural. We have "chairs" but not "talls." Another difference is that the negation of a sortal predicate is not itself a sortal predicate. So while "is a cat" denotes a sortal, "is not a cat" does not, since the property it denotes has none of the three features characteristic of a sortal. Knowing that something is not a cat tells us nothing about what sorts of changes it can survive. By contrast, the negation of a quality predicate is a quality predicate. For instance, "is tall" and "is not tall" both denote qualities instantiated in individuals. Strawson offered the following more general linguistic characterization of the distinction between sortal properties (or "universals") and what he called "characterizing universals."

> Roughly, and with reservations, certain common nouns for particulars introduce sortal universals, while verbs and adjectives applicable to particulars introduce characterizing universals.   (Strawson 1959, 168)

What he says makes sense of common nouns like "chair," "cat," "proton," "galaxy," and so on. And it is right that adjectives like "is tall" and "is short" are qualities. The same is true of physical terms like "weighs 150 kilograms," "is moving at 10 kilometers per hour," and "is positively charged." Those terms and phrases all denote qualities. But Strawson might have exaggerated a bit in suggesting that all verbs denote qualities. Some do, like those for mass and movement. But causal verbs, like "burn," "cut," "tear," and "bite" seem to denote properties that are sortal-like, since we can count and distinguish the burnings, cuttings, tearings, and bitings in a room, and since in knowing that an action is a tearing we know something about when it starts and ends. This is no doubt connected to the fact that actions are events and events are countable and have starts and ends. But we won't need to sort all of this out.

Some psychological properties, such as being happy and being angry, are qualities. We can't count a person's states of happiness, even if she is happy about both her job and her marriage. Anthony Kenny drew attention to this by noting that it is a mistake to ask how many senses of humor Oliver Cromwell had. But it is not a mistake in counting. It is not that, as a contingent matter, Cromwell only had one sense of humor, whereas someone else might have five or twenty-seven. The mistake is in thinking that having a sense of humor is a sortal property instead of a quality. In this sense, it is a category mistake (Kenny 1989, 72). It is worth noting that ability properties are also not sortals. We can count the people in a room who are able to speak Portuguese or who can play piano. But there is no such thing as counting the *havings* of those abilities. If there were, then it would make sense to ask whether Marco's ability to speak Portuguese is the very one he had yesterday, whether perhaps his ability has been replaced from one moment to the next without our noticing, and whether he has three abilities to speak Portuguese. This point about abilities is important because, on one standard view anyway, to believe something is to have a certain ability.

Let's turn now to belief properties. If the property of believing that the 504 stops at Garden were a sortal, then it should make sense to count instantiations of it.[9] That is, we should be able to count *believings*. But, perhaps unsurprisingly, the idea of counting believings is odd. Jones believes that the 504 stops at Garden. How many believings by her of this are there? It is tempting to say just one. But is this just a contingent matter? Could she in fact have two believings of it, in the way she has two lungs? She might have two reasons for believing it, but would this generate two believings? It seems to me not to make much sense to ask how many believings of it by her there are. This is like asking how many senses of humor Oliver Cromwell has. Nor does it make much sense to ask whether her believing of it now is numerically identical to her believing of it five minutes ago, or whether an evil demon might be replacing one believing of it with another every few minutes. But if belief properties were sortals, then these questions would make sense. It should make sense to ask if Jones has two or three believings that the 504 stops at Garden and whether her believing it now is numerically the same as her

---

[9] The property of being water and the property of being gold are not sortals, since we cannot count the golds or the waters. Gold and water are stuffs, and while we cannot count them, we can measure them, and this distinguishes them from qualities. There can be more or less water or gold, but not more or less red or more tallness. Here again, believing is not a stuff, since there cannot be more or less believing that the 504 stops at Garden.

believing it five minutes ago. We should able to count and distinguish those believings. That we cannot suggests that belief properties are not sortals.

That belief properties are not sortals can be hard to see. One reason is that there *are* things we can count when we ask how many beliefs a person has. We can do this by counting the propositions that would be true if she were right (or the possibilities that would then obtain). Since the proposition that the 504 stops at Garden is distinct from the proposition that it stops at Fern, we can say that Jones believes at least two things. So we *can* count the things a person believes, and this can make it seem easy to count their believings of them. What is more, as the Oxford English Dictionary notes, the word "belief" is ambiguous. It can be used to refer both to a certain sort of mental state and to *what* someone believes. This makes it easy to slide from counting beliefs, in the sense of the things a person believes, to counting their believings.

I find an analogy with ownership helpful here. For questions about the individuation of ownership states and about their survival through time are not as easily answered as questions about the individuation and survival of chairs and tables. Suppose Sarah owns twenty books. She thus has at least 20 possessions. But how many possessings by her are there? Two answers suggest themselves. Perhaps there is one possessing for each book, and so twenty possessings. Alternately, perhaps there is one possessing of twenty books. How are we supposed to decide? Suppose that, in her case, it is one owning of twenty books. Could her brother own the very same books but have twenty ownings instead? What might account for that difference? It seems to me that nothing in our ordinary understanding of ownership helps us answer these questions. And it is not that we are ignorant of some fact about ownership whose discovery could settle the matter.

Now consider ownership states through time. We know how to answer the question whether the copy of *War and Peace* that Sarah owns today is the same as the one she owned yesterday. In knowing what a book is we know something about how to tell when a book at one time is the same as a book at another. We can imagine what it would be for someone to replace one copy with another. But none of this is straightforward if we ask about ownership states. Is Sarah's owning *War and Peace* the very same owning as yesterday, or has it perhaps been subtly replaced by someone? Of course, she might own the book twice, once as a teen and again as a retiree. But should we then say she was in a single ownership state twice or distinct ownership states? Our ordinary understanding of ownership, in contrast to our understanding of such sortal properties as being a chair and being a bicycle, does not yield easy answers to these questions. This is not to deny that Sarah can own thousands of things. It is only to deny that owning thousands of things involves being in thousands of states of ownership. What we need to resist is the urge to think there need be an answer to the question how many ownings by her there are. The property of ownership is not the right sort of property to yield an answer.

I find this analogy between believing and owning helpful in part because both believing and owning involve objects. Indeed, both belief properties and ownership properties are individuated by an object. I will have more to say about the individuation of belief in the next chapter. But notice that while we have the familiar ambiguity in "belief" between believing and what is believed, there is no analogous ambiguity with ownership. There is no word in English that can mean both the thing owned and the owning of it. We have "possession" for the thing owned, and this naturally takes a plural. The word "possessing" can be used for the act of taking or keeping possession of something. But there is no form of "possessing" or "owning" that is used for the state one is in when one owns something and that takes a plural. That is why there is no ambiguity in "possession" as there is in the case of "belief." And this, it seems to me, is instructive. We should think of believing the way we do of owning. Belief properties, like ownership properties, may be individuated by an instantiation of a sortal property, but they are not themselves sortal properties.

I have been relying on an analogy between owning and believing. Ownership properties and belief properties are alike in being qualities. And they are alike in being individuated by an object. I think we can see things about the nature of believing by attending to these logical similarities. I'll return to this analogy a few more times. But there are also differences. Ownership is at least in part a legal matter dependent on contingent decisions and practices of a community. It is not just that it is a contingent matter what some person owns, for it is also a contingent matter what some person believes. And it is not just that what a person owns depends on facts about her social environment, for I agree with Burge (1978) that what a person believes also depends on such facts. The difference I have in mind between owning and believing is that facts about ownership seem somehow to be a *result* of our decisions and practices. People own the things they do because of decisions people made. I do not think that believing is dependent in this way on our decisions or practices. Indeed, I think believing and knowing must predate such decisions and practices. So I recognize that there are important differences between believing and owning. But the logical similarities are, I think, instructive.

In saying that knowledge and belief must predate social practices and decisions I don't mean to deny that social practices and decisions can affect the *status* of someone's belief and knowledge. It is one thing for a person to know some fact and another for others to recognize that they do. As Miranda Fricker (2009) argues, one form of injustice involves a failure to acknowledge that someone else knows something. Such failures can flow from, and in turn perpetuate, racial and social biases and prejudices. We can be mistaken about whether someone knows a fact and this mistake can be both wrong and harmful. As Dale Turner (2006) argues, recognizing this is especially important in countries like Canada that are working towards reconciliation with Indigenous peoples and their historically devalued knowledge and epistemic practices. Accepting all of this is compatible

44 THE ONTOLOGY OF BELIEVING

with insisting that facts about whether a person believes something are not a result of our practices and decisions in the way facts about ownership are.

It might be tempting to think that some future discovery could show us how to answer questions about the individuation and survival of belief states. In particular, it might seem that a discovery about human neurology might shed light on this. Couldn't we learn that when a person's beliefs change there is an observable change in the states or activity of some set of neurons? I don't doubt that such a discovery is possible. And nothing on my account of belief conflicts with the idea that our believing what we do has something to do with our having the neural systems we do. As I said in Chapter 1, I take it that believers are agents, some of whose responses are up to them, and it seems to me that our being such agents is a natural biological fact about us. But I don't see how a neurological discovery could settle the questions I raised about the individuation and persistence of belief states. Think again about ownership. It seems plausible that the fact that Sarah owns a book has something to do with her neurons. But should we expect that a future discovery in neurology might tell us whether Sarah has one state of owning twenty books or twenty states of owning a single book? This does not seem likely to me. Nor, it seems to me, does it seem likely that a future discovery in neurology will reveal that Jones is in one state of believing many things or many states of believing one thing. Accepting that belief properties are qualities poses no threat to investigating the neurological basis of cognition and the mind. But unless we understand what believing itself involves we can't understand what that basis is a basis for.

It will be important in what follows to keep in mind this difference between sortals and qualities. For the tendency to hypostasize beliefs—to put them in the same ontological category as lungs and hearts and chairs—seems to come naturally in philosophy. Such tendencies can be hard to spot, and even harder to block. It is now fairly common, for instance, for philosophers to speak of belief "tokens." This leads naturally to the idea that belief states can be true or false, can be causes, can be things we consider and manipulate, and can be the bearers of various normative properties. In chapters to come, I will resist these ideas, and suggest that they make it harder for us to appreciate the nature of believing.

2.3 Belief States and Realizers

When Jones believes that the 504 stops at Garden, where is her belief state located? If we keep our eye on the fact that belief properties are qualities, we will find it plausible to say that belief states are not the sort of thing that have locations. Cromwell's sense of humor does not have one either, and neither does his height or weight. A person can be in a belief state, but the belief state itself is not in anything. But some philosophers, and especially those who are happy to talk about belief tokens, say that a person's beliefs are located in her head. David Armstrong, for instance, famously said that the concept of a belief state is the concept of an *internal* state that is apt to have certain causes and certain effects (Armstrong 1981, 23). Belief states, he said, are inside people's brains. To sort this out, we need to separate two claims.

Some say that a person's beliefs are *realized* by states of her brain. The notion of mental realization is a technical one and the details won't matter for my purposes, so I will make some simplifying assumptions. I will assume that realization is a relation between states, so the idea is that a belief state is realized by a brain state. And I will assume that a brain state consists in some part of a brain (or maybe an entire brain) having a certain property. In the case of Jones' belief, let's call the relevant part of her brain, "B," and let's call the property in question, "being N." The idea, then, is that 3 is realized by 3_B.

3. Jones' believing that the 504 stops at Garden

3_B. B's being N

We now face two questions. The substantive one is whether 3 *is* in fact realized by 3B. The terminological one is whether, if it is, we should call 3 or 3B the belief state.

I won't try to settle the substantive question here.[10] The rough idea is that it is, in some sense, in virtue of B's having the property of being N that Jones has the property of believing that the 504 stops at Garden. Spelling out this sense is an ongoing research project. Much also depends on what property N is. It is not the property of believing that the 504 stops at Garden, since no brain or brain part has that property. It is also not the property of being an organ of someone who believes that the 504 stops at Garden, for although Jones' brain has that property, so does her heart. I take it that N is meant to be a property that is not a belief property and that only a brain could have. But it need not be a narrowly neurological property. It might be a property that a brain has only if something outside the brain has some other property. That is, it might be that neurologically identical brain or brain parts can differ in whether they have N. This supervenience idea is thus compatible with what some call the externalism of mental states.

I said that the idea that 3 is realized by 3B is attractive if one thinks that belief states are causes. But this is not essential. Anthony Kenny (1989) holds that belief states are not causes but he agrees that there must be some neural "vehicle" for a person's mental states. As Kenny sees it, to believe something is to have a certain sort of ability, and he rejects Armstrong's view that beliefs are causes. Still, he thinks this is compatible with there being some brain state that realizes that ability, just as there is some brain state that realizes Sarah's ability to play the piano. As I said, all of this is the subject of current study and I won't take a stand on it here.

---

[10] I develop the idea that beliefs are states a person is in and not states inside a person in Hunter (2001).

46 THE ONTOLOGY OF BELIEVING

My interest, here anyway, is in a second question. Suppose that there *is* a 3_B that realizes 3. Should we say that 3_B is Jones' belief state? If we do, then since her brain is inside her, we could then say that her believing is inside her, or anyway that it is a state of something that is inside her. But we don't need to speak this way. We could instead say that 3 is the belief state, and that 3_B realizes it. We would then say that the believing is a state that Jones, the person, is in and is not a state of something inside her. I don't think it matters much which way we speak, though the second way is closer to our ordinary way of talking. Since it remains an open question whether there is a 3_B that realizes 3, I will adopt the second way of speaking.

I won't take a stand on whether a person's believing something is realized by a state of her brain. But that claim says more than just that a person's internal states are relevant to her believing what she does. A believer is alive and her internal states are surely relevant to this. The claim that an internal state realizes a person's believing something is the stronger claim that there is a natural correlation between believing something and some state of an internal part of the believer. This is an empirical matter that we should leave to scientists. I am persuaded, though, by the externalist arguments Putnam (1975) gave about linguistic meaning and that Burge (1979) extended to psychological states that physiologically identical people might mean and believe different things if their environments are different. But I do reject a concessive externalism that says that internal realizers have semantic and causal properties, not in virtue of their intrinsic states, but in virtue of relations they contingently bear to facts in her social and natural environments. I reject this, not because I reject the internal realizers, but because I deny that believing is a representational or causal state. Believing is a matter of being in a certain position relative to how things in one's environment are and could have been. That position is not a representation of that environment and it does not cause the believer to do, think, or feel things. Perhaps this makes my view a more radical form of Externalism.

2.4 Believing Is Not an Action or Activity

I have said that to believe something is to be in a certain sort of mental or psychological state. But some have said that to believe something is to be performing a mental *act* of assenting, judging or affirming. And others have said that to believe something is to bear a cognitive *relation* to it. Both views are meant to capture important aspects of believing, but I think these features can be better captured by the state view. I will consider the act view in this section and the relation view in the next.

Matt Boyle and Pamela Hieronymi have independently articulated versions of the act view. They suggest that only it can acknowledge the distinctive sort of agency a person has with respect to their beliefs. This agency, they say, is reflected

BELIEVING IS NOT AN ACTION OR ACTIVITY 47

in the responsibility we have for our beliefs and for the fact that we know in a special way what we believe. Here is how Boyle describes the responsibility characteristic of believing.

> We expect . . . subjects, not merely to hold various beliefs, but to be cognizant of what beliefs they hold; and we expect then, nor merely to have their beliefs regulated by the presence or absence of grounds, but to be able themselves to discuss the grounds, to be able themselves to discuss the grounds on which they hold the beliefs they do . . . . We do not merely suppose that cognitively mature human beings can, in the normal case, give expert testimony on what they believe and why. We treat them as in some sense *in charge* of what they believe and why, not merely specially knowledgeable about these topics.   (Boyle 2009, 122–3)

One idea here is that believing involves self-knowledge. If Jones believes that the 504 streetcar stops at Garden Avenue, then she knows that she believes it. What is more, Jones knows something about *why* she believes it, at least in the sense that if we ask her why she believes it, she will be ready with an answer. A second idea is that believing involves self-determination. People are able to make up their own minds and are held to account when they do and are expected to change their minds when doing so is called for. We are, as Boyle puts it, in some important sense, in charge of the fact that we believe what we do. One main task facing a theory of epistemic responsibility is to flesh out what this being-in-charge comes to.

Boyle and Hieronymi claim that we cannot understand epistemic responsibility if we think of believing as a mental state. Instead, they suggest, we need to think of it as a special sort of act or an activity, one that is not intentional or voluntary. According to Boyle, "belief (i)s an enduring, non-occurrent act of assenting to a proposition" (Boyle 2009, 142, n. 31). Hieronymi suggests that "believing is an activity done for reasons, though not something that can be completed or finished" (Hieronymi 2009, 174). I find much to value in their positive proposals about mental responsibility. But I think their diagnosis of the problem they are responding to has not been radical enough. Contemporary philosophy of mind has made epistemic responsibility seem mysterious, not because it has overlooked the ways that believing is like an action, but because its standard conception of mental states leaves no room for the subjects of belief. To understand mental responsibility we need to bring the believer back into focus, by showing the errors in the standard story about the metaphysics of believing. That's my aim in this chapter and the next two. I will discuss self-knowledge in Chapter 6, our responsibility for believing in Chapter 7, and the norms of believing in Chapter 8.

The state view of belief can allow that there acts of judging or affirming or assenting, and neither Boyle nor Hieronymi deny this. Indeed, on a traditional

48   THE ONTOLOGY OF BELIEVING

view, acts of judgment cause or bring about beliefs. Boyle quotes the following passage from Shoemaker.

> [B]elieving something—having the standing belief that so and so is the case—is not an act. Judging, thought of as a mental occurrence rather than a standing state, *is* an act.   (Shoemaker 2009, 36; italics in original)

Boyle and Hieronymi aim to challenge this contrast between acts of judgment and states of belief. On their view, believing is itself a sort of act or activity.[11]

From a purely linguistic point of view, it might seem that believing is unlike being in a state. Compare believing something with being generous.

Jones is generous.

Jones believes that the 504 stops at Garden.

Being generous is not something a person does, but believing is. Being generous or being six feet tall is something we are or can be, but believing is something we do. People do it, some think that cats and dogs do it, and everyone agrees that trees and rocks don't do it. You cannot *do* being generous, nor can you *do* solubility, being six feet tall, or being late for an appointment. The fact that believing is something we do is reflected in the linguistic fact that "to believe" is a transitive verb. So it might seem, on its linguistic face anyway, that believing is more like an act or an activity than like a state.

To see why believing is a state, it is helpful to compare it to events of various kinds. There are different ways to categorize events, and it won't matter too much for our purposes which we adopt. Mourelatos (1978) distinguishes activities (as in "Jones was riding the streetcar"), accomplishments (as in "Jones was riding the streetcar to Dundas West Station"), and achievements (as in "Jones arrived at Dundas West Station"). Believing is like each of these in some ways, but also unlike them in others. In the end, though, I think we should agree with Ryle and Armstrong that believing is a state.

Let's start with accomplishments.

Jones believed that the 504 stops at Garden.

Jones was riding the streetcar to Dundas West Station.

---

[11] Ernest Sosa develops a similar view. "Belief is a kind of performance, which attains one level of success if it is true (or accurate), a second level if it is competent (or adroit), and a third if its truth manifests the believer's competence (or it is apt.)" (Sosa 2011, 1) Mathew Chrisman (2016) suggests that Sosa's view is best understood as that the *formation* of a belief is a sort of performance that can be assessed at these three levels.

One difference between believing and an accomplishment is that, unlike believing, an accomplishment takes time. Jones' riding to Dundas West Station might have taken twenty minutes, but his believing did not take any time, though it might have lasted for twenty minutes. It takes time to accomplish something, but it takes no time to believe something, and not because believing is an instantaneous accomplishment. It is not an accomplishment at all. In this respect, believing is like the state of being six feet tall, which takes no time, but can last for some time.

Another difference between believing and an accomplishment is that accomplishments are either completed or unfinished. Jones either completed (hence, "accomplishment") his ride to Dundas West Station or he did not. But believing is not something we can finish doing or leave incomplete. Jones cannot complete his believing that the 504 stops at Garden, and nor can he stop halfway through. When a person believes something his believing it is, as it were, complete at each moment that he believed it. In this respect too, believing is like being six feet tall, which is not something one can complete or leave undone. If one is six feet tall for ten years, then one is fully six feet tall at each moment in those ten years. So in this respect, too, believing something is unlike an accomplishment and like a state.

Let's next consider achievements.

Jones believed that the 504 stops at Garden.

Jones arrived at Dundas West Station.

As this example suggests, the completion of an accomplishment is an achievement. Jones' arriving at Dundas West Station is the completion of his riding the streetcar to Dundas West Station. But not all achievements are completions. Starting an accomplishment is also an achievement. Jones' starting to ride the streetcar to Dundas West Station is one. And maybe there are achievements that are neither starts nor completions of accomplishments. Now, unlike accomplishments, achievements take no time. This can be hard to notice, since we *can* ask how long it took for his achievement to occur, but here we are asking how long it took for the accomplishment to complete, not how long its completion itself took. This point is easiest to see if we ask how long his starting the ride lasted: it lasted no time. Achievements are, as it were, instantaneous. In this respect, believing is unlike an achievement, since believing, like being six feet tall, can last for some time, whereas an achievement cannot.

Finally, consider activities.

Jones believed that the 504 stops at Garden.

Jones was riding the streetcar.

50 THE ONTOLOGY OF BELIEVING

Unlike accomplishments, activities can be neither completed nor left unfinished. It makes no sense to ask whether Jones ever finished his activity of riding the streetcar. When we ask someone engaged in an activity whether she is done or finished, we are asking whether she is about to stop the activity, not whether she has completed it. Nor does it make sense to ask how long his riding the streetcar took. It might have *lasted* twenty minutes, but it did not *take* twenty minutes. In these two respects, believing is like an activity. For, as we have seen, believing cannot be completed or unfinished and does not take any time, though it can last for some time. As we have also seen, the same is true for being six feet tall: it can be neither completed nor unfinished and it takes no time. So an activity is like a state in these respects.

But an activity is unlike a state in another respect. Activities can be in process, whereas states cannot.

Jones is riding the streetcar.
*Jones is being six feet tall.

Throughout the time that Jones was riding the streetcar, he was in the process of riding it. But Jones was never in the process of being six feet tall or of being generous. This reflects, perhaps, the fact that being six feet tall and being generous are not things one can do, and so are not things one can be in the *process* of doing. Believing is like a state in this respect.

*Jones was believing that the 504 stops at Garden.
One cannot be in the process of believing something.

It is tempting to say that the fundamental difference between an activity and a state is that one is active while engaging in an activity, but not while being in a state. This is fine, so long as we note two qualifications. One is that being active is not the same as being in motion. One can be in the process of standing still or of imagining a soccer match, but neither activity involves motion. A second qualification is that a person can be the patient of an activity, such as aging or being rained on. It is closer to the truth, perhaps, to say that being the agent of an activity in process involves control whereas being in a state does not. Still, it is not perfectly clear what it is for a person to be in control while doing something, but it is clear enough anyway that standing still requires control and so does imagining a soccer match. But it takes no control to be six feet tall, and even if *remaining* generous takes control, simply *being* generous does not. So engaging in an activity requires agential control while being in a state does not.

Mark Richard says that to "believe that there is snow in the street is to represent the state of affairs that there is snow in the street, with the representation playing a certain role in one's cognitive economy" (Richard 2013, 704). This formulation suggests both that believing is (i) an act of representing or (ii) a representation. If what I have said is right, the first suggestion must be wrong. I take it that to represent, say, the 504 as stopping at Garden is an act that one can do intentionally and voluntarily. Asserting that the 504 stops there is one way to do it. Drawing a complete and accurate map of Toronto's transit system is another. But believing that the 504 stops there is not an act of representing. I suspect that Richard really has in mind the second suggestion, that believing is a representation. If this means that believing is a state that is true or false, then I will argue against it in Chapter 3.

I have been arguing that believing is not an action or activity. Recently, some have argued that propositions are acts. Scott Soames considers them to be "purely representational cognitive acts or operations" (Soames 2013, 481). Peter Hanks develops a similar view. And both hold that the primary bearers of truth and falsity are not propositions at all, but rather particular acts. Here is how Hanks puts the idea.

> [T]he primary bearers of truth-conditions are actions that subjects perform in thinking and speaking about the world. More specifically, they are acts of predication, in which, in the simplest cases, subjects attribute properties and relations to objects. Someone performs an act of predication when she judges that a is F or when she asserts that a is F. These actions are the proper source of truth conditions. Propositions are types of these actions, and they owe their truth-conditions to them.   (Hanks 2013, 559; for a similar statement by Soames, see Soames 2015)

On this view, propositions are act-types, and they inherit their truth-conditional properties from their tokens. Their accounts of the nature of propositions are rich and interesting, but the details won't matter for my purposes.[12]

Soames does not argue that acts can be true, aside from a general argument that his account of propositions provides a better explanation of intentionality than its alternatives. Hanks does acknowledge that some consider it a category mistake, but counters that the "mere fact that we have the adverbs 'truly' and 'falsely' in our language shows that we recognize properties of truth and falsity that apply to actions" (Hanks 2013, 561). This consideration is, I think, inconclusive. Hanks is right that we can say that Jones truly asserted that the 504 stops at Garden. And he may be right that the adverb "truly" modifies the asserting. But what is the modification? Is it that the asserting was true or that the asserting was *of* a truth? Both options modify the act, but Hanks needs it to be the former to support his view that acts themselves are true. The latter strikes me as equally plausible.

---

[12] For discussion, see the articles collected in Rattan & Hunter (2013) and (King, Soames, & Speaks (2014).

52   THE ONTOLOGY OF BELIEVING

And think of a comparison case: "Jones accurately painted a portrait of Sarah." Here, I think, it is the portrait that is accurate, not the act of painting it. The act might be good in various ways, it might be careful and delicate, but it cannot be accurate (or inaccurate). Likewise, what Jones asserted might be true, but his asserting it, or so it seems to me, is not the right sort of thing to be true or false.

Let me summarize. Believing is like an activity in that it is something we do. But it is more like a state in several respects: it can last for a time; cannot be completed; cannot be in process; and can be neither voluntary nor intentional. For these reasons, believing is best considered to be a state, and not an act or an activity. But I agree that believing is tied to agency in a way that other states are not. The image of believing something as being in a certain position can help us locate this tie and so can the analogy with being in a spatial location. There is nothing essentially active about, say, being in London. People can be in London, but so can rocks and pebbles. Unlike rocks and pebbles, Jones is an agent some of whose responses are up to her. This means that when she is in London she is in a certain position from which she can exercise her capacities and manifest her dispositions, and being in that position can make a difference to what she is likely to do. One disanalogy between believing and being in a spatial location is that only an agent some of whose responses are up to her can believe something. But this difference is traceable, not to believing itself, but to being a thing some of whose responses are up to her. It is not the believing that is active; it is the believer.

2.5 Believing Is Not a Relation

Some hold that to believe something is to bear a certain cognitive relation to the belief's object. Since the standard view is that the object of belief is a proposition, the standard version of this idea is that believing is a relation to a proposition. For Jones to believe that the 504 stops at Garden is for her to stand in a "cognitively real" relation to that proposition.[13] I think we should resist this idea.

I will first explain why the standard arguments offered in support of it are unpersuasive and how we can reject it without adopting an instrumentalist view of the objects of belief. I will then show that believing differs in important ways from paradigmatic examples of relations. While this won't prove that believing is not a relation, it will I think shift the burden onto someone who claims that it is. In Section 2.6, I will consider an idea that often accompanies the idea that believing is

---

[13] This is the dominant view, by far. Fodor (1978) offers the classic case for the relational view. But it is denied by some, notably Davidson (1991), Dennett (1987a), Churchland (1979), Field (2001), and Stalnaker (1984). The first four denied it partly because they denied the existence of propositions. Stalnaker accepts that there are propositions but denies that believing is a relation in favor of what he calls a pragmatic conception of belief. For arguments against the relational view that draw on ordinary-language considerations, see White (1972), Rundle (2001), and Hacker (2004).

a relation, namely that believing requires grasping or understanding its object. I think we should accept this, but, as I will argue, it does not support the idea that believing is a relation. To grasp or understand the object of a belief, I will suggest, is to know how things would be if a certain possibility obtained, and to know this is to be in a certain cognitive state. Knowing is no more a relation than is believing.

But we need to start by clarifying the idea of a relation. The idea that believing something is standing in a relation to a proposition is meant to contrast with the idea that believing something is having a certain monadic property, but this contrast is elusive. This makes it hard to draw a sharp distinction between the state view and the relation view. It might be, at the end of the day, that the question of whether believing is a relation is merely terminological. Still, the added idea that believing is a *cognitive* relation is not meant to be terminological, and so it is worth trying to get clear on the issues.

I will assume that there is a real distinction between monadic properties and relations. Some cases are clear. I will assume that *being next to* is a relation and not a monadic property. One thing might bear that relation to another, but there is no such thing as an object's simply *being next to*, for there is no such property. In contrast, *being round* is a monadic property and not a relation. A thing might be round and its being round is not a matter of its standing in a relation to some other thing. So, some cases are clear.

But what about *being a father*? On one hand, it looks like a monadic property since, as with *being round*, we can correctly say of a thing that it is a father without referring to anything else. But it also looks like a relation, since one is a father only if one stands in a certain relation—*being a father of*—to something else. So is it a property or a relation? Perhaps we should say that *being a father* is a "relational property"; it is a monadic property that an object has (only) in virtue of standing in some relation to something. I take it that if believing something is a property, then it is a relational one, for it is hard to see how a person could believe something without bearing *some* relation to *something*.[14] So one initial clarification I want to make is that I will take the idea that believing is a relation to be that believing is a genuine relation like *being next to* and not just a relational property, like *being a parent*.

One more clarification is needed. It concerns the things that the relation idea claims are related by the believing relation. On one side of the relation would be believers like Jones, you, and me. But what is on the other side of the relation? On the propositional version of the idea, it would be propositions on the other side. Propositions are objects, and so the right sort of entity to be on that other side. But what about possibilities? On my view, possibilities are the objects of belief, in the sense that belief properties are individuated by possibilities. But I am going to suggest (in Chapter 3) that possibilities are properties, and not objects. They are

---

[14] The classic arguments for this are in Putnam (1975) and Burge (1979).

54 THE ONTOLOGY OF BELIEVING

properties of actual things. Jones is not a lawyer but she could have been. The fact that she could have been consists in her having the property of having possibly been a lawyer. It is a property I have too. What kind of property? It seems to me that possibilities are qualities, not sortals. Possibilities are not things or stuffs. Rather, they are properties of things and stuffs. In this respect, talks of possibilities is like talk of beliefs, and I think that we should resist hypostasizing possibilities for the very same reasons that we should resist hypostasizing beliefs. If we do, then I think the relation idea will seem much less plausible, since it won't be clear there is an object fit to be on the other side of the alleged believing relation. Still, these reflections assume a controversial view about modality and about the metaphysics of properties. And I think it is anyway worth pursuing the question whether believing is a relation to a proposition.

Here is how Jerry Fodor puts the idea that believing is a relation.

> Propositional attitudes should be analyzed as relations. In particular, the verb in a sentence like 'John believes it's raining' expresses a relation between John and something else, and a token of that sentence is true iff John stands in the belief-relation to that thing. Equivalently, for these purposes, 'it's raining' is a term in 'John believes it's raining'.   (Fodor 1978, 502)

Fodor denies that believing is a relation to a proposition, holding instead that it is a relation to a representation inside the believer's brain, but this won't matter for my purposes, as my target is the idea that to believe something is to bear a certain relation to some other entity (520). Fodor offers three reasons to accept the relation idea, though he admits that none is conclusive.

Fodor's first reason turns on the surface grammar of sentences like this.

Jones believes that the 504 stops at Garden.

The idea that believing is a relation is, Fodor says,

> [I]ntuitively plausible. 'believes' *looks* like a two-place relation, and it would be nice if our theory of belief permitted us to save the appearances.   (502, emphasis added)

It is true that "to believe" is a verb and that it looks like a term for a relation. It has a place for a subject term and another for an object term. But, as many have noted, this surface appearance does not show that believing is a relation.[15] This point is

---

[15] See the references in footnote 13.

often made by considering the verb "weigh," which also looks like it expresses a relation, in this case between a person and a number.

Jones weighs 75 kilograms.

But this sentence states that Jones has a certain property and not that he bears a relation to a certain number. Indeed, the property of having a certain mass is an intrinsic property and not even a relational one. The verb "weighs" in this sentence functions as a *relational predicate,* and the complex phrase "weighs 75 kilograms" names an intrinsic property, and it does this by reference to a number. Fodor's opponents held that we ascribe belief states to people in the same sort of way. Though believing something is not an intrinsic property of a person, we use a complex phrase to identify the belief state by reference to an abstract object, a number in the case of mass, and a proposition in the case of belief. So the fact that "to believe" functions grammatically as a relational predicate does not show that it refers to a relation.

Fodor's second reason for accepting the relation idea—which, to be fair, he calls but a "straw in the wind"—is that it can explain the fact that from:

Jones believes that the 504 stops at Garden.

we can validly infer:

There is something that Jones believes.

It is true that relations allow for this sort of valid existential generalization.

Jones is next to Sarah.
There is something Jones is next to.

So, perhaps grounding valid existential generalization is necessary for relations. But Fodor needs it to be sufficient, not merely necessary. And it is not obvious that existential generalization is valid only when relations obtain. For the following inference is also valid, even though weighing 75 kilograms is not a relation.

Jones weighs 75 kilograms, so there is something that Jones weighs.

So, Fodor's second reason for thinking that believing is a relation is also unpersuasive.

Fodor's third reason is that "the only known alternative to the view that verbs of propositional attitude express relations is that they are (semantically) 'fused' with

56 THE ONTOLOGY OF BELIEVING

their objects, and that view would seem to be hopeless" (503). According to the fusion view, phrases like "believes that the 504 stops at Garden" have no internal logical or grammatical structure that might help explain how it refers to a certain state of belief. I agree that such a view is implausible. Surely any plausible account of the semantics of that phrase will see its meaning as partly a function of the meanings of its parts. But one can reject the idea that believing is a relation without adopting the fusion view. In the mass case, one can say that which intrinsic property the phrase "weighs 75 kilograms" picks out is in part a function of the meanings of the phrase's parts, and that, in the belief case, the non-intrinsic property picked out by the phrase "believes that the 504 stops at Garden" is in part a function of the meanings of that phrase's parts.

Some who have denied that believing is a relation on the basis of this comparison with mass properties have further held that the objects of belief play only an instrumental role in belief ascriptions. The idea is that while we may refer to a number in order to identify an object's mass, that number is not itself essential to the identity of that physical property. Rather, numbers are part of a framework that is useful for identifying and distinguishing physical properties but different such frameworks would serve equally well. The property identified by the phrase "weighs 75 kilograms" has nothing essentially to do with the number 75, for it is also identified by the phrase "weighs 165.347 pounds." Indeed, so long as we adjust the units, *any* number could be used to identify that same mass. In this sense, reference to numbers in ascribing physical properties is merely a convenience.

Donald Davidson suggests that the same is true when we say what someone believes.

> The entities that we mention to help specify a state of mind do not have to play any psychological or epistemological role for the person in that state, just as numbers play no physical role. (Davidson 1991, 205–6)

The view that reference to an object plays only an instrumental and dispensable role in belief ascriptions is called the Measurement Theory of Mind.[16] I won't consider whether such an instrumentalist view is right in the case of such physical properties as mass. But I think we ought to reject it for the case of mental states. For it seems to me that belief states are individuated by their objects. That is, if O1 is the object of Simon's belief and 02 is the object is Jane's belief, then Simon and Jane are in the same belief just in case 01 = 02. We have no other systematic way to identify or distinguish among different belief states other than in terms of their object. And unlike with mass, we cannot adjust units of measurement. It is essential to the state of believing that the 504 stops at Garden that it has the

---

[16] See Mathews (2007).

object it does. This is so whether the object of belief is a proposition, as the standard view maintains, or a possibility as I maintain. So denying the relation idea does not force one to hold that the objects of belief play only an instrumental and possibly dispensable role in our psychological theories.

In the end, then, the arguments Fodor offers for the idea that believing is a relation are unpersuasive. Of course, this does not show that believing is *not* a relation between a person and a proposition. Fodor's considerations all turned on the properties of belief sentences, but a different approach would be to see whether believing something has features that are common to relations. Anthony Kenny identified several characteristics that he argued relations generally share. He then argued that actions are not relations because they lack those characteristics.[17] I won't consider whether Kenny is right about actions. But it is interesting to note that believing lacks three of the characteristics he says are common to relations. For simplicity, I will assume that the object of belief is a proposition, though everything I say will apply equally to possibilities.

Relations are reversible. When two things stand in a relation, it is (in general) possible for the relation to have been reversed. This is clear in the case of symmetric relations, such as *being next to* and *being as smart as*.

a. Jones is next to Smith.
b. Smith is next to Jones.

If a is true, then not only is it possible that b could have been true, b must be true, for the relation by its nature runs both ways. But asymmetric relations are generally reversible too.

c. Jones is to the left of Smith.
d. Jones is smarter than Smith.

If these are true, then the following are false, but only contingently so.

c'. Smith is to the left of Jones.
d'. Smith is smarter than Jones.

Smith could have been to the left of or been smarter than Jones. These examples illustrate the general rule that relations are reversible.

There are exceptions to this reversibility rule. In some cases, when a relation obtains its reverse not only fails to obtain, but could not have obtained. Here is an example.

---

[17] Kenny (1963); see also Hyman (2015).

58 THE ONTOLOGY OF BELIEVING

e.   Jones is a parent of Jane.

e'   Jane is a parent of Jones.

If e is true, then e' is not just false, it is impossible. No child could have been her parent's parent. But in this case, the nature of the relation itself explains the failure of reversibility. It is in the very nature of being a parent that if it holds between two individuals, then it could not have been reversed. We could say that *being the parent of* is by its nature irreversible. In general, when a relation fails to be reversible this failure is explainable by the nature of the relation itself. Notice, too, that even if e' is necessarily false, it remains a grammatically fine sentence. What I mean is that we could make it mean something true simply by changing the referents of the proper names to other things of the same category (in this case, people) while leaving the meaning of the remaining parts alone.

Compare now the case of believing.

f.   Jones believes that the 504 stops at Garden.

f'.   That the 504 stops at Garden believes Jones.

If "believes" were a relation, then it would plainly be asymmetric, since f is true but f' is not. But it is not just that f' is contingently false. It is either nonsense or else necessarily false. No proposition can believe anything. And notice that the case here is importantly unlike the exceptional case involving e and e'. For even if Jane cannot be Jones' parent, because she is Jones' child, she is nonetheless the right sort of thing to be Jones' parent. But propositions are not the right sort of thing to be believers. We might say that f' is trivially false because of this category mistake. What is more, Jones is not the right sort of thing to be believed. (She can be trusted, and so in this sense can be believed, but this is not the sense of "believe" at issue in f.) So f' is necessarily false because it involves a category error at both ends: it has the wrong sort of thing in both its subject and object positions.

Relations have a fixed number of terms. Some relations are between two terms (e.g., *being smarter than*), some between three terms (e.g., *being half-way between .... and....*), and etc. It is essential to a relation what number of terms it relates. No relation could in some cases hold between three things and in other cases hold between four things. Relations thus have a "fixed polyadicity." This is reflected grammatically in the fact that removing a term from a sentence stating that a relation obtains yields nonsense.

Jones is next to Sarah.

Jones is halfway between London and Oxford.

*Jones is next to.

*Jones is halfway between London (and).

By comparison, dropping the noun-clause from a propositional attitude report does not yield non-sense.

Jones believes that the 504 stops at Garden.
Jones believes.
Jones hopes that it will rain tomorrow.
Jones hopes.

The results might even be true. To be sure, we get nonsense if we drop the subject term:

Jones believes that the 504 stops at Garden.
*Believes that the 504 stops at Garden.

But with a paradigm relation we get nonsense when either term is dropped. If "believes" named a relation in the way that "is next to" does, then we'd expect it to have a fixed polyadicity that is reflected grammatically. But it does not.

Complements do not modify relations. We can add a complement clause to a sentence that states that a relation obtains.

a.   Jones is next to Smith.
b.   Jones is next to Smith in the garden.
c.   Jones is next to Smith with a knife.

In general, adding the complement clause does not modify the relation being ascribed. That is, the relation between Jones and Smith said to obtain in b and c is the very same relation said to obtain in a. In each case, it is the relation, *being next to*. The reason for this is that there is no such relation as *being next in the garden to* or *being next to with a knife*. If there were, then the following sentences ought to make sense, but they do not.

*Jones is next in the garden to Smith.
*Jones is next with a knife to Smith.

So the complement clauses in b and c do not modify or characterize the relation that is said to obtain between Jones and Smith. In the first case, rather, it specifies where the relation obtains; it thus modifies the obtaining of a relation, that is, it modifies a fact. In the second case, it modifies Jones. It tells us that he has a knife. This is true of all relations. Adding a complement clause to a sentence stating a relation can modify one or all of the relata or can specify temporal, spatial, or

60   THE ONTOLOGY OF BELIEVING

other facts about the obtaining of the relation. But it does not tell us more about the relation itself.

By contrast, consider the following.

Jones believes that the 504 stops at Garden without good evidence.

In this sentence, the complement modifies the believing. It tells us that the believing is not based on good evidence. This is clearer, perhaps, if we make the complement a prefix.

Without good evidence, Jones believes that the 504 stops at Garden.

And it is very clear if we put the complement inside the sentence.

Jones believes without good evidence that the 504 stops at Garden.

This complement informs us about Jones' state. As we saw above, in the case of paradigm relation sentences, complement clauses cannot be placed in the middle like this.

In these three respects, the verb "believes" does not look like a paradigm relation. It is not reversible, has no fixed polyadicity, and admits modification. As I noted, however, there are exceptions to these rules, and one might insist that believing is an exceptional sort of relation. Still, the onus is on one who insists that believing is a relation. For the alternative, that sentences like the following ascribe properties to believers, does not entail that "believes" is exceptional in any way.

Jones believes that the 504 stops at Garden.

So, it seems to me, we don't need to accept the idea that believing is a relation.

2.6 Believing and Understanding

The idea that believing is a relation is often accompanied by a second idea, namely that believing requires grasping or understanding the belief's object. Gurpreet Rattan, who accepts this second idea, adds that grasping or understanding is a "cognitively real relation" to a proposition (Rattan 2016, 4).[18] I think we ought to accept this second idea, but it does not entail that grasping is a cognitive *relation*.

---

[18] Rattan is opposing the Measurement Theory of Mind, arguing that it cannot explain the normativity of belief or the perspectival character of intentional explanation. I return to these in later chapters.

It is, rather, a cognitive state: to grasp or understand P is (putting it roughly for now) to know what it would be for P to obtain, and to know this is to be in a certain state.

We should start by noting that the idea that believing involves grasping its object does not entail that believing is a relation. Suppose that believing does involve grasping and, further, that grasping is a real cognitive relation to the object of the belief. It would still not follow that believing is also a relation to that object. All that would follow is that believing is a *relational property*: one a person can have only by bearing the grasping relation to the object of the belief. So even if, as Rattan claims, one needs to bear a real cognitive relation to an object in order for it to be the object of one's belief, it would still not follow that believing is also a relation.

But in any event, we should resist the idea that grasping the object of a belief is a relation. The reasons I gave above for thinking that believing is not a relation apply equally well to grasping. Here again, I will assume for convenience that the object of a belief is a proposition. Unlike paradigmatic relations, grasping is not reversible.

Jones grasps the proposition that the 504 stops at Garden.
*The proposition that the 504 stops at Garden grasps Jones.

It lacks fixed polyadicity.

Jones grasps the proposition that the 504 stops at Garden.
Jones grasps.

And it admits modification.

Jones incompletely grasps the proposition that the 504 stops at Garden.

In these three respects, grasping is unlike paradigmatic relations. It seems to me, then, that we can resist the view that grasping a proposition is itself a cognitive relation to a proposition.

But we can nonetheless say that grasping the object of a belief is something *cognitive*. It seems to me that believing something requires grasping or understanding a certain possibility. To believe that the 504 stops at Garden, for instance, requires understanding what it would be for the 504 to stop at Garden. It requires, in other words, knowing what it would be for a certain possibility to obtain.

This can be accepted by one who holds that the object of belief is a proposition. For on a traditional idea, grasping a *proposition* requires knowing its truth conditions. On this view, to understand a proposition one must know a way

62 THE ONTOLOGY OF BELIEVING

that things might be, a certain possibility. The idea is sometimes put picturesquely: to grasp a proposition is to know the distinction it draws in a space of possible worlds. It is tempting to generalize this idea as follows.[19] *To grasp the object of belief is to know how things would be if it were true.* But the semantic ascent here is misleading. It suggests that understanding a proposition is a matter of knowing, *with respect to that proposition*, that it has certain truth conditions. In terms of the picturesque idea, the suggestion is that to grasp a proposition is to know, of it, that it draws a certain distinction among possibilities that one might know independently, as if one could know the possibilities in the space without knowing that a certain proposition draws a distinction among them. But this is misleading because knowing those possibilities *just is* knowing the distinctions among them. And, at least according to the traditional idea, knowing such a distinction *just is* grasping a proposition. This point is clear, I think, if we focus on particular cases. To grasp the proposition that Jones loves Mary is to know what it would be for Jones to love Mary. It is to know what possibility that is. Someone who does not know what it would be for Jones to love Mary does not grasp or understand the proposition that Jones loves Mary. These object-level formulations avoid the impression left by semantic ascent that grasping a proposition is knowing something *about* that proposition.

What I have said points to an important connection between believing and knowing. In fact, there are two connections. First, believing that P requires being able to know whether P. This is because believing a proposition requires knowing what it would be for it to be true, and this in turn requires being able to know whether it is true. One can of course have a capacity to know whether P without in fact knowing whether P. I can have an ability to know whether Caesar shaved the day he crossed the Rubicon, even if I won't ever know whether he did. I can even believe he did without knowing whether he did. But I cannot believe that he did without being able to know whether he did. Insisting that believing cannot outstrip our capacity for knowing may be a form of Verificationism, but it would be a modest form, since it places no restrictions on what we can believe. Indeed, it allows for omniscient beings, so long as what they believe cannot outstrip what they can know. This is the first point.

The second point is that believing that P is *characteristically* a product of a capacity to know whether P. That is, believing that P is one of the characteristic results of an investigation into whether P. Of course, our cognitive capacities are fallible. Someone who tries to figure out whether the 504 stops at Garden may end up undecided, or believing it without really knowing it, or, if she is really unlucky,

---

[19] The objects of belief are always general in a way I will sketch in Chapter 5. Each possibility has many potential witnesses. Grasping a possibility requires knowing something about this variety. Charles Travis has argued that this knowing is a form of conceptual understanding, and he argues that this marks a fundamental difference between believing and perceiving. For discussion of this, see Travis (2014).

believing that it does not. This second point is not that believing that P results only from a *successful* exercise of a capacity to know whether P. Nor is it that believing that P can only results from an exercise of that capacity—there may be other ways to generate that belief. The idea, rather, is that it is in the nature of believing that P that it is a *characteristic* result of the exercise of a capacity to come to know whether P.

This chapter has been about the ontology of believing. I suggested that to believe something is to have a belief property and I argued that belief properties are qualities and not sortals. Seeing this helps us to avoid hypostasizing belief states, treating them as if they were entities in their own right. In this respect, believing something is like owning something. I argued that this view of the ontology of belief is compatible with the idea that belief states are realized by states of the brain, but I took no stand on this idea. I then argued that believing is neither an action nor a relation. I ended the chapter by accepting the idea that believing requires knowing how things would be if one were right, but that this knowledge is also not a relation. In the next two chapters I will argue that believing is not a form of representing. I will first suggest, in Chapter 4, that belief properties are individuated by possibilities and not by propositions. In Chapter 5, I will argue that belief states are neither true nor false. Seeing all of this will, I hope, flesh out the idea that believing is being in a certain position among the ways things are or could have been, and not a matter of representing them.

3
The Objects of Believing

On my view, a person is right or wrong in believing something depending on whether a certain possibility obtains. But believing is not representing. In believing something, one does not represent the world. Nor does believing involve a representation. I'll argue for this in two steps. In this chapter, I'll argue that the objects of belief are possibilities, just as the objects of knowledge are facts. I will call this the *modal view* of believing.[1] It is meant to contrast with a *propositional view*, according to which the objects of belief are things that are by their very nature true or false.[2] In Chapter 4, I will then argue that belief states and properties are neither true nor false. I don't deny that there is a close connection between belief and truth. When a person believes something, she is right or wrong depending on how things are, but this does not entail that believing is a form of representing. The image I offered at the end of the introduction, of believing as being positioned in a world of possibilities, is meant to suggest an alternative. Believing, like knowing, is a way of being at home in the world, in position to have the ways things are or could have been throw light on one's actions, thoughts, and feelings.

The idea that believing is representing has deep roots in philosophy. It is encouraged by a combination of ideas I mentioned at the start of Chapter 2. One is a rationalist idea that our minds are better known than our bodies or our surroundings and the other is an empiricist idea that the "contents" of our minds are all elements in a stream of consciousness. This combination encourages treating beliefs as like entities of a certain sort, and I argued against this in Chapter 2. But it also encourages thinking of beliefs as like pictures or

---

[1] Many philosophers have espoused something like the modal view of the objects of belief. It has roots in Wittgenstein's *Tractatus Logico-Philosophicus*, though he never developed it. In Wittgenstein 1958, 35–40) he rejected the idea of an intermediary—a "shadow" between an expression of a mental state and the facts. Moore reports that Wittgenstein also rejected the idea of a "shadow" lying between a person's belief and the fact (if any) that "verifies it" (Moore 1954, 13). But Wittgenstein's primary concern is arguably with linguistic representation, not with believing. Ruth Barcan Marcus sketched a version of the modal view (Marcus 1993), and it is similar in some respects to the Situation Semantics of Barwise and Perry (1999). More recently, Mark Richard (2013) has defended it. And, of course, it is similar in some respects to the idea that propositions are sets of possibilities, as developed by Stalnaker (1984).

[2] Alan White (1972) and Bede Rundle (2001) offer ordinary-language critiques of the propositional view, though they don't consider the modal view. In their critiques they argue that believing is not an attitude to an object of any sort, but I think what they have in mind is that believing is not a relation. I agree and discussed this in chapter 2. But whether believing is a relation to an object is independent of how belief properties are individuated. On my view, belief properties are individuated by possibilities even though believing is not a relation to a possibility.

On Believing: Being Right in a World of Possibilities. David Hunter, Oxford University Press. © David Hunter 2022.
DOI: 10.1093/oso/9780192859549.003.0004

representations, and this is a persistent view in analytic philosophy. Many contemporary philosophers in the analytic tradition who might insist they reject those two early modern ideas still take beliefs to be representations. (See, for instance, the quote from Bermúdez in Chapter 2.) Some of them take language to be essential to belief, or at least to our human form of believing, and think of believing as like inner asserting. It is of course true that language extends our cognitive reach. We use it when we step back and reflect on ourselves and our place in the world. This self-reflection extends what we are able to believe and know and it is hard to imagine doing it without linguistic or representational means. But this does not show that believing is itself a form of representing. For one thing, representing is an action or activity and can be done intentionally, whereas believing and knowing are states and cannot be intentional. More importantly, we can use language to reflect on ourselves only if we already know something about its representational features. This sort of self-reflection using language thus presupposes that we know and believe things and so cannot be a precondition for our knowledge or belief.

In this chapter, I'll develop the modal view of the objects of belief and sketch some of its virtues. I'll start, in Section 3.1, by contrasting the modal and propositional views and by getting clearer on where they disagree. In Section 3.2, I will consider familiar puzzle cases that many think doom the modal view from the very start. These cases are standardly taken to show that there are more belief properties than there are possibilities, but I will argue that the cases do not show this. In Section 3.3, I will further clarify the modal view by contrasting believing with certainty, probability, and agnosticism. In Section 3.4, I'll argue that the modal view can account as well as the propositional view for the fact that objects of belief can be objects of speech acts and for the way they are about things in the world. In Section 3.5, I'll suggest that a primary virtue of the modal view is how it fits natural accounts of knowledge and inquiry. The propositional view can be made to fit but, I argue in Section 3.6, the fit is comparatively poor. The modal view has largely been neglected and in Section 3.7 I will sketch its history. I'll end, in Section 3.8, by considering Mark Richard's recent view that beliefs are representational in a thin sense.

3.1 Individuating Belief Properties

The idea that the objects of belief are possibilities is meant to contrast with the view that they are propositions, things that are by their very nature representations. By the objects of belief, I have in mind what grammarians call the "accusative." When Jones believes that the 504 stops at Garden, the grammatical accusative of her belief is *that the 504 stops at Garden*. The modal and representational views disagree about what sort of entity it is. We need to get a bit clearer on what this disagreement is about.

66 THE OBJECTS OF BELIEVING

One thing that obscures the disagreement is the fact that some have used "proposition" as a name for *whatever* the grammatical objects of belief turn out to be. (e.g., Richard 2013) On this usage, it is just a terminological fact that propositions are the objects of belief. If so, and if I am right that possibilities are the objects of belief, then it would be a mistake to think that propositions are true or false. But I take it to be a substantive question whether the objects of belief are representations or not. Since this is the question I am interested in, I will continue to assume that propositions are by their very nature representational, and so capable of being either true or false.

The disagreement is also obscured by the separate question whether believing is a cognitive relation between a person and the object believed. Believing is commonly said to be a "propositional attitude" and this certainly suggests the relational view. In Chapter 2, I cast doubt on the standard arguments offered in support of the relational view and offered some reasons against it. But I also suggested that there may be little more than a terminological matter here, one that needs to be settled by decision. And, in any event, the question whether believing is a relation is independent of the question whether the object of belief (and so one of the terms related) is a possibility or a proposition. My interest in this chapter is on this latter question.

More specifically, my interest is in how belief properties are individuated. I will take it that all sides accept the following.

INDIVIDUATION: Believing O1 = believing O2 if and only if O1 = O2.

The idea is that there is no difference in belief properties without a difference in the object. In this respect, belief properties are like mass properties.

Weighing N kg = weighing M kg if and only if N = M.

There is, according to INDIVIDUATION, nothing more to distinguish two belief properties than a difference in their object, just as there is nothing more to distinguish two mass properties than a difference in their numerical value. In Chapter 2, I distinguished belief properties from what I called belief states. A belief state consists in a person's having some belief property. The following is a belief state.

Jones' believing that the 504 stops at Garden

I take it that this belief state is individuated by two things: Jones and the property of believing that the 504 stops at Garden. So, more generally, I take it we should accept the following.

S1's believing that O1 = S2's believing that O2 if and only if S1= S2 and O1 = O2.

There is, as I see it, nothing more to the fact that a person believes something than the identity of that person and of the relevant belief property.[3]

As I said, the modal and propositional views disagree about what individuates belief properties. It is worth reminding ourselves how propositions and possibilities differ. A proposition is an abstract object that has truth conditions essentially. It is either true or false, or at least is capable of being either true or false. There are different accounts of their nature, but I don't think these differences will matter much for my purposes. What is important is that propositions are essentially representational: they are capable of being either true or false.[4]

What is a possibility? I am inclined to think that possibilities are properties of the actual world or of actual things. Jones is not a lawyer but she could have been. Her being a lawyer is a possibility for her, though one that does not obtain. It is also an unrealized possibility for me, too. What kind of property is a possibility? It seems to me that possibilities are qualities, not sortals. The instantiation of a possibility is not itself a thing or a stuff. Rather, possibilities are properties that are instantiated in things and stuffs. In this respect, talk of possibilities is like talk of beliefs, and I am inclined to think that hypostasizing possibilities is as risky as hypostasizing beliefs.[5] But I don't think this will matter for what follows, so I will take the risk and speak as if possibilities were entities.

Some philosophers appeal to sets of possibilities to help model similarities, differences, and relations among propositions. Every proposition determines a set of possibilities: those that would obtain were the proposition true. The following determine different sets of possibilities.

The proposition that the 504 stops at Garden

The proposition that the 504 stops at Fern.

This difference in the possibilities they determine is part of what makes these distinct propositions. Most theorists think an adequate modeling of propositions will need more than just sets of possibilities. As they see it, propositions are individuated more finely than possibilities. If there is more than one necessarily true proposition, then the differences between them cannot be modeled by sets of

---

[3] John Perry (1979) rejects this. As he sees it, two people can be in the *same* belief state even though they have different belief properties. This more complicated view is needed, he says, to make sense of the puzzle cases I will discuss in Section 3.2. Since I think these cases do not constitute an objection to the modal view, I won't consider Perry's view.

[4] Jeff Speaks argues that propositions have truth conditions but are not representational (Speaks 2014). What matters for my purposes is that, unlike propositions, possibilities do not have truth conditions, and so can be neither true nor false.

[5] As I understand it, Irad Kimhi (2018) holds that propositions are facts, and that facts are not objects, and he concludes that propositions cannot be objects of thought. I suspect he would also say that possibilities are not objects and so would likewise insist that they cannot be objects of thought and belief. But it would not follow that propositions and possibilities cannot individuate belief properties. And this is my interest here.

68 THE OBJECTS OF BELIEVING

possibilities, since all necessarily true propositions determine the same set. The same is true if there is more than one necessarily false proposition, or if distinct contingent propositions can determine the same set of possibilities. Maybe, for instance, there are essentially first-personal propositions that are equivalent to ones that are essentially impersonal. Some have suggested that propositions are best modeled, not by a simple set of possibilities, but by a set of possibilities each of which is assigned a probability value.[6] These *probability spaces* are better, they say, for modeling propositions about how probable something is given a body of evidence. To motivate these more complicated models these theorists point to the sorts of puzzle cases I will discuss in the next section. I agree that modal beliefs, beliefs about how likely something is, pose a challenge for an account of believing. I am confident a modal view can help us understand these cases, and I will say something about them in the Section 3.3, though I won't offer a full defense of this claim here.

But here is an important point worth stressing. Even if I am wrong that the objects of belief are possibilities, it would not follow that they are propositions. Even if there are more belief properties than there are possibilities, we would still need an argument for the propositional view, since alternatives would need to be ruled out. For instance, a slightly modified modal view might hold that the objects of belief are complex entities consisting of a possibility and something else. Maybe when Jones believes something that she would put by saying "I am here now," the object of her belief is neither a proposition nor a possibility but is instead a complex entity consisting of a possibility, a person, a time, and a place. I am not endorsing such a modified view. In fact, I think the simple modal view has all the resources we need to understand cases of first-person belief. My present point is simply that even if I am wrong about this, an independent argument for the propositional view would be needed. We would still need an argument that believing involves representations.

3.2 Pure Cases and the Modal View of Belief

According to many philosophers, there are more belief properties than there are possibilities. If so, then possibilities cannot be the objects of belief, or at least not the only ones. To support this, they point to familiar and puzzling cases of people who are mistaken or confused about which thing is which, or what is what, or who, where, or when they are. These cases are usually taken to be decisive counter-examples to the modal view. In this section, my aims are purely defensive. I will argue that these cases do not show that there are more belief properties than there

---

[6] See Yalcin (2016) and Moss (2018). For more on the nature of propositions, see Merricks (2015). For more on possible worlds, see Divers (2002).

are possibilities. They are not counter-examples to the modal view. I know this part of my view is the most controversial, and might strike many as not just wrong but wrongheaded. I will end this section by offering a concession or two. The main one is that most of what else I say in this work is independent of the idea that the objects of belief are possibilities. The other is that the puzzle cases arise because there are limits to belief and not because of where the modal view locates those limits. So even if the modal view gets those limits wrong, we can't avoid the puzzles just by rejecting it.

Here is what a case would have to be like to show *decisively* that the modal view of the objects of belief is false. It would be one where two people agree on which possibilities obtain and yet differ in what they believe. (Or where one person changes her beliefs without changing her view on which possibilities obtain.) One person would then have a belief property that the other lacks, even though every possibility that is believed to obtain by one is believed to obtain by the other. A case like that would show that there are more belief properties—and hence, more to believe—than the modal view allows. I will call such a case a pure case.

This methodological point should not be controversial. Suppose we wanted to show that size is not just a matter of shape. To do this, we'd find two things that share a shape but not a size. Such a pure case would show decisively that even if everything that has a size has a shape, there is more to size than just shape. Or, again, suppose we wanted to show that there is more to being an ophthalmologist than just being a doctor. We'd look for two doctors, only one of whom is an ophthalmologist. Such a pure case would show decisively that there is more to being an ophthalmologist than just being a doctor. The cases would not have to be real ones, they could be imaginary. But to be decisive, they have to be pure.

It seems to me that the usual cases put forward against the modal view are not pure cases. Let's start with Frege's astronomer. She believes, as she would put it in English, that Hesperus and Phosphorus are different stars or planets. After extensive study, she makes a discovery that she would put in English by saying that Hesperus *is* Phosphorus, after all. This is a familiar kind of story, and it is easy to tell variants of it. I think we can all agree that the discovery involved a change in what she believed. She believed something before the discovery that she does not believe after it. How do we get from this to a conflict with the modal view?

For this to be a pure case, it would have to be one where the astronomer's discovery did not involve a change in belief about which contingent possibilities obtain. But this is not plausible. Before the discovery, the astronomer believed that the names "Hesperus" and "Phosphorus" referred to different entities. After the discovery, she believes that they co-refer. What is more, the discovery changed the astronomer's beliefs about how many stars or planets there are. After the discovery, she thinks there are fewer stars or planets than she thought there were before the discovery. (And she knows she has changed her mind on this.) So the astronomer's discovery did involve a change in belief about which contingent

70 THE OBJECTS OF BELIEVING

possibilities obtain. I don't think anyone can deny this. This is simply part of any plausible telling of the story. But this means it is not a pure case. So it is not a case that can decisively show that the modal view is false.

More evidence that it is not a pure case emerges if we imagine the astronomer's post-discovery reflections. After the discovery, the astronomer might say the following: "I was wrong. But had I been right, that would have explained many of the gravitational observations we made." Set aside whether the astronomer is right about this counterfactual. What is she suggesting in its antecedent? She is not suggesting that the obtaining of a certain *im*possibility would have explained the gravitational observations. An impossibility could not have obtained, so we can't cite its obtaining to explain anything. Here is a more plausible suggestion. Before the discovery, the astronomer believed that a certain general possibility obtained, one whose obtaining required that of a more specific possibility, what we might call its witness. The following illustrate the distinction I have in mind.[7]

(1) The possibility that someone is at the streetcar stop
(2) The possibility that Jones is at the streetcar stop
(3) The possibility that Sarah is at the streetcar stop

For (1) to obtain a possibility like (2) or (3) must also obtain. There cannot be someone at the streetcar stops unless a particular person is there. In this sense, the obtaining of (2) or of (3) would be a witness for the obtaining of (1). That is what I mean in saying that (1) is more "general" than either (2) or (3). If one believes that (2) obtains, then one also believes that (1) does. One cannot believe that Jones is at the streetcar stop without believing that someone is there. Importantly, though, one can believe that (1) obtains without believing that either (2) or (3) do, since one can believe that someone is there without believing of any particular person that they are that someone. This idea of one possibility being a witness for another can help us understand what the astronomer is suggesting in that post-discovery counterfactual. Before her discovery she believed that a possibility obtained that witnessed a more general one. She might have put that more general one this way: the heavenly body in that location (pointing to where in the evening we see Hesperus) is distinct from the heavenly body in that location (pointing to where in the morning we see Phosphorus). This more general possibility does not obtain, though she believed prior to her discovery that it did. It is contingent that it does not obtain, since (or so I will assume) distinct entities might have been in those locations. What she is suggesting in her post-discovery counterfactual is that had that more general possibility obtained, then the obtaining of its witness would have explained the gravitational observations they made. It is a contingent matter

---

[7] What I say here follows (Stalnaker 2011, 14–19).

whether this general possibility obtains, and she and her colleagues disagreed about it. She believed it did, they believed it did not. After the discovery, she no longer believes that it obtains. The fact that in making her discovery she changed her mind on this contingent matter is still more reason to think that the case is not a pure one. (I will say more in Chapter 5 about the idea that the obtaining of one possibility is a witness for that of another.)

Consider a slight variation on the counterfactual. Suppose that the astronomer said this: "I was wrong. But had Hesperus not been Phosphorus, that would have explained the gravitational observations we made." Again, set aside whether this counterfactual is true, and focus on what the astronomer would be suggesting in the antecedent. Here too, it is not plausible to think she is suggesting that the obtaining of a certain impossibility would have explained the observations. Instead, she would be saying the same thing as in the first counterfactual: if a certain general possibility had obtained, one she believed prior to her discovery did obtain, then its witness would have explained the observations. She is using "had Hesperus not been Phosphorus" to identify, not an impossibility, but a general and contingent possibility. And this is how her colleagues would interpret her.

This might seem like a misleading or unhelpful choice of words if her intention is to identify a general possibility. But her choice actually makes good conversational sense. For there are, as she might put it, many ways that it could have been the case that Hesperus was not Phosphorus. Describing each of them would be very difficult. Indeed, she might not even know enough about the variety to easily characterize all of them. Plausibly, she knows this. (Compare someone who missed a streetcar saying: "Had it arrived on time, I'd have not been late to the meeting." The speaker need not have a specific streetcar in mind; she may merely wish for relief from streetcarlessness.) And she does not intend her counterfactual claim to be restricted to a specific general possibility, but to be open to the wide variety of them. An easy way to respect this openness is to use the phrase "had Hesperus not been Phosphorus" to identify, not a specific general possibility but a *kind* of general possibility, each one of which would have been witnessed by something correctly describable, had it obtained, by "Hesperus is not Phosphorus." I don't mean to say that the speech act here is a simple one, or that the linguistic and conversational facts that make it reasonable are easy to understand. To the contrary: they are surely among the most complex of human actions. But thinking of the speech act in this way shows that the modal view has rich resources to understand and explain the familiar cases.

An important theme in Wittgenstein's work was how sentences that express necessities or impossibilities can play a useful dialectical role. In the right context, saying one can help resolve certain kinds of disagreement and remove certain kinds of confusion. Arguably, this theme runs throughout his career, though only in his later work did he stress that this usefulness amounts to a kind of

72 THE OBJECTS OF BELIEVING

meaningfulness. Whether, as Anscombe insisted, Wittgenstein also held that using such sentences can yield a sort of knowledge—though of facts that one cannot state or even really believe—is another matter.[8] I won't try to decide whether she was right about Wittgenstein. But for my part, I can't share this view. It seems to me that when we use such sentences to help someone overcome a confusion or error (what I will call in Chapter 5 a "credal illusion") the result is not a mystical insight, but rather a mundane alignment with the ways things are or could have been. The image of knowing and believing as like being more or less at home in a world of possibilities is meant to evoke this idea of alignment.

Another case widely considered to be a counter-example to the modal view is John Perry's (1979) case of the shopper. As he tells the story, the shopper is walking through a grocery store following a trail of sugar he believes is spilling out of someone else's cart. After a little while and some reflection, the shopper discovers what he would put by saying that he, himself is the one spilling the sugar. We can all agree that this story involves a change in what the shopper believes. He believes something after the discovery that he did not believe before it. How do we get from this to a conflict with the modal view?

For this to be a pure case, it would have to be one where the shopper's discovery did not involve a change in belief about which contingent possibilities obtain. But this is not plausible. The discovery changed the shopper's beliefs about how many people are in the store. After the discovery, the shopper believes there are fewer people in the store than he thought there were before the discovery. (And he knows he has changed his mind on this.) It is a contingent matter how many people there are in the store. So the shopper's discovery involved a change in belief about which possibilities obtain. I don't think anyone can deny this. It is simply part of any plausible telling of the story. But this means that the case is not pure. And so it is not a counterexample to the modal view.

This case is often taken to show that there is something essentially subjective about believing. Some say that there must be essentially personal belief properties, ones that only a single person can have. I don't deny that there is something essentially personal about each of our states of belief, something that marks off your perspective as your own. But I deny that it involves essentially personal belief properties. The essential subjectivity, as I see it, is not a matter of *what* a person believes. Rather, it concerns what I will call credal necessities. For each of us, there are possibilities that we and we alone must believe obtain. Because these credal necessities are unique to each person, they constitute the essential subjectivity of belief. I discuss this in Chapter 6.

---

[8] My views in this paragraph are influenced by Diamond (2019) and Kremer (2001). Anscombe's discussion of Wittgenstein is in Anscombe (1959). This was also an important theme in the early work of Hilary Putnam; see especially Putnam (1962). I am indebted here to conversations with Charles Travis.

PURE CASES AND THE MODAL VIEW OF BELIEF   73

I'll mention one final puzzling story thought to be a counter-example to the modal view of the objects of belief. 1979) introduced his case of the omniscient Gods in order to craft a pure case against the modal view. We are to imagine two Gods who are omniscient, who know all the contingent matters of fact. They do not differ or disagree about which possibilities obtain. But, Lewis says, we can imagine one of the Gods being or becoming uncertain about which of the two Gods he himself is. As He might put his uncertainty: Am I the one on the tallest mountain or the one on the coldest mountain? This is supposed to be a case where the Gods have different beliefs without differing over which possibilities obtain. So isn't this a pure case against the modal view?

Philosophical scruples differ. I find stories about the cognitive and practical lives of omniscient and omnipotent beings deeply puzzling. I find I lose my grip on what it is for them to believe and act. My sense is that it is more likely that our telling of this story is confused or distorted somehow than that it really shows that the modal view is wrong. I would be more comfortable rejecting the modal view if we could craft a pure case involving astronomers, shoppers, or streetcar drivers. But I have not been able to. So I will stick with the modal view.[9]

I have argued that the familiar puzzling cases are not counter-examples to the modal view of belief. One might reply that I have missed the point of the stories. One might say this: "The astronomer believes, before the discovery, that Hesperus is not Phosphorus. But this is not a possibility, it is an impossibility. And so the fact that the astronomer believes this shows that there *are* more belief properties than there are possibilities. At the very least, we need to allow that impossibilities can be objects of belief too. And this is a problem for the modal view, which says that only possibilities are objects of belief."

While I feel the pull of this reply, I think we should resist the idea that someone can believe an impossibility. It seems to me this would make our account of belief more puzzling, not less.[10] How are we supposed to identify and distinguish impossibilities? How are we supposed to say how a person who believes an impossibility takes things to be? The sentence "Hesperus is not Phosphorus" is not true of anything, so it is not a true description of an impossibility or of a way anyone could take things to be. We should not treat talk of impossibilities as just a straightforward extension of talk of possibilities. Think about making a list of all

---

[9] Benson Mates (1952) drew attention to puzzling sentences with iterated belief operators. Though his primary interest was in synonymy it is tempting to draw from his cases morals about the individuation of belief properties. But the puzzling sentences are complicated and so is the way we use our linguistic resources to ascribe beliefs to others, especially in cases when we think the other is suffering what I will call a credal illusion. I won't consider his cases here, but for discussion, see Burge (1978).

[10] One point to note is that allowing that impossibilities can be objects of belief does not support what I called the propositional view, that the objects of belief are representations. Impossibilities are not representations. So a concessive friend of the modal view might be happy to embrace belief in impossibilities, if her real opponent is the propositional view.

74 THE OBJECTS OF BELIEVING

the objects there are. We know how to add possible objects to the list, those that don't exist but might have, like the younger brother I don't have. But how are we to add impossible ones? There aren't any impossible objects, and there could not have been. Talk of impossible objects is not just a straightforward extension of talk about objects, or even of possible objects. It seems to me that talk of impossibilities is the same.

The point I have tried to make in this section is a small one. It is that the sorts of cases usually put forward to show that there are more belief properties than there are possibilities do not show this. But this standard may seem too high. One might think that the cases anyway *suggest* or *indicate* or provide *some* reason to think that the modal view is mistaken. I don't have an argument against this more moderate criticism. I am not even sure how, at the end of the day, to prove that the modal view is true. But I think it is worth getting as clear as we can on the dialectical situation, especially since it is often taken as a bit of data that the cases show that the modal view is wrong.

More importantly, any account of the individuation of belief will face the sorts of puzzle the modal view faces. Or at least, any account will that takes it to be an objective matter what there is to believe. On any such account, it will be possible for a person to think they believe something when in fact they don't. It is helpful to compare belief to perception. It is an objective matter what there is for a person to see. This means a person can think she sees something when in fact she does not. Such visual illusions are the price one pays for the objectivity of perception. The same is true, I think, of belief. If there are limits to belief, then it will be possible for a person to suffer a credal illusion. The modal view may be wrong about where these limits are located. But because it is clear about where it locates them, it helps us to think clearly about the fact that there are limits and about the illusions they engender. That it helps us to see all of this is not an argument in favor of the modal view. But it is a reason to adopt it if only to help us think about the nature of believing. And, most importantly, we can't avoid the puzzles just by rejecting the modal view, because the puzzles emerge from the fact that there are limits to belief. (I return to this topic in Chapter 5 when I consider credal illusions, and then again in Chapter 7 when I consider valid inference.)

One final point. The claims I develop in this book about how belief states explain, about their ontology, about belief and representation, about the objective and subjective limits to belief, about inference, and about the ethics of belief are all independent of the claims I make about how to individuate belief properties. Whether there are more things to believe than there are possibilities has no bearing, it seems to me, on the underlying nature of belief or on the links between belief, action, and rationality. I am more wedded to those claims than I am to the modal view, though I also think that the modal view is helpful at formulating these claims about belief's underlying nature. I hope you will find those claims worth studying even if you think I am utterly wrong (-headed) about how to individuate

CERTAINTY, PROBABILITY, AND AGNOSTICISM   75

beliefs, even if you think (as most philosophers do) that there is more to believe than there are possibilities.

3.3 Certainty, Probability, and Agnosticism

The modal view says that the objects of belief are possibilities, but I don't mean that when a person believes something she believes that it *is* possible. I mean that she believes that that possibility obtains. To clarify this, it is helpful to consider closely related epistemic phenomena. A person can be more or less certain about something, her belief in it can be more or less strong, she can believe that some possibility is more likely to obtain than another, and she can be undecided about some matter. The connections between believing, on the one hand, and certainty, strength, probability, and indecision, on the other hand, are complicated, and I won't try to sort it all out here. But sketching these connections can help flesh out the modal view.

We can start by noting that while certainty comes in degrees, believing something does not. To believe something is to have a property, and one person cannot have that property more than another, or have more of it than another. A person can be more or less certain about something she believes, and her belief can be stronger or weaker, but she cannot more or less have the property of believing it.[11] A person either has the property or she doesn't.[12]

This is not a special fact about belief properties. It is a surface fact about all properties. No matter what property we consider, one thing cannot have it more than another, or have more of it than another. John can't have the property of being a father more than Simon does. Nor can someone have the property of being PM of Canada more than someone else. One person can, of course, be taller or stronger than another, but this is not because the one has more of the property of being tall or of being strong than the other does. If Jones is six feet tall and Simon is five feet tall, then Jones is taller than Simon. But this does not mean that he has more of the

---

[11] Eric Schwitzgebel (2001) argues that there can be cases of in-between believing, where it is not quite true that a person believes something and not quite true that she does not believe it. I agree that the cases he considers are suggestive, and I discuss some of them in the Appendix. On his view, to believe something is to have enough of a weighted set of dispositional and affective properties. It is a vague matter, he thinks, just how many of them a person needs to have. But he does not, so far as I can see, think that one person can have the property of believing something more than someone else, or have more of that property. (Jones does not have more of the property of being 6'1", or have it more than Simon, just because he is closer to being 6'1" than Simon.) I am inclined to think of Schwitzgebel's cases as revealing the context-dependence of the sentences we use to ascribe belief properties. I discuss that in my 2009b and 2011b, but won't pursue it here.

[12] For more on this, see Moon (2017) and Hacker (2004). What I say in this section is indebted to Moon's discussion. For a recent survey and discussion of the connections between belief, certainty and strength, see Jackson (2018). Jackson argues that believing and being certain are distinct attitudes irreducible one to the other.

76 THE OBJECTS OF BELIEVING

property *being tall* than Simon does. (Jones has more height that Simon; but this is not because Jones has more of the property *height* than Simon does.) The same is true of belief properties. No one can have that property more, or have more of it, than another. So unlike certainty, believing does not come in degrees.

Some say we can measure certainty on a scale from 0 to 1.[13] Sarah's certainty, or "credence," that the 504 stops at Garden might be 0.85 while her credence that she was born in Toronto might be 0.99. Her certainty in the latter is then higher than her certainty in the former. And some say that believing just is sufficient credence: that a belief state is a credence state. I don't think this can be quite right, since certainty comes in degrees and believing does not. But it might be that a person believes something just in case they are sufficiently certain about it. Being in a belief state might, that is, be correlated with having a sufficient level of credence or certainty. Still, theorists disagree both about whether it make sense to measure certainty in this way and about whether belief involves a threshold of certainty. I won't try to settle these issues here.[14]

We should distinguish certainty from the strength of a person's belief. I have in mind how inclined a person is to change her mind. Gopal might believe that the 504 stops at Garden and that it stops at Fern, but he might believe the former more strongly than the latter. And a person who is undecided on some matter may be more or less inclined to believe it. I take these both to involve dispositions. The first is a disposition to *stop* believing something, while the second is a disposition to *start* believing something. Many theorists have suggested that believing something is itself a disposition. On this view, belief states are dispositional states. But it is worth separating these two ideas. Even if there are dispositions to start and to stop believing something, this would not entail that believing is *itself* a disposition. In Chapter 1, I argued that it is not. On my view, to believe something is to be in a certain position to manifest the dispositions and to exercise the capacities one has. It is not itself a disposition or capacity.

The stronger a person's belief, the less inclined (prepared or likely) she is to change her mind about it, and the weaker the belief, the more inclined (prepared or likely) she is to change it. How inclined a person is to change her mind can depend on how strong she takes her evidence to be and where that evidence came from. If Gopal thinks his observational evidence is very strong, then his belief will likely be very firm. But, human nature being what it is, the inclination can also depend on the person's character. A gullible person is likely to change her beliefs easily, even if she thinks her evidence is strong. If she is very gullible, her assessments of that evidence might also easily change. She might easily decide that her observations were not to be trusted. And a stubborn person might strongly believe something even though she thinks her evidence for it is weak.

---

[13] For a collection of recent papers on this, see Huber & Schmidt-Petri (2009).
[14] For a clear discussion of these debates, see Jackson (2018).

So while there is some connection between the strength of a person's belief and her assessments of her evidence, the connection is not simple.

The connection between strength and certainty is also not simple. Like certainty, strength comes in degrees. And as a general rule, when a person's belief is strong their certainty is high. But if Sarah is gullible or easily persuaded, then her belief that the 504 stops at Fern might be comparatively weak or fragile (it is hard to know how to describe it) even though she is quite certain that it stops there. It might take only a small amount of new information to shake her belief, even though she now feels quite certain about it. And someone might feel relatively uncertain about something while clinging to it stubbornly. So the strength of a person's belief seems to be independent of her certainty about it.

Part of what makes this complicated is the variety of ways we have in English for conveying our assessment of our evidence. Suppose Gopal thinks he has fairly good evidence that the 504 stops at Grenadier, but not enough to be sure. He might convey this with the following.

I am inclined to believe that the 504 stops at Grenadier, but I am not sure.

Here, Gopal conveys his view on the matter by describing the likelihood of his believing it. This way of putting it conveys that while he does not believe it, he has more reason to believe it than not. But Gopal might instead say the following.

The 504 probably does stop at Grenadier, but I am not sure.

This way of putting it suggests that he does believe something, namely that the obtaining of a certain possibility is more or less probable. He might instead convey his position by identifying a possibility whose obtaining would settle the matter for him.

If the 504 stops between Fern and Howard, then it stops at Grenadier.

Here he seems to express a conditional belief: a readiness to come to believe something if a certain condition is met. I don't mean that these are three ways of saying or conveying the same thing. There is considerable debate about how best to understand the semantic and pragmatic aspects involved in the use of such sentences. I won't try to sort it all out here.[15]

But I think we can abstract from these linguistic matters and consider what sort of information a person might want to assert or convey about their evidence or about their assessment of probabilities. There is debate, of course, over the nature

---

[15] What follows relies on the discussion in White (1975) and Bennett (2003). For a variety of recent views, see the papers in Egan & Weatherson (2011).

78 THE OBJECTS OF BELIEVING

of probability itself. If determinism is true, then every future possibility is either certain to obtain or certain not to obtain. This would be an objective matter, in the sense that a person could be wrong in thinking that some possibility is certain to obtain. It would also be a contingent matter, since had past circumstances been different, then a different set of future possibilities would have been guaranteed to obtain. If determinism is not true, however, then a given possibility can be more or less likely to obtain. This too would be an objective matter, in the sense that a person could be mistaken about it. And it would also be contingent, since the probability of some possibility's obtaining depends on the facts and a difference in the past might make some future possibility more or less likely to obtain. As circumstances change, the probability of some possibility's obtaining can change too. Before the pandemic it was very likely that I would be in Vermont this January, but the travel bans effectively ruled that out. This is not the place to try to decide whether determinism is true and anyway my interest is in trying to understand what someone believes when she thinks that some future possibility is more likely to occur than another.

The determinist and indeterminist can agree that a body of facts provides more or less evidential support that some possibility will obtain. The stronger the support, the more probable that it will, given those facts. Recent discoveries in climate science, for instance, indicate that Miami will very likely flood in the next hundred years. I take this to be an objective matter too, again in the sense that a person can be mistaken about how likely some body of facts makes some outcome. Scientists can agree that recently discovered facts in climate science make it very likely that Miami will flood, while disagreeing about just how likely they make it. These scientists might also disagree about whether determinism is true. One might think that Miami's flooding is either certain to happen or certain not to happen while holding that recent discoveries strongly indicate that it will. And an indeterminist could agree with her about how likely it is that Miami will flood while denying that one outcome is already guaranteed. Both the determinist and the indeterminist look to the facts when making these assessments, and they can agree on how likely the facts make some outcome.

Our scientists' shared belief about how likely it is that Miami will flood is *based on* facts they know (or think they know). But that belief is not *about* those known facts and nor is it about the support those known facts provide for their belief that Miami will likely flood. I take it to be a contingent matter how likely it is that Miami will flood. That likelihood is fixed or settled by the relevant facts. But we need to distinguish belief in some likelihood from belief about what makes it likely. The distinction is a general one. I am an uncle because I have a nephew. It is contingent that I am an uncle, even though the fact that I have a nephew makes it certain that I am an uncle. We need this same distinction when it comes to belief in probabilities. It is a contingent matter how likely it is that Miami will flood, even if it that likelihood is made certain by the facts.

CERTAINTY, PROBABILITY, AND AGNOSTICISM 79

Our scientists have beliefs about those facts and about how likely they make it that Miami will flood. But what they are trying to get right, in formulating their assessment, is how likely it is that Miami will flood given all the *relevant* facts, not just all the ones they think they know. And the scientists should concede that they might not know all the relevant facts. This too is an objective matter. One can be mistaken about which facts are relevant and about whether those facts are known. The scientists should agree that new discoveries (both about relevant facts and about which ones are relevant) might reveal that they were wrong about the likelihood that Miami will flood. Not that they were wrong about how likely it was given the facts *they knew*, but that they were wrong about how likely it was given *the facts*. They will adjust their belief in light of those newly discovered facts. But their belief is not *about* those discovered facts. It is about how likely it is that Miami will flood. And this is an objective matter about which they can be mistaken.

Of course, the determinist will insist that the outcome is guaranteed one way or the other, given *all* the (present) facts. The indeterminist disagrees. That disagreement is what defines the one as a determinist and the other as an indeterminist. But the scientists should make one additional concession that lessens the significance of this disagreement and provides something more for them to agree on. They should concede that some relevant facts might be beyond our knowledge. The concession is not just that humans might never know all the facts relevant to whether Miami will flood. It is that humans might not be *able to* know them all. This is just a modest acknowledgment of our cognitive limits. Even the indeterminist should agree that some of the facts relevant to settling how likely it is that Miami will flood are beyond our knowledge, even if she insists that all the facts leave it open whether it will flood. So in making their assessment the scientists should admit that they aim to base it on all the present relevant facts *they can come to know*. And this too is an objective matter, since one can be mistaken about which facts are within our ken, and which are not.

This concession allows them to agree on something objective while continuing to disagree about determinism. They can agree on how likely it is that Miami will flood *given all the facts that we can know*. They can continue to aim to be right about how likely it is, given all the present relevant facts, that Miami will flood. Their concession is simply that what they have to go on might be less than all the relevant facts. And they can agree on this concession while continuing to disagree over determinism. For the concession is not about whether it is already guaranteed whether Miami will flood, but about whether we can know all the facts that are relevant to whether it will flood. This concession effectively diminishes the significance of their disagreement over determinism. The determinist can insist that it is already settled whether Miami will flood, while agreeing with the indeterminist that, given the facts, it is very likely to flood. This is agreement

80 THE OBJECTS OF BELIEVING

over an objective and contingent matter.[16] It is a further matter (one that is to my mind less important for an account of belief) how the scientists might use their linguistic resources to say and convey this shared belief.

One last point is worth mentioning. It concerns agnosticism. Jane Friedman argues that in addition to believing something and disbelieving it there is a third mental state, one of suspending judgment about it. I will call this being agnostic about it. As Friedman points out, being agnostic about something is not the same as neither believing it nor disbelieving it.

> We don't come into the world agnostic or suspending judgment about whether bumblebees hibernate during the winter or about whether a drought killed the dinosaurs or about whether an American invented the light bulb, even though we are in states on non-belief with respect to the propositions expressed by these sentences. Cavemen hadn't suspended judgment about whether the Large Haldron Collider would find the Higgs boson and my great grandparents did not suspend about whether Google Chrome is better than Firefox, despite the fact that the relevant people lacked the relevant beliefs. One cannot count as agnostic about P if one cannot even grasp P.   (Friedman 2013, 168)

If a person knows that something is possible, then she either believes that it obtains, believes that it does not obtain, or else is agnostic about it. But there may be a possibility she knows nothing about, in which case she will neither believe it, nor disbelieve it, nor be agnostic about it. What it is for a person to know that something is possible is a complex matter, and I won't have much to say about it here.

Let me take stock. To believe something is to have a certain belief property, and this does not come in degrees. A person either has the property or she does not. But she may be more or less certain about something she believes. And her believing it may be more or less strong. Both certainty and strength can depend on the person's assessment of her evidence, but they can also flow from her character. Strength of belief is a dispositional matter, concerning how likely or inclined a person is to change her mind. And a person who is undecided on some matter can be more or less inclined to believe it. Even if these inclinations are dispositions, it would not follow that belief states are themselves dispositions.

---

[16] What I am suggesting is that the following (using numbers to help clarify thing) is possible. The probability that Miami floods in the next hundred years is 1; the probability, given all the facts that humans can now know, is 0.8; the probability, given what our scientists actually know, is 0.9; those scientists' own assessment of the probability given what they actually know is 0.6. In making their predictions, our scientists are trying to get some things right. They are trying to get right how likely what they now know makes it that Miami will flood. But they are also trying to get right how likely what *can now be known* makes it, and that is an objective matter. Dorothy Edgington (1986) and (1995) argues that while these are objective matters, the predictions our scientists make and the beliefs those predictions convey are neither true nor false. For discussion, see Stalnaker (2019), chapter 11.

3.4 Speech Acts and Aboutness

Any account of the objects of belief should accommodate two plausible ideas. One is that the objects of belief are also objects of speech acts. The other is that the objects of belief are, in some sense, about things in the believer's world. The modal and propositional views accommodate these facts equally well, but in different ways. Seeing this will help clarify the differences between the two views.

Let's start with speech acts. Zeno Vendler called "the near universal identity of the objects of speech and thought" a "staggering perspective" (Vendler 1972, 36). Here is how he described it.

> [T]he same things that can be asserted, suggested, or denied in words, can be realized, and understood, believed, suspected, or doubted in thought; things regarded, considered, looked upon, and recognized to be such and such in thought, can also be characterized, described, and defined in the same way in words... To put it briefly: you can say whatever you think, and you can think almost whatever you can say.   (Vendler 1972, 36)

(The final qualification marked by "almost" concerns certain performatives and is not relevant for my purposes.) The point is that the objects of belief and of certain other mental states can also be the objects of various speech acts.[17]

The propositional view can accommodate this. It holds that to believe that P is to believe that P is true. And a person who believes that P can usually also assert that P, and the accommodating idea is that to assert that P is to assert that P is true. Likewise, to assume that P is to assume that it is true; to consider whether P is to consider whether P is true; to suggest that P is to suggest that P is true; to deny P is to deny that P is true; and so on. So, the propositional view can easily accommodate Vendler's point.

But so can the modal view. It holds that to believe that P is to believe that P obtains. And a person who believes that P obtains can usually also assert that P, and the accommodating idea is that to assert that P is to assert that P obtains. Likewise, to assume that P is to assume that it obtains; to consider whether P is to consider whether it obtains; to suggest that P is to suggest that P obtains; to deny that P is to deny that P obtains; and so on. So Vendler's point won't help us decide between the modal view and the propositional view of the objects of belief.

---

[17] It is another matter whether the objects of belief are also the meanings or semantic values of sentences. This can't be so for all sentences, of course, since some are context-dependent. I am inclined to think this context-dependence is pervasive. In any case, though, my interest in the text is on the plausible idea that a person can say what she believes. How she uses her linguistic resources to do this, and what gives those resources the properties they have, are complicated issues I won't pursue.

82 THE OBJECTS OF BELIEVING

The modal and the propositional views can also both accept the fact that what a person believes is, in some sense, about things in the world.[18] When Sarah believes that the 504 stops at Garden, her belief is about Garden Avenue and about the 504 streetcar. A person's beliefs are about objects, properties, and relations in her environment. Plausibly, it is the object of a person's belief that fixes which objects, properties, and relations a person's beliefs are about. Both the propositional and the modal view can accept this.

Consider the proposition that the 504 stops at Garden. That proposition is about Garden Avenue, but it is not about Regent Street, in London. Why not? I think a plausible answer is that the proposition is about Garden Avenue because whether it is true depends on how things are with Garden Avenue. In particular, it depends on whether the 504 streetcar stops there. By contrast, whether it is true has nothing, I think, to do with how things are with Regent Street in London. So, this is a clear sense in which the proposition is about Garden Avenue but not about Regent Street. The propositional view of the objects of belief can say that when Jones believes that the 504 stops at Garden, she is believing something about Garden Avenue because what she believes—that proposition—is about Garden Avenue in this sense.

But all of this is available for the modal theorist too. For the possibility that the 504 stops at Garden Avenue is also about Garden Avenue. Likewise, the fact that the 504 stops at Garden is also about Garden Avenue. The fact that Trump is President is a fact about the United States. And notice that the possibility that the 504 stops at Garden is not a possibility about Regent Street. And the modal view can say an analogous thing as was said by the propositional story. The possibility that the 504 stops at Garden is about Garden Avenue because whether the possibility obtains depends on how things are with Garden Avenue—in particular, it depends on whether the 504 does stop there. So the modal theorist can say that Jones' belief is about Garden Avenue because what she believes—the possibility that the 504 stops at Garden—is about Garden Avenue.

Thus, both the modal and the propositional views can accommodate a clear sense in which a person's beliefs are about things in the world. But one might think that another aboutness fact needs explaining. One might think that in addition to the proposition's being true or false, Jones' *believing* that the 504 stops at Garden is true or false depending on how things are with Garden Avenue. And one might think that this is best explained by the propositional view. The thought would be that her believing is true or false depending on whether the proposition is true or false. I think this is a double mistake. A friend of the modal view could just as easily say that Jones' believing is true or false depending on whether a certain possibility obtains. So it would be a mistake to think that only

---

[18] For a recent discussion of aboutness, see Yablo (2016).

KNOWLEDGE, INQUIRY, AND ACTION   83

the propositional view could explain the truth of Jones' belief state. But the more fundamental mistake is to think that belief properties and belief states have semantical properties at all. The property of believing that the 504 stops at Garden is neither true nor false and nor is the fact of Jones' having that property. Mental states are not representations or representational, at least not in the way that propositions are. This will be the topic of Chapter 4.

3.5 Knowledge, Inquiry, and Action

Let me turn now to one virtue of the modal view. The idea that the objects of belief are possibilities fits elegantly with an independently plausible account of the objects of knowledge, and with a plausible picture of rational inquiry and action. Let me explain this.

Let's start with the objects of knowledge. It might seem that they cannot belong in the same ontological category as the objects of belief. On a traditional view of knowledge, when Jones knows that the 504 stops at Bloor, what she knows—that is, the object of her knowledge—is a certain fact. It is the fact that the 504 stops at Bloor. And it is also plausible to think that states of knowing are individuated by facts.

Knowing that F1 = Knowing that F2 if and only if F1 = F2.

But not every belief can have a fact as its object, of course, since a person can believe something and be wrong. If Jones believes that the 504 stops at Fern, then the object of her belief cannot be the fact that the 504 stops at Fern, for there is no such fact. The 504 does not stop there. But Jones believes that it does, and her belief is individuated by something, so the object of her belief must not be a fact (or at least not that fact).

Though the 504 does not stop at Fern, it might have. Had it, then Jones would have been right in believing that it did. And I take it that the object of her belief in that case would have been the same as the object of her belief in the case where she is wrong.[19] The difference in the two cases is not a difference in what individuates her belief. She believes the same thing in both cases, namely, that the 504 stops at Fern. The difference, rather, is in whether what she believes to obtain does obtain.

---

[19] Armstrong (1973, 43–4) reports that John Anderson (1962) held that the object of a true belief is a fact (or state of affairs) and that a false belief has no single object, but involves rather a multiple relation between the believer and whatever objects, properties and relations the belief concerns. Likewise, Alan White says that there may be no general answer to the question what is the object of belief. He then adds: the object of belief "is something which exists when the belief is not mistaken and does not exist when it is mistaken" (White 1972, 83). I won't pursue this, since the modal and propositional views that I am contrasting both disagree with Anderson and White.

84 THE OBJECTS OF BELIEVING

This is a difference in which possibilities obtain, not a difference in what she believes. So, in believing that the 504 stops at Fern, Jones got hold of a possibility such that, had it obtained, she would have been right, though as a matter of fact, given that it does not obtain, she is wrong. The obtaining of that possibility is thus both necessary and sufficient for her to be right in believing that the 504 stops at Fern. And indeed, had it stopped there, then she might well have known and not just believed it.

This suggests the following elegant picture. A fact is the *obtaining* of a possibility.[20] The object of a belief is a possibility and the object of knowing (at least when knowing entails believing) is the obtaining of a possibility. This allows us to capture the idea that both knowing and believing concern a contrast between how things are and how they could have been, between actuality and possibility. The difference between knowing something and believing it is clearest when we contrast knowing with incorrectly believing. The person who believes incorrectly that P has got hold of a possibility, a way that things could have been. Because that possibility does not obtain, it is not a fact that P. Had it obtained, then she would have been correct in believing it. The object of her belief would then have been a possibility whose obtaining is a fact. Knowing that fact requires more, I take it, than correctly believing in it. But had she known it, then what she would have known would have been the obtaining of what she believed when she incorrectly believed that P. The possibility that P is the object of her belief when she incorrectly or correctly believes that P *and* its obtaining is the object of her knowledge when she knows that P. The elegant picture is of a deep uniformity between knowing and believing: both are positions individuated within a space of possibilities. This is one of the modal view's virtues.

The modal view of the object of belief also fits neatly with an idea about how inquiry yields knowledge. In investigating some subject matter, one starts with a set of open possibilities—ways that the subject matter might be given what one thinks one knows. Susan knows that the 504 travels along Roncesvalles, and believes that it stops at either Garden or Galley but not both. Inquiry proceeds by ruling out possibilities or by uncovering additional ones. Susan learns that the 504 does not stop at Galley, and so concludes that it stops at Garden. Or perhaps she learns that she had overlooked the possibility that it stops at *both* Garden and Galley, or that it might also stop at Fern. As inquiry proceeds, the set of open possibilities changes, shrinking or growing with changes in one's information. The general idea is that coming to know the subject matter consists in ruling out ways that it is not but could have been and identifying the way that it is. Ruling out some possibility consists in starting to believe that things are not that way. This

---

[20] I take this idea from Hyman (2017) though he uses it for a different purpose. I discuss this in the next section.

sort of disjunctive reasoning is not the only inferential method used in inquiry. But it is a central one, and the modal view of the object of belief fits it neatly.

Finally, the modal view fits neatly with an independently plausible view about action. The view I have in mind says that when a person knows some fact then they are positioned to do, think, and feel things in the light of that fact. That fact can be their reason. The modal view allows us to say something similar in cases when a person merely believes something, either because they don't know it or because they are mistaken. In such cases, when the person acts on their belief, they are not acting in light of a fact, since that is reserved for one who knows. But they are, we might say, acting in the light of a possibility. If the believer is right, but just doesn't know, then the possibility actually obtains, and so is a fact. If the believer is mistaken, then they are acting in light of a way things could have been. In this way, the modal view allows us to say neatly how knowing and believing relate to reasons.

3.6 Making the Propositional View Fit

There are two ways to try to make the propositional view of the objects of belief fit the idea that the object of knowing is a fact and this picture of inquiry. One concerns the relation between propositions and possibilities, and the other concerns the nature of facts. In both cases, however, the fit is comparatively poor. I'll take them in turn.

One way to make the propositional view fit is to add to it that each proposition determines a possibility. For instance, the proposition that the 504 stops at Garden is true just in case the possibility that the 504 stops at Garden obtains. More generally:

DET: For every proposition P, there is a possibility p*, such that P is true just in case p* obtains.

A proponent of the propositional view who accepts DET can then say that the object of belief—a proposition on their view—fits the idea that the object of knowledge is a fact—a way that things are—because every proposition determines a way that things might be. The fit is not as neat though, for this proposal raises two questions that are not easily answered.

First, why do belief and knowledge have such different sorts of objects? On this proposal, the objects of belief and knowledge belong to different ontological categories. The object of belief is a representation while the object of knowledge is a fact in the world. Given that knowledge and belief are both cognitive states, why are their objects so very different?

The second question is related to this. Given that there are facts and possibilities, and given that the object of knowledge is a fact, why isn't there a mental state

86   THE OBJECTS OF BELIEVING

whose object is a possibility? It certainly seems like there could be. But if there is, what is it and how does it differ from belief? If there isn't one, then why not? I am not aware of good answers to these questions, so I won't pursue them.

And in any case, virtually no proponent of the propositional view endorses DET. For it entails something that propositionalists typically reject. I have in mind the following.

LIMIT: S believes that P only if it is possible that P.

The modal view also entails this. For it says that the object of belief is a possibility. What a person can believe is, on the modal view, limited to what is possible. More specifically, the modal view entails that one cannot believe what is impossible. Most philosophers who have published views on the nature of belief deny LIMIT. They hold that a person can believe something impossible. It is, for instance, impossible that Sam Clemens not be Mark Twain. Yet many philosophers hold that a person can believe that Sam Clemens is not Mark Twain. The object of that person's belief cannot be a possibility, since there is no such possibility as that Sam Clemens is not Mark Twain. Rather, the object must be (or anyway it must determine) an impossibility. So, these philosophers say, the object of a belief cannot be, in all cases anyway, a possibility. And so they reject DET.

It is worth noting that denying DET raises further problems.[21] It is not clear how we are to understand rational inquiry if the options we start with include impossibilities. To engage in inquiry we need to be able to describe and distinguish the live options. But it is not clear how we are to describe an impossibility. Are we supposed to use a contradiction? But a contradiction is not true of anything, and so is not true of an impossibility. And if we cannot describe an impossibility, then how can we distinguish among them in our deliberations? How can we distinguish one impossibility from another, or any of them from a possibility? If we can't distinguish them, how can we rule them out? Moreover, rational progress is usually made in an inquiry by ruling out or adding possibilities in response to new information. But what sort of *new* information would justify ruling out an impossibility? What sort of discovery might give one reason to rule out the impossibility that Twain and Clemens are distinct? And what would justify adding an impossibility to our set of options? There are still other problems. How does conditional reasoning work, when their antecedents are impossible? Why wouldn't adding more impossibilities count as progress? What is more, we also need to be able to describe how those we reason with take things to be and what options they believe remain open. To say what others believe is to say how things

---

[21] For more discussion of this, see Stalnaker (1996).

MAKING THE PROPOSITIONAL VIEW FIT   87

would be if they were right. But an impossible belief cannot be right, so there is no way to say how things would be if a person who believes something impossible were right. It is no good to reply: If she were right, then Sam Clemens would not be Mark Twain—for that is not a coherent description of anything. The following *is* a coherent description: there could have been two people, each with some of the properties that Mark Twain actually had but differing in other ways, and perhaps one of them is named "Mark Twain" and the other is named "Sam Clemens." But this is not a description of an impossibility: it is a description of a general possibility, one that can obtain only if a more specific one obtains. A person might believe that this general possibility obtains. But this is not belief in the obtaining of an impossibility; it is belief in the obtaining of a general possibility that lacks a possible witness.

A proponent of the propositional view who also rejects DET thus owes us an account of rational inquiry and of belief ascription that make sense of belief in impossibilities. They may insist, in reply, that the modal view cannot make sense of what actually happens during inquiry where people make certain kinds of mistakes. I reject this charge. I think the modal view actually has the resources to make good sense of this, though it won't fully remove the sense that reasoning has broken down in such cases. What I said about how one possibility can be a witness for another is part of the story, and I will also argue in Chapter 5 that we need to recognize the possibility of a certain kind of credal illusion. But even if I am wrong about that, it would not follow that the objects of belief are propositions. And it would not remove the need for accounts of rational inquiry and belief ascription if we deny DET.

There is a second, and more radical, way to make the propositional view fit. It is to hold that a fact is a true proposition.[22] But here too the fit is comparatively poor. I have been assuming that facts are concrete, as opposed to abstract, entities. Here is how J.L. Austin put the idea.

> Phenomena, events, situations, states of affairs, are commonly supposed to be genuinely-in-the-world [...] Yet surely of all these we can say that they are facts. The collapse of the Germans is an event and is a fact—was an event and was a fact. (Austin 1979, 104)

Bertrand Russell had the same idea. He added that facts are "the kind of things that makes a proposition true or false" (Russell 1918, 182). In arguing that the propositional view of the object of belief fits poorly with the idea that the object of knowing is a fact, I have been assuming this conception of fact. But some hold that

---

[22] What I say here follows the discussion in Hyman (2017); see also White (1972).

88 THE OBJECTS OF BELIEVING

facts are a kind of proposition. More specifically, they hold that a fact is a *true* proposition. Here is how Strawson put this view.

> A proposition, an intensional abstract item, may have many properties: it may be simple or complex; it may entail or be incompatible with this, that, or the other proposition. It may also have the property of being true; and then it may properly be called 'a truth': and this is what a fact is—a truth. (Strawson 1998, 403)

On this conception, the proposition that the Germans collapsed is a fact. It is a fact because it is true. Facts, on this view, just are true propositions. If a fact is a proposition, then it may appear easy to make the propositional view fit the idea that the object of knowledge is a fact. For the objects of knowledge would be the same as the objects of belief. In both cases, the objects would be propositions.

I called this a more radical way to make the propositional view fit. It is radical in two respects. First, it requires that we change our ordinary ways of talking about facts. We would not ordinarily say that a fact is true. It seems a mistake, and not just somehow redundant, to say that the fact that the 504 stops at Garden is true. The proposition that it does is true, and maybe so is a sentence expressing that proposition. But we would not ordinarily call the *fact* that it does true or false; we would say, rather, that the fact obtains. Moreover, we ordinarily think of facts as what we can discover or forget. Sonia might, for instance, discover (or forget) that the 504 stops at Bloor. But in discovering (or forgetting) this, she did not discover (or forget) a proposition. Indeed, she might have known that proposition long before her discovery. So adopting the idea that a fact is a proposition requires a more or less radical change in the way we speak about facts.

This proposal is radical in a second respect. Suppose that the fact that the 504 stops at Garden is a proposition and not, as Austin put it, a situation or state of affairs in-the-world. Still, there would presumably be some state of affairs or situation in-the-world that obtains given that that proposition is true. It would be the state of affairs or situation whose obtaining makes it a fact that the 504 stops at Garden. (I suppose an even more radical propositionalist might deny this. This strikes me as desperate.) But now if there is such a state of affairs, why can't it be the object of a mental state? The object of knowing is, on the view we are now considering, a proposition. But why couldn't there also be a mental state whose object is, not the true proposition that the 504 stops at Garden, but rather the state of affairs that makes that proposition true? Why must the objects of knowledge and belief be representations, when there are perfectly well-suited entities in-the-world to be the objects of our mental states?

Indeed, we can now see that conceiving of facts as true propositions won't really make the propositional view of belief fit the idea that the object of knowing is a fact. For that idea was, I take it, that the object of knowing is something, as Austin put it, in-the-world. And once we allow that a fact is a proposition made true by a state of affairs or situation in-the-world, then we can put that original idea by

A HISTORY OF NEGLECT 89

saying that the object of knowledge is a state of affairs or a situation.[23] What Jones knows when she knows that the 504 stops at Bloor is not the (true) proposition that it does, but rather the state of affairs whose obtaining makes that proposition into a fact. What she acts on, when she acts on what she knows, is not a certain proposition, but rather, a certain state of affairs or situation in-the-world. That is the attractive view of knowledge, and we can't make the propositional view fit it simply by deciding to call a true proposition a fact.

John Hyman has recently argued against the idea that a fact is a true proposition. But he also denies that the object of knowledge is what Austin called a state of affairs or a situation in-the-world. The object of knowledge, on Hyman's view, is not a true proposition, but rather the *truth* of a proposition.[24] Hyman does not say much about the truth of a proposition.

> The truth of a proposition is not a true proposition, any more than the beauty of a place is a beautiful place, or the goodness of a man is a good man. It is an abstract particular, a trope or mode, albeit with an abstract bearer, an instance of the property of being true. But of course if the fact that P is the truth of the proposition that P, then there is such a fact if, and only if, the proposition that P is true.   (Hyman 2017, 17)

As he sees it, this proposal captures the best of two views: it allows facts to be abstract entities while denying that they are propositions. But it seems to me to carry the same costs as the radical move I just considered. In particular, we are left wondering why there cannot be a mental state whose object is the thing-in-the-world whose obtaining explains the existence of that fact.

I mention Hyman's view, though, not in order to critique it, but in order to steal it for my own purposes. The modal view says that the object of belief is a way that things might be. I suggested that this view fits neatly the idea that the object of knowing is a way that things are. The object of belief is a possibility, while the object of knowing is a fact. We can make this combination elegant if we add that a fact is the *obtaining* of a possibility. The obtaining of a possibility is not an abstract entity; it is an entity in the world.

3.7 A History of Neglect

Despite fitting so neatly the attractive accounts of knowledge and inquiry the modal view has largely been neglected. Some of the initial neglect stemmed from

---

[23] Indeed, Armstrong made this proposal hoping to recapture the attractive view of knowledge in response to the prevalence of the idea that a fact is just a proposition.
[24] He credits Slote (1974) and Fine (1982).

90   THE OBJECTS OF BELIEVING

discomfort and suspicion about metaphysical modality. More recently, the neglect seems due to an inertia and the sense that there is no alternative.

We can start this history lesson with Frege, who held that the objects of belief are propositions, and that propositions are abstract entities that exist in a "third realm" (Frege 1918). He did not have much to say about modal notions, but what he did say suggests that he considered them to be psychological or epistemological notions, and not metaphysical ones.

> If a statement is presented as possible, then *either* the speaker is refraining from judgement, by indicating that he knows no laws from which its negation would follow; or else he is saying that the statement's negation in its universal form is false. In the latter case we have what is usually called a *particular affirmative judgement* (see §12). 'It is possible that the Earth will one day collide with another heavenly body' is an example of the first case, and 'A cold can result in death' an example of the second.   (Frege 1952, 4–5, emphases in original)

To say that something is possible, Frege seems to be suggesting, is to say something about one's evidence or grounds for a certain proposition. It is not to make a metaphysical claim. And he famously held that a fact—the object of knowledge— is nothing but a true proposition. It is thus no surprise that Frege never considered the idea that the object of belief might be a metaphysical possibility.

Russell too viewed modality with suspicion.

> [T]here seems to be no true proposition of which it could be said that it might have been false. One might as well say that redness might have been a taste rather than a colour. What is true, is true; what is false, is false, and there is nothing more to be said. Necessity seems to be a psychological rather than a logical notion.   (1990, 257)

Russell is denying that any true proposition could have been false, but it seems clear that he has in mind a more general doubt about necessity and possibility. He's not claiming that every true proposition is also necessarily true. Rather, he thinks that necessity and possibility are epistemological and not metaphysical notions. This is a little puzzling, since he considered the notion of a fact to be a metaphysical and not an epistemological one. Why treat ways things are so differently from ways they could have been?[25]

---

[25] Russell famously decried the idea of a negative fact. "There is implanted in the human breast an almost unquenchable desire to find some way of avoiding the admission that negative facts are as ultimate as those that are positive" (Russell 1919, 4). Perhaps his breast felt the same about unobtaining possibilities.

In any event, Russell recognized that the object of belief cannot in every case be a fact, since a person can be mistaken in what they believe. His example is Othello's believing that Desdemona loves Cassio. The object of Othello's belief cannot be the fact that Desdemona loves Cassio (or, as Russell put it, Desdemona's love for Cassio), since there is no such fact.

> It might be said that his belief is a relation to a different object namely 'that Desdemona loves Cassio'; but it is almost as difficult to suppose that there is such an object as this, when Desdemona does not love Cassio, as it was to suppose that there is 'Desdemona's love for Cassio'. Hence it will be better to seek for a theory of belief which does not make it consist in a relation of the mind to a single object. (Russell 1912, 72)

Russell did not explain the difficulty he has in mind here, and instead went on to develop the view that believing has no single object, but is rather a multiple relation between a believer and whatever objects, properties, and relations the belief concerns.[26]

Moore seems to have seen the same difficulty as Russell. Having abandoned the idea that the object of a belief is a proposition, he then considers whether it might be a fact. But this raises an immediate problem.

> If you consider what happens when a man entertains a false belief, it doesn't seem as is his belief consisted merely in his having a relation to some object which certainly *is*. It seems rather as if the thing he was believing, the *object* of his belief, were just the fact which certainly is *not*—which certainly is not because his belief is false. This, of course, creates a difficulty, because if the object certainly is *not*— if there *is* no such thing, it is impossible for him to or anything else to have any kind of relation to it. (Moore 1953, 263)

Faced with this difficulty, Moore recommended abandoning the idea that believing has any object at all.[27]

---

[26] For a recent development of this multiple relation view, see Moltmann (2003). For a critique, see Soames (2010).

[27] Alan White (1972) agreed with Moore that there is a problem. After rejecting the propositional view, White says that there may be no general answer to the question what is the object of belief. He then adds: the object of belief "is something which exists when the belief is not mistaken and does not exist when it is mistaken" (White 1972, 83). He has in mind facts as what exist when the belief is not mistaken. But if we replace "exist" with "obtain," then we get the modal view that the objects are in all cases possibilities. Irad Kimhi (2018) also claims to see a problem understanding what could be the object of a belief or thought that is mistaken. He is happy with facts in his ontology, though he counts them syncategorematic. But it seems to me that we need to admit not just facts but also possibilities, not just ways things are but also ways they could have been. We can count possibilities as syncategorematic too. And surely part of the power of thought and reason is precisely that it can range over the possible as easily as over the actual (though within limits in both cases).

92 THE OBJECTS OF BELIEVING

But why did Russell and Moore not say that the object—or better, entity—is a certain possibility, in Russell's case, that Desdemona loves Cassio. After all, she might have loved him, even though she did not. And what Othello believed was precisely that she did. He was convinced that possibility obtained. Russell was driven to the multiple relation theory of judgment, and Moore to the idea that belief has no object, in part anyway, because they found it too difficult to believe that there are such things as possibilities.

Carnap did not share this skepticism about modality, but this was because he thought modal notions could be reduced or explained in terms of truth and meaning. So while he was not exactly skeptical of possibility, he did not grant it an explanatory role. As for propositions, Carnap was, at least in *Meaning and Necessity*, fairly open-minded. He was prepared to identify true propositions with structured complexes of a certain sort, and to identifying these with facts. But, like Russell, he felt there was something odd about false propositions. Perhaps, he suggested, they can be thought of as "unexemplified" complexes, a little like an unexemplified property. But he also suggested that all propositions might, for theoretical purposes anyway, be identified with sets of sentences (Carnap 1947, section 6). So far as I know, he never entertained the idea that the object of a belief might be a possibility, and he always held that propositions are true or false.

Quine was no friend of modality, but he was also no friend of abstract objects, and for this reason was suspicious of propositions. He held instead that the objects of belief are sentences or sets of sentences or (though this view never really drew a fanbase) sets of nerve-ending stimulations (Quine 1960). Gilbert Ryle said that beliefs have a "propositional hook," though what he probably had in mind is a linguistic sense of "proposition," and he anyway never considered the idea that the object of belief might be a possibility (Ryle 1949). Skepticism about modality waned in the final third of the twentieth century, but by then the propositional view was firmly entrenched. David Lewis (1986) and Robert Stalnaker (1976), who appealed to modal notions to understand belief and other attitudes, nonetheless took the objects of belief to be propositions. They modeled propositions using sets of possible worlds, and some of what they say even suggests they identified propositions with these sets. But, so far as I can see, they never abandoned the idea that the object of belief must be a representation, something that is or can be true or false.

Interestingly, one of the founders of modern modal logic, Ruth Barcan Marcus, once sketched a view on which the objects of belief are not propositions.

> Believing is understood to be a relation between a subject or agent and a state of affairs that it is not necessarily actual but that has actual objects as constituents. We may think of states of affairs as structures of actual objects: individuals as well as properties and relations. The structure into which those objects enter need not be an actual world structure. (Marcus 1993, 240)

Marcus does not elaborate on this idea. And she does not identify these structures with possibilities, but this would, I think, be a natural extension of her sketch.

3.8 Representation without Propositions

The propositional view of the object of belief is so standard that it is rarely argued for. I suspect that a certain idea about belief explains its popularity, even among those who are not skeptical of metaphysical modality and so might have been open to the modal view. It is the idea that belief states are representations, that they true or false. If one thought this, then one might also think that the objects of belief must be propositions, since propositions are representational. But this line of thought should be resisted.

This connection between the propositional view and the idea that beliefs are true is neatly expressed by Scott Soames.

> It is a truism that a belief, assertion, hypothesis, or conjecture represents the world as being a certain way, and so is capable of being true or false. Ordinarily, what we mean by this is that *what is believed, asserted, hypothesizes,* or *conjectured* represents the world and so is true or false. Using the familiar name 'proposition' for these things, we may ask "*In virtue of what are propositions representational, and hence bearers of truth conditions?*"
>
> (Soames 2010, 63–4; italics in original)

The idea is that only the propositional view can make sense of the truism that beliefs are true or false. If the object of a belief is not a representation—is not capable of being true or false—then how could a belief itself be representational? If this is right, then of course the object of belief cannot be a possibility, for possibilities are not representations. They are not capable of being true or false. I suspect that something like this line of thought explains the dominance of the propositional view.

Soames says that it is a truism that a belief is a representation or that it represents. This way of putting the truism hypostasizes beliefs, treating them as in the same category as paintings and painters. A painting might be a representation and a person might be a painter. But belief states belong in a different ontological category than paintings and painters. Belief properties are qualities, not sortals. Their instantiations are not the right sorts of things to be representations. Still, there is a truism in the neighborhood: If S believes that P, then S is right if P is the case, and otherwise she is wrong.[28] Jones is right in believing that the 504

---

[28] Arthur Collins offered the following analysis of believing: S believes that P just in case S is right if the proposition that P is true, and S is wrong if the proposition that P is false (Collins 1988). On this analysis, S's belief is not true or false, except perhaps in some derivative sense.

94   THE OBJECTS OF BELIEVING

stops at Garden, because it does, and Sarah is mistaken in believing that it stops at Fern, because it does not. But in believing what they do, Jones and Sarah do not *represent* the world as being some way, at least not in the sense in which to assert something is to represent. Asserting something is an action, and believing is not an action. A painting might be a representation of a street scene, but Jones and Sarah are not representations of anything, certainly not of the 504.[29] So I am not sure Soames is right about the truism.

But even if Soames were right that belief states are representational, it would not follow that the objects of belief are themselves representations. One might hold that belief states are representational even though their objects are possibilities. One could even accept the modal view and say that a believing is true if its object obtains. Indeed, this is Mark Richard's view. He calls the objects of belief "propositions," but here is what he says about them.

> We invoke propositions in an account of mind and language as the semantic values of complement clauses. An account of propositions that sees them as states of affairs—ways for things to be, ways individuated in terms of the objects and properties they involve—is adequate for this purpose.   (Richard 2013, 716)

As I understand it, his view is that the object of belief is a possibility—a way that things might be. I take it he thinks these possibilities are entities in-the-world in Austin's sense.

Richard says that a proposition is a representation, but only in "a lame and watered-down sense" (Richard 2013, 710).

> What are true or false in the primary sense of 'true' and 'false' are acts of representation. It is useful and harmless to extend truth talk beyond this primary sense. We do extend truth talk in this way. So there is a lame, watered down sense in which objects of the attitudes are true or false and hence representational. It is hard—well, it is hard for me, at least—to see what the point of insisting that propositions need to be representational in some stronger sense might be.
>
> (Richard 2013, 710)

For what is true or false in the primary sense, according to Richard, are "actual and possible acts or events of representation."

---

[29] To be clear, I do not deny that the proposition that the 504 stops at Garden is true if Jones is right; and it is false if she is wrong. I am not denying the existence or the representational nature of propositions. I take no stand on whether there are propositions, though it is not clear to me why we need them to understand the nature of believing.

> To believe that there is snow in the street is to represent the state of affairs that there is snow in the street, with the representation playing a certain role in one's cognitive economy.   (Richard 2013, 704)

> I don't envision a one-size-fits-all account of what it is to represent a state of affairs....I think it's as close to analytic as it gets, that if one represents John's throwing a ball, one has a representation of John's throwing a ball. So if you or I or the dog believe that John threw a ball, we have a representation of the state of affairs, John's throwing a ball.   (Richard 2013, 705)

Richard moves in the first passage from the idea that believing is an act of representing to the idea that believing is itself a representation. In the second passage, he suggests that believing requires *having* a representation. He does not explain why he thinks that to believe is to represent. And he does not say whether the believing is itself the representation, or whether the representation is somehow inside the believer.

I agree with Richard that the objects of belief are ways that things might be, possibilities. I also agree with him that possibilities are not representational in any interesting sense. And he may be right that it is harmless to call possibilities representational in a watered-down sense. But it is hard—well, it is hard for me, at least—to see what point there is in insisting, as Richard does, that *believing* is representational in a full-strength sense. This is the topic of the next chapter.

This chapter has been about the individuation of belief properties. In Section 3.1, I suggested that they are individuated by their objects. On my view, these objects are possibilities, ways that things are or could have been, and not propositions. I argued, in Section 3.2, that familiar puzzling cases often considered counter-examples to this view are not in fact counter-examples. I argued that they all involve a change or difference in which contingent possibilities the believers take to obtain. This means they are not pure cases, and so do not decisively tell against the modal view of the individuation of belief properties. In Section 3.3, I discussed agnosticism, certainty, strength of belief and what it is to believe that some possibility is more or less likely to obtain. In Sections 3.4 and 3.5, I described some virtues of this modal view that I then argued, in Section 3.6, the propositional view lacks. In Section 3.7, I very briefly sketched the way 20th-century thinking about belief neglected the modal view. The idea that the objects of belief are not representations is the first part of my argument that believing is not a sort representing. But this idea leaves open whether belief properties or states are themselves in some interesting sense representational. The aim of Chapter 4 is to argue that they are not.

4
Believing without Representing

On my view, believing is a mental or psychological state but it is not a representational one. A person who believes something is right or wrong depending on the facts, but in believing that things are some way she is not representing them as being that way. In Chapter 3, I argued that the objects of belief are possibilities and not propositions. In this chapter, I will argue that belief properties and belief states are neither true nor false. In this sense, beliefs are not mental representations.

To see this, it helps to consider the distinctions we drew in Chapter 2 between propositions, belief properties, and belief states. I assume that propositions can be true or false. But I will argue, in Sections 4.2 and 4.3, that neither belief properties nor belief states can. In Section 4.4, I will detail some of the ways our ordinary talk encourages the idea that they can. This will involve adding items to the list I made in Chapter 2. In Sections 4.5 and 4.6, I will consider how to rethink certain philosophical claims and projects that seem to presuppose that belief states and facts can be true or false. In Section 4.7, I will extend the lesson about belief to desire. But I will start by trying to get clearer on what it might mean to say that belief is representational.

4.1 Believing and Truth

When a person believes something, she is either right or wrong depending on whether things are as she believes them to be. Jones is right in believing that the 504 stops at Garden, since it does. Sarah is mistaken in believing that it stops at Fern, since it doesn't. This gets to the very heart of believing. It is what distinguishes believing from other mental or psychological states. Whether a person is correct or mistaken when she hopes for, imagines, or wants something has nothing to do with whether things are as she hopes, imagines, or wants them to be. It is distinctive of believing that whether one is right or wrong in believing something depends in this way on the facts.

Let's call this idea CORRECT.

CORRECT.   A person who believes that P is correct only if P; otherwise, she is mistaken.

On Believing: Being Right in a World of Possibilities. David Hunter, Oxford University Press. © David Hunter 2022.
DOI: 10.1093/oso/9780192859549.003.0005

BELIEVING AND TRUTH 97

Here are two related theses.

CORRECT$_{\text{PROPOSITION}}$. A person who believes that P is correct only if the proposition that P is true; otherwise, she is mistaken.

CORRECT$_{\text{POSSIBILITY}}$. A person who believes that P is correct only if the possibility that P obtains; otherwise, she is mistaken.

I think they are both true as well. But CORRECT$_{\text{PROPOSITION}}$ has played a far more central role in philosophical treatments of believing. Indeed, CORRECT$_{\text{POSSIBILITY}}$ has largely been neglected.

One reason for this neglect is that propositions are standardly considered the *objects* of belief. Belief, on this view, is a *propositional* attitude, in the sense that propositions are the things that are believed. In Chapter 3, I offered reasons to think instead that possibilities are the objects of belief. But perhaps the primary support for the centrality of CORRECT$_{\text{PROPOSITION}}$ is the idea that there is a special link between belief and truth.

Many philosophers have said that when a person believes something their *believing* it is itself true or false, too. Here are some examples.

> Among the characterizations we may assign to human mental states and actions, there are two which stand out as specially important. We may characterize certain states as true (or false); we may characterize others as good (or evil). Beliefs, most obviously, may be described as true or false; desires, most obviously, may be described as good or evil. Those states and activities which can be evaluated on the true/false scale belong to the cognitive side of the soul; those states and activities which are evaluated on the good/evil scale belong to the affective, volitional side of the soul. At the highest level, the truth-bearing (or falseness-bearing) items are actualizations of the intellect; the goodness-bearing (or badness-bearing) items are actualizations of the will. (Kenny 1989, 75)

> As they are conceived and spoken of in our folk theory, both beliefs and the objects of beliefs can have semantic properties. Thus we may say either

> Maggie's belief is true.

> or

> What Maggie believes is true. (Stich 1985 31)

> Belief is ... a propositional attitude. But if belief states are relations to propositions, they are automatically truth-evaluable. They are true if the proposition that is their object is true' (Braddon-Mitchell and Jackson 1996, 177)

> [A]ccording to physicalism, beliefs are states of people's brains. So if Bloggs's beliefs are about things, it follows that states of his brain are about things. But how does a state of someone's brain get to be about Mt Everest?
> (Ravenscroft 2005, 125)

98   BELIEVING WITHOUT REPRESENTING

I will view a psychology as being commonsensical about the attitudes – in fact, as endorsing them—just in case it postulates states (entities, events, whatever) satisfying the following conditions:

(i)   They are semantically evaluable.
(ii) They have causal powers.
(iii) The implicit generalizations of commonsense belief/desire psychology are largely true of them.

In effect, I'm assuming that (i)–(iii) are the essential properties of the attitudes.

(Fodor 1987, 17)

These passages all express the idea that when a person believes something, the related proposition is not the only thing that is true or false. The person's believing it is also true or false. Let's call this TRUTH$_{\text{BELIEVING}}$.

TRUTH$_{\text{BELIEVING}}$ When a person who believes that P is correct, their believing that P is true; otherwise, it is false.

My aim in this chapter is to argue that we should reject it.[1]

This idea that believing is itself representational plays a central role in two influential philosophical projects. Some have argued that being capable of truth is part of what makes a belief the sort of thing it is. And they draw from this a normative moral: beliefs *aim* at being true, or a true belief is a better belief than a false one.[2] Here is how Bernard Williams put the idea in an influential essay.

[B]eliefs aim at truth. When I say that beliefs aim at truth, I have particularly in mind three things. First: that truth and falsehood are a dimension of an assessment of beliefs as opposed to many other psychological states and dispositions … [W]hen someone believes something, then he believes something which can be assessed as true or false, and his belief, in terms of the content of what he believes, is true or false.   (Williams 1973, 137)

If beliefs are not true or false, then claims like this about the nature and normative character of belief will need to be rethought. This rethinking need not involve denying a special link between belief and truth, for we can still hold that a person who believes that P is right or wrong depending on whether the proposition that

---

[1] Richard Floyd (2017) also rejects the idea that a person's believing something can be true or false, though he does not offer an argument against it. He notes, correctly in my view, that the idea is encouraged by hypostasizing believing. If one thinks that belief states are entities of some kind, then it may seem more natural to think of them as potential bearers of semantic properties.
[2] See, for instance, Williams (1973) and Velleman (2007).

BELIEVING AND TRUTH   99

P is true. But more care will be needed to describe the distinctive and peculiar relations linking belief and truth. (In the final chapter, I will argue that believing is not inherently normative. No belief state, I will argue, is a better belief state than any other.)

The idea that beliefs can be true or false also fits naturally into various explanatory projects. If a person's beliefs can be true or false, then beliefs must have informational or propositional or semantic content, and one can then ask how a mental state gets its content. The task here is akin to that of explaining how a bit of language comes to have its semantic properties. Here is how Jaegwon Kim puts the task in the case of belief.

> You hope that it will be a clear day tomorrow, and I believe that it will ... [T]hese states, though they are states of different persons and represent different attitudes (believing, hoping, ...), have the same content, expressed by the sentence "It will be a clear day tomorrow." And this content represents (or is) a certain state of affairs, namely, its being a clear day tomorrow.... *But in virtue of what do these intentional states have this content and represent the state of affairs they represent?* It can't be a brute fact about these states that they have this particular content and not some other; it must have an explanation. This is the basic question about mental content.   (Kim, 1996, 184; italics added)

The problem of explaining mental content, according to Kim, is the problem of explaining how a person's belief state gets the content it has.[3] Jackson and Braddon-Mitchell, in the passage I quoted earlier, suggest that a belief simply inherits the semantic properties of the relevant proposition, but in suggesting this they are admitting that some explanation is needed. And if, as the passage from Ravenscroft suggests, a person's beliefs are realized by states of her brain, then we may also feel a need to explain how a person's brain states can have propositional contents. But if, as I contend, belief states are not true or false, and so lack informational content, then these explanatory projects rest on a false presupposition. There may of course be real problems in the vicinity, ones that do call for explanation, and I'll mention them briefly at the end of Section 4.4. But to say the problems involve explaining how a belief state gets its content would be, if I am right, to mischaracterize them.

---

[3] I find it hard to place Robert Brandom's views in my story. He says he rejects representationalism, but he also says that this project's "animating thought is that the meaning of linguistic expressions and *the contents of intentional states,* indeed, awareness itself, should be understood, to begin with, in terms of playing a distinctive kind of role in *reasoning*" (Brandom 2000, 11; first italics added). I am not sure how to reject representationalism about belief without rejecting the idea that belief states have a content, and the best way to do this, it seems to me, is to deny that they are the right sorts of things to have contents.

100 BELIEVING WITHOUT REPRESENTING

4.2 Belief Properties and States Are Neither True Nor False

I now want to argue that believing is not representational. Let's start by asking whether belief properties can be true or false.

1. The proposition that the 504 stops at Garden.
3. The property of believing that the 504 stops at Garden.

Can 3 be true or false?

As Stich notes, if we answer Yes, then we face a second question: does 3 have the same truth value and, more generally, the same *semantic properties* as 1? Stich holds that propositions are the objects of belief, in the following sense: where P and Q are propositions, the property of believing that P is the property of believing that Q just in case P = Q. Stich thinks that this would explain why 3 has the same semantic properties as 1. But I think he is mistaken about this.

For it is not generally true that a property individuated by an object inherits that object's properties.[4] Consider the property of having a mass of 7 kg. That property is individuated by the number 7, for where N and M are numbers, the property of having a mass of N kg is the property of having a mass of M kg just in case N = M. Just as, according to Stich, propositions individuate belief properties, so numbers individuate mass properties. But the property of having a mass of 7 kg does not inherit the properties of the number 7. That number is odd and prime, but that mass is not odd or prime. 7 is the successor of 6 and is a factor of 21. But that mass property is not a successor of 6 nor a factor of 21. So, it is not in general true that a property individuated by an object inherits that object's properties. So, contra Stich, the fact that 3 is individuated by 1 could not by itself explain why 3 has the same semantic properties as 1.

In fact, this example helps us to answer our original question. It is not just that the property of having a mass of 7 kg does not share the arithmetic properties of the number 7. That property has no arithmetic properties at all. It is not even or odd or prime. And it bears no arithmetic relations to other mass properties. That property of having a mass of 7 kg is not one half the property of having a mass of 14 kg. Arithmetic relations do not hold between properties; they hold between numbers.

The point is not that mass properties cannot themselves have properties, for they can. Having a mass of 7 kg has the property of being a physical property, and it has the property of being an example in this book. The point is that they do not have *arithmetic* properties and do not stand in arithmetic *relations* to one another,

---

[4] What follows echoes points made in Matthews (2007) and Stalnaker (1984), though neither denies that beliefs can be true or false.

even though they are individuated by objects that do have such properties and that do stand in such relations to one another. To think otherwise is to confuse a property with the object that individuates it.

It seems to me that the idea that mental properties have semantic properties makes the same confusion. Belief properties like 3 do not have semantic properties, are not true or false, and do not bear semantic relations to other belief properties. This is not because they cannot have properties, for they can and do. It is rather, that they are not the right sort of entity to have semantic properties. To think they do is to confuse a property with the object that individuates it.

I have argued that we should resist the idea that belief properties can be true or false. But what about the fact or state of affairs that consists in a person's having a belief property, such as Jones's believing that the 504 stops at Garden? Is that state of affairs true?

I suspect that putting the question this way already makes clear that the answer is no. The fact that Jones believes that it stops there—that fact or state of affairs—is not true or false. That fact is not about Garden Avenue. It has no semantic properties.

And the reasons are basically the same as those for resisting saying that 3 is true. As we saw, the property of having a mass of 7 kg does not share the properties of the number 7. It is not odd or prime and is not a factor of 21. Now consider a book that weighs 7 kg. The fact that it weighs 7 kg is not odd or prime and is not a factor of 21. That fact is not larger than 6 or smaller than 25. The general point is that an instantiation of a property that is individuated by an object need not inherit the properties of that object.

4.3 Tokens, Types, and Confusing Nominals

I have suggested that belief properties and belief states are not true or false. One might think that there is some other entity—*the* belief, or *Jones'* belief, or her *token* belief—and that it can be true or false. But what might such an entity be, if it is neither a property of believing something nor a state that consists of someone's having such a property? I don't deny that propositions can be true or false. And if there are representations inside our brains then they can be true or false, I suppose. And I don't deny that belief properties can be individuated in terms of such entities. But neither propositions nor these representations are themselves belief properties or states, any more than a number is a mass, even though mass properties and states are individuated by numbers. A person's believing something is not itself a proposition or a neural representation.

This conclusion may be surprising to someone who holds that there are belief tokens. For talk of "mental state tokens" is very familiar, and it plainly suggests that beliefs are a sort of particular which would make them candidates for having semantic properties. But just what sort of particular would a belief token be? It

102 BELIEVING WITHOUT REPRESENTING

could not be what I have called a belief property, such as believing that the 504 stops at Garden, for a belief token would surely be an instantiation of a belief property. Perhaps a belief token is what I have called a belief state, such as the fact that Jones believes that the 504 stops at Garden. But then belief tokens would not be true or false, for (or so I have argued) belief states are not true or false. I am not sure what else there is for a belief token to be.

But we have anyway already seen reason to resist the idea that there are belief tokens. A token, I take it, is an individual we can count. I have three subway tokens in my bag, and two tokens of Quine's *Word and Object*. But as we saw in Chapter 2, there is something odd in the idea of counting beliefs. Like all of us, Jones believes many things, but how many believings by her are there? To answer this, we might try counting her beliefs, but then we are counting the *things* she believes, not her believings of them. In this respect, believing something is like possessing something. If Sarah owns twenty books, she has twenty possessions, but how many possessings by her are there? Is there one possessing for each book, and so twenty possessings? Our ordinary understanding of "possession" does not yield answers to these questions. This, together with the fact that the plural "possessings" sounds so odd is reason, I think, to resist saying there are any token possessings at all. Resisting this is compatible with saying that Sarah has many thousands of possessions. I suggest we say the same about belief: we can count the things a person believes, but we cannot count her believings of them. The instantiation of a belief property is not a particular, and so not a token.

I suspect that the idea that there are belief tokens is encouraged on a subtle linguistic slide. Notice how Stich formulates what he takes to be common-sense about belief.

> As they are conceived and spoken of in our folk theory, both beliefs and the objects of beliefs can have semantic properties. Thus we may say either
>
> Maggie's belief is true.
>
> or
>
> What Maggie believes is true.
>
> However, the truth value of a belief must be the same as the truth value of the object of the belief. Thus common sense finds nothing but paradox in a claim like
>
> John's belief is true, though what he believes is false.   (Stich 1985)

To refer to Maggie's mental state, Stich uses the derived nominal "Maggie's belief," rather than the gerundive nominal "Maggie's believing."[5] Here is the distinction using my example.

---

[5] This use of the terms "derived" and "gerundive" are due to Chomsky (1975). For discussion of their differences, see Steward (1997), chapter 4.

TOKENS, TYPES, AND CONFUSING NOMINALS   103

(a)   Jones' believing that the 504 stops at Garden

(b)   Jones' belief that the 504 stops at Garden

(c)   The belief that the 504 stops at Garden

I claim that a noun like (a) refers to a certain state of affairs or fact. A noun like (c), in contrast, is most naturally understood as referring to a proposition. This is noted by the OED, which says that the word "belief" can mean: "[s]omething believed; a proposition or set of propositions held to be true."

But a noun like (b) sits confusingly between (a) and (c). It can be used to refer to what I am calling a belief state, as in the following.

Jones' belief that the 504 stops at Garden is unjustified.

Jones's *believing* something can be unjustified, but the *property* of believing it cannot be unjustified, and neither can the proposition in question. But (b) can also be used to refer to what I am calling a belief property.

Jones' belief that the 504 stops at Garden is widely shared.

The fact that Jones has the property of believing it cannot be widely shared, though many can share that property. Likewise, my being tall cannot be widely shared, though many can share my height. And we cannot share propositions any more than we can share numbers. So, a noun like (b) can be used to refer to properties as well as to facts. And just to add to the complexity, (b) can even be used to refer to a proposition.

Jones' belief that the 504 stops at Garden has never been denied.

This is most naturally understood as saying that the proposition Jones believes has never been denied. One can deny *that* she believes it, but this is not what that sentence says. And of course you cannot deny the property of believing it. So, a noun like (b) can be used to refer to all three members of our original trio: propositions, properties and facts.

The upshot is that it is not at all clear that in addition to propositions, belief properties, and belief states, there is a further entity—Jones' belief—that might be true or false. All of this applies equally well to assertions. It is commonly said that assertions are true, but consider the following.

(a2)   Jones' asserting that the 504 stops at Garden

(a3)   Asserting that the 504 stops at Garden

(a4)   The assertion that the 504 stops at Garden

104 BELIEVING WITHOUT REPRESENTING

(a5)   Jones' assertion that the 504 stops at Garden

I take it that (a3) is a type or sort of speech act of which (a2) is a case or an instance. An act is an event, and events are countable. We can ask how many times someone asserted something. But I find it odd to suppose that an act (or an event of someone's performing an act) can have semantic properties or can be true or false. *What* a person asserts might be true, but the act of asserting it cannot be true and nor can someone's performing that act. Of course, a person who asserts that P is right depending on whether the proposition that P is true. So, there is a close link between assertion and truth even if, as I suspect, acts of asserting are neither true nor false.

4.4 Beliefs and Realizers

Some say that a person's beliefs are realized by states of her brain and that those brain states can be true or false. Ian Ravenscroft gives a clear statement of this view.

> Bloggs's belief that Mt Everest is 8,848 meters high is about Mt Everest and represents Everest as being a certain height....Now, according to physicalism, beliefs are states of people's brains. So if Bloggs's beliefs are about things, it follows that states of his brain are about things. But how does a state of someone's brain get to be about Mt Everest?   (Ravenscroft 2005, 125)

If this is right, then an explanation is needed of how a brain state gets its content. This is one version of what Kim called the problem of mental content. To assess all of this, it is helpful to note that Ravenscroft's view has two parts.

One is that a person's beliefs are realized by states of their brain. I will assume that this mental realization is a relation between facts, and that the idea is that a belief state is realized by a brain state. And I will assume that by a brain state we mean that some part of a brain (or maybe an entire brain) has some property.[6] Let's call the relevant part of Jones' brain, "B," and let's call the relevant property "being P." The first part of Ravenscroft's view, then, is that the fact that Jones believes that the 504 stops at Garden is realized by the fact that B is P.

The second part of the view is that the brain state that realizes Jones' belief can be true or false. Why should we think this? Here is a natural line of thought:

(i)   Jones' believing that the 504 stops at Garden is true.

(ii)   Jones' believing that the 504 stops at Garden is (realized by) B's being P.

---

[6] For more discussion of this, see Steward (1997).

So, (iii) B's being P is true.

The argument is not sound, though, since its first premise is false. Or at any rate, I contend that it is false. So I think we should reject this argument.

What is more, I think we already have good reason to reject the argument's conclusion. Indeed, the reasons I gave for thinking that Jones' believing that the 504 stops at Garden is neither true nor false apply equally well to the state of affairs of B's being P. Remember that B is a part of Jones' brain, and P is some property. Is the state of affairs that consists in B's having that property true? I suspect that put this way most would agree that the answer is no. That state of affairs is not the right sort of entity to have semantical properties, any more than is the state of affairs that consists in Jones' having the property of believing that the 504 stops at Garden. And nothing here turns on just what part of Jones' brain B is or on what property P is. An object's having a certain property is simply not the right sort of entity to be true or false. So even if Jones' belief is realized by a state of her brain, I suggest that we reject the idea that that state of her brain can be true or false.

This means that Kim's account of the problem of mental content rests on a mistake. Even if a person's beliefs are realized by states of her brain, we do not need to explain how her brain states can be true or false, for they are not true or false. There is no problem of explaining how belief states get the contents they do, since belief states have no contents.

I don't deny that there are, though, genuine problems in the vicinity that do need explaining. It is a fact, after all, that Jones believes that the 504 stops at Garden, and as with any fact, we may need or want to explain how this fact came to be. We already know some of the possibilities: maybe she saw the street signs, or studied the transit map, or learned it from her parents. A careful study of Jones might reveal the answer. There is also a more general problem in the vicinity. How is it that a being like Jones can have such a property as believing that the 504 stops at Garden? After all, trees and rocks cannot, so what is it about Jones that makes her capable of having it? More work needs to be done, I think, to sharpen this problem. But its answer might draw on facts about Jones' biological constitution and her causal and social relations to her environment. And perhaps these are the very sorts of facts one might have drawn on if one hoped to explain how Jones' brain states can be true or false. So my point is not that there are no genuine explanatory projects in the vicinity, but only that it is a mistake to think of them as aiming to explain how belief states get their content.

4.5 Derivative Truth

One might agree that belief properties and belief states cannot strictly speaking be true or false but insist that they can be true or false in a derivative sense. Perhaps

106 BELIEVING WITHOUT REPRESENTING

we could say that the property of believing that P is *derivatively true* just in case the proposition that P is true. Likewise for belief states. Of course, there can be no objection to introducing a derivative sense of truth, so long as we clearly define it. But doing so carries some risks and won't help with the normative projects I mentioned at the outset.

Here is how J.L. Austin put the idea that while we *call* beliefs true or false, strictly speaking, only *propositions* are true or false.[7]

> Some say that "truth is primarily a property of beliefs." But it may be doubted whether the expression "a true belief" is at all common outside philosophy and theology: and it seems clear that a man is said to hold a true belief when *and in the sense* that he believes (in) something which is true, or believes that something which is true is true. Moreover if, as some also say, a belief is "of the nature of a picture," then it is of the nature of what cannot be true, though it may be, for example, faithful.   (Austin 1950, 112; italics added)

We see the same idea in this passage from Scott Soames.

> It is a truism that a belief, assertion, hypothesis, or conjecture represents the world as being a certain way, and so is capable of being true or false. Ordinarily, what we mean by this is that *what is believed, asserted, hypothesizes, or conjectured* represents the world and so is true or false.
>
> (Soames 2010, 63–4; italics in original)

Whether Austin and Soames are right that this is what philosophers have meant, or perhaps should have meant, in calling beliefs true, it is worth making clear why the so-called truism is actually false. For the idea that a belief can be true or false fits naturally into a wide variety of familiar philosophical views and projects that will need to be rethought if, as I have argued, beliefs are not true or false.

For many purposes, it is probably harmless to speak of the semantic properties of a belief property or fact in this derivative sense. But if our goal is to understand the metaphysics of mental things it is best, I think, to avoid derivative senses introduced merely for the sake of convenience. As I said above, I think most would agree that properties and facts are not the right sorts of things to have semantic properties, or to be true or false. Objects are. If our goal is to understand the various ontological categories populating our mental lives, then it is best to make explicit what sorts of things can be true of belief properties and belief states.

---

[7] David Armstrong is another of the rare philosophers who explicitly denied that beliefs are true or false, insisting that only propositions are genuinely true or false. Armstrong suggested that perhaps we should allow beliefs to be true in a derivative sense (Armstrong 1973, chapter 4).

DERIVATIVE TRUTH   107

More importantly, though, admitting this derivative sense would make it more difficult to specify the special relation that belief bears to truth. Recall the passage from Bernard Williams, who said that unlike other mental states, belief by its very nature aims at being true, which suggests that a false belief is in some way defective *qua* belief. A derivative sense of truth would make it more difficult to capture this idea. For this derivative sense would apply equally well to *all* propositional mental things. Hoping that P would also be true in this derivative sense just in case the proposition that P is true, as would doubting that P, imagining that P, and wishing that P. But Williams meant to capture something peculiar to belief. And he also meant to capture the idea that a false belief was somehow defective. We would then have to explain why a derivatively false belief is defective but a derivatively false imagining or hoping is not, since there is nothing defective in imagining or hoping something false. A derivative sense of true would thus blur the differences between belief and other propositional mental facts and so obscure whatever normative links obtain between belief and truth. (Insisting that only beliefs and not imaginings or hopings are derivatively true simply begs the question that an appeal to derivative truth was meant to help answer: what is distinctive about believing.) In short, it would make it harder, not easier, to capture any special relations between belief and truth.

As I said at the start, I do not deny that there is a special relation between belief and truth. When a person believes that P, they are right if the proposition that P is true, and they are wrong if that proposition is false. This link is missing when a person imagines or supposes or hopes something. So we can still recognize a special link between belief and truth even if we deny that beliefs are themselves true or false. And this link is no accident: it is part of what it is for a person to believe something that they are right or wrong in believing it depending on the truth of a proposition. In this sense, it is a constitutive link.

Perhaps we can also capture the normative claims without presupposing that beliefs are true or false. We might say that in believing something, a person aims to be right. A person who believes that P when P is false has made a mistake or is mistaken. And we could say that it is better to be right than to be wrong in what we believe. These sound to me like plausible generalizations. But they involve assessing the believer, and one might hope to be able to assess the belief states themselves. Could we say that if P is true and q is false, then S's believing that P is better than S's believing that q? This would be an assessment, not of the believer, S, but of one of S's believings. I will return to this in the final chapter.

But it is worth considering once again the analogy I noted between believing and owning. We can assess what Jones believes, and likewise we can assess what Sarah owns. Some of her books might be much better than others. But can we also assess her owning of the books? Would we say that her owning of *War and Peace* is better than her owning of *Cat's Cradle* on the grounds that the first is a better book? Of course, it can be better to own some things than others, and it might be

108 BELIEVING WITHOUT REPRESENTING

quite good to own *War and Peace*. But these are assessments of the owner or of her possessions, they are not assessments of her possessings. For my part, I can't see what it could be for one owning of a thing to be a better owning than another. Likewise, while it might be better to believe and be right than to believe and be wrong, I can't see what it could be for one believing to be better than another. But if there is sense to be made here, it won't help to talk about beliefs as if they were true or false. For beliefs are neither true nor false.

4.6 On Wanting

The idea that beliefs are true or false fits neatly with an equally common idea about desire. The idea is that desires can be satisfied or not, that while beliefs have truth conditions, desires have satisfaction conditions. Anthony Kenny puts the idea in terms of a contrast between truth and falsity on one side and good and evil on the other.

> Beliefs, most obviously, may be described as true or false; desires, most obviously may be described as good or evil. Those states and activities which can be evaluated on the true/false scale belong to the cognitive side of the soul; those states and activities which are evaluated on the good/evil scale belong to the affective, volitional side of the soul.   (Kenny 1989, 75)

An asymmetry here between beliefs and desires would be odd. Why would desires be good or evil if beliefs were not true or false? What would account for this difference?[8] In fact, however, there is no asymmetry. For I think that it is also wrong to suppose that a person's desires are satisfied or that they have satisfaction conditions. When a person gets something they want, it is the person and not their desire that is, in the primary sense, satisfied. Only in a derivative sense can we say that a person's desires are satisfied.

As general rule, it is pretty satisfying to get or do something one wants to get or do.[9] Suppose Jones wants a martini. And suppose she makes herself one. Very likely, if it is a good martini anyway, Jones will be satisfied, for she got what she wanted. And we can say what would satisfy Jones in this case: having a good martini. So there is a condition such that being in it would satisfy Jones when she

---

[8] Thanks to Peter Hanks for forcing me think about this point.

[9] Actually, it is satisfying to get what *one thinks* one wants, regardless of whether one really does want it. In other work (Hunter 2021) I argue that wanting is just lacking something one needs, and that one can believe that one wants something and be wrong. Wanting, I argue, is not a mental or psychological state, though believing that one wants something is, and it is this sort of belief that is relevant in explaining rational action. Developing all of this here would take us too far afield, so for present purposes I will set this aside.

wants a martini. To this extent, when a person desires something there is an associated satisfaction condition.

Of course, people are rarely completely satisfied. For one thing, you can't always get what you want, and sometimes what you get is not good enough. People ordinarily want a lot of things, and it is hard to be satisfied when you only get some of what you want. Something similar is true of belief. It is rare for someone to be completely right about how things are. They will be right about some things and wrong about others. In this respect, desires are like beliefs. No one is ever completely right or completely satisfied.

But desires differ from beliefs in important ways. For one thing, a person can have incompatible desires. Jones might want to see the new *Star Wars* movie and also to stay at home and work, knowing she cannot do both. In that case, if she sees the movie, then she may be a little dissatisfied, even though she got one thing she wanted, because she didn't get something else she wanted. What is more, a person may want something while wishing she did not want it. Peter might crave a donut while wishing he did not crave it, or anyway while wishing it did not move him to act, and he may even end up unhappy when he gets the donut. The sorts of psychic complexity possible with desires are largely absent in the case of belief.[10]

Still, as a general rule, a person is satisfied when she gets what she wants. Should we also say that when a person gets what she wants, her *desire* is satisfied? If we do say this, then we mean something different by "satisfied." The person is satisfied because they got what they wanted. But a person's desires do not want anything. They don't have desires of their own. So whatever we might want to mean in saying of a person's desire that it is satisfied cannot be what we mean when we say of a person who gets what she wanted that she is satisfied.

It seems to me that what we mean when we say that a person's desires are satisfied is that she got something she believed that she wanted and (so) is satisfied. And when we say her desire has a satisfaction condition, what we mean is that there is a condition such that she will be satisfied just in case she believes that it is met. The primary sense of satisfaction here is one that applies to persons. Only in a derivative sense, I think, do we speak of a desire as satisfied. Likewise, the primary notion in the case of belief is that of a person being right or wrong, and only in a derivative sense do we speak of a belief's being true or false.

Again, it might be harmless to say that when a person is right their belief is true. Likewise, it might be harmless to say that when a person is satisfied so is her desire. But I think these short-hands carry real risks. For starters, if our goal is to get clear on the nature of our mental lives then it is best to avoid the short-hands. What is

---

[10] Largely, but not entirely. In other work, I have argued that a person can believe something while wishing they did not believe it, not (just) because they wish it were not so, but because they wish they were the sort of person who could, in the face of the evidence they have, not believe it. But such cases are necessarily the rare exception. Incompatible and alienated desires are far more common and can last longer. (Hunter 2011a)

more, it is all too easy to commit the homuncular fallacy of supposing that desires and beliefs have a psychic life of their own. More seriously, though, these short-hands can distort the genuine explanatory problems we face in trying to understand the mind. Explaining how people but not trees or rocks can have beliefs and desires is a real explanatory task, even though I think it is hard to make it precise. But the idea that we need to explain how a person's beliefs and desires get truth and satisfaction conditions is a pseudo-problem, one that is fostered by an inattentive reliance on this sort of short-hand.

Most importantly, though, these short-hands can make the person who has the beliefs and desires disappear from view. This complaint is familiar from action theory, where Jennifer Hornsby (1995) and others have said that thinking of actions as bodily movements leaves out the agent. Whether this is so in the case of action theory is not my concern here. But I do think that in the philosophy of mind the idea that beliefs are true or false and that desires are satisfied or not does risk making the subject disappear. Returning our focus, as I have tried to do in this chapter, to the more fundamental ideas of a person's being right or wrong in believing something and being satisfied or not in desiring something can, I think, help us keep the person in view. This is important, I think, if we are to understand the normative dimensions of these attitudes, which is a point I will return to in my final chapter.

In these first four chapters, I have described the ontology of believing. On my view, to believe something is to be in position to do, think, and feel things in light of a possibility whose obtaining would make one right. Beliefs are not themselves causes, capacities or dispositions. Rather, in believing something, the believer is set to exercise and manifest the capacities and dispositions she already has or will acquire in light of the reasons she takes there to be. The image of knowing and believing as like being more or less at home among the ways things are is meant to evoke this idea of a position. What is more, believing something is not a way of representing the world. The objects of belief are possibilities, ways that things are or could have been, and not representations of such ways. And while one's belief states are not true or false, there is a tight connection between belief and how things are, for whether one is right or wrong in believing something depends only on whether the possibility that is the object of that belief obtains. That logical aspect of belief, as Anscombe called it, is at the heart of believing and distinguishes it from other mental states. It also grounds the limits of belief, and exploring them is the task of the next two chapters.

5
Objectivity and Credal Illusions

My first four chapters focused on the ontology of believing, on what it is to believe. These next two focus on the limits of belief, on what there is to believe. I said that the core logical aspect of believing is that a person who believes something is right or wrong depending on the facts. This is connected to two other features. One is that there is something essentially objective or impersonal in a person's beliefs, since it is an objective fact that she has the beliefs she does. The other is that there is, at the same time, something essentially personal or subjective about a person's beliefs, something that marks her perspective as her own. Both the objectivity and the subjectivity of belief concern limits to what a person can believe, limits to what she can be right or wrong about, and this is how they are connected to the logical aspect of belief. Perhaps the primary virtue of the modal view of the objects of belief is that it allows us to see all of this very clearly. The aim of this chapter and the next is to develop these ideas.

The objectivity and subjectivity I have in mind both concern limits to what a person can believe. Some limits are objective because they apply to everyone but others are subjective because they are different for each person. The objective limits give rise to credal illusions, where a person thinks she believes something when, in fact, she does not. The subjective ones give rise to credal necessities, possibilities a person cannot help but believe obtain. The modal view of belief can help us to describe these limits, to understand their sources, and to appreciate their puzzling nature. This chapter is about the objective limits. The next is about the subjective ones.

The credal illusions I will discuss are illustrated by the puzzling cases I mentioned in Chapter 3. Many theorists take those puzzles to show that the modal view of the objects of belief must be mistaken, that there must be more belief properties than there are possibilities. In effect, the objection is that the modal view gets the *limits* of belief wrong, that there is more to believe than the modal view allows. In Chapter 3 I explained why I disagree with this, but I acknowledged that the cases teach us something important about the nature of believing. As I see it, they teach us something about what happens when we cross the limits of belief, and they illustrate the different grounds or sources of these limits. This chapter explores this.

In Section 5.1, I will introduce the notion of a credal illusion, where a person thinks she believes something when, in fact, she does not. I will then show how certain of the familiar puzzle cases involve just such illusions, and what the cases

---

On Believing: Being Right in a World of Possibilities. David Hunter, Oxford University Press. © David Hunter 2022.
DOI: 10.1093/oso/9780192859549.003.0006

reveal about the various grounds or sources of the limits to belief. I will first consider, in Section 5.2, credal illusions involving possibilities that are beyond our cognitive reach. I'll illustrate these with cases from Russell and Frege. Section 5.3 looks at credal illusions involving future possibilities, illustrated by the so-called Sleeping Beauty puzzle. In Section 5.4, I will consider credal illusions involving mere possibilities, and I will discuss Twin-Earth cases. One point that will emerge is that credal limits are contingent: had things been different in various ways, a person could have believed things that she cannot now believe. But not every theorist agrees that belief is objective in this way, and the very idea of there being such limits is itself puzzling. While I agree that the limits are puzzling, I don't think they are a problem that an account of the nature of believing needs to solve. Rather, I think the risk of credal illusions is the price we pay for believing anything at all. I'll discuss this in the final two sections.

But before turning to that, I want to say something about the limits of the modal view itself. The modal view of believing is silent on what possibilities there are, just as an account of knowledge should be silent on what facts there are. My examples have involved my character Jones and her belief that the 504 stops at Garden Avenue. But the modal view can allow that we have beliefs about ethical, religious, and aesthetic matters too. If there are contingent facts about such matters, possibilities that obtain but need not have, then those possibilities can be the objects of belief. It strikes me that there are such possibilities, and that we can and do believe in their obtaining. Jones ought to stop at Garden Avenue, and she may know this and so believe it, and she may believe that Sarah is not a very good streetcar driver. She may believe that God gave Sarah poor eyesight, and that the Mona Lisa is a more beautiful painting than any of Rothko's works. These beliefs concern contingent matters of fact, I take it, since it is contingent whether Jones ought to stop at Garden, whether Sarah is a good driver, whether God gave Sarah poor eyesight (assuming he did), and whether Da Vinci created beautiful paintings. It may be a tricky matter understanding what makes these possibilities obtain. And friends of the modal view can agree that possibilities are the objects of belief while disagreeing on whether there are such possibilities. It is best, I think, for the modal view itself to be silent on this.

What does the modal view say about *non*-contingent ethical, religious, and aesthetic matters? I said in Chapter 3 that I doubt anyone ever believes an impossibility. Or, more cautiously, I know of no pure case of someone believing one. This applies to ethical, religious, and aesthetic impossibilities too. Necessities are complicated too. The modal view does not entail this, but I'm inclined to think that every believer is already in position to act in light of how things must have been, and so already believes them. To test this, we'd need a pure case of someone changing her mind about some necessity without changing her mind on contingent matters. I know of no such case. At the same time, I doubt those necessities cast any light on what people do, think, or feel. Why the world is one way rather than another cannot be explained or rationalized by how it had to be. I'll say a little more about this in Chapter 7 when I discuss inference and deductive validity. But I am afraid that all of this is matter for another book.

5.1 Objectivity and Credal Illusions

I take it that if there are limits to what a person can believe, then these limits are objective. In calling them objective, I mean that a person can be mistaken about them. She can think she is believing something when, in fact, she is not because she has crossed beyond the limits. In such a case, the person would be suffering what I will call a *credal illusion*. Before looking at cases, I want to describe at a general level what such illusions would be like.

It is helpful to start with visual illusions. A person can think she is seeing an object when, as a matter of fact, there is no object there to be seen. It is not up to her what there is to see. This is set by the world. The existence of such limits is part of what makes visual perception objective. And this explains why a person can suffer a visual illusion. It is also a contingent matter what there is for a person to see. It depends on how she is positioned in the world, and on what visible things there are, and both of these are contingent matters. She might have occupied a different position, and other things might have existed. The limits of visual perception are thus objective and contingent.

Two features of visual illusions are noteworthy. First, they can be *persistent*. It can continue to look as if there is a puddle on the road ahead, even once one has realized it is an illusion. Second, visual illusions are usually *accompanied* by non-illusory vision. One actually sees the road when one thinks one sees a puddle. And it seems likely that this accompanying genuine vision plays some role in encouraging the original illusion. Credal illusions display these same two features. They can persist even after one spots them, and they are usually accompanied by genuine beliefs. The cases I will consider all involve these two features.

In describing these cases, I will be assuming that the objects of belief are possibilities. But this is inessential. The question whether there are limits to belief is independent of the question what the objects of belief are. One could accept the propositional view of belief and hold that what propositions there are for a person to believe is an objective matter set independently of us. One could add that it is a contingent matter what propositions there are, or anyway, what propositions a person can believe. And one could also accept the possibility of credal illusions. One would then hold that a person can think she has got hold in belief of a proposition when, in fact, she has not, either because there is no such proposition or because she is not able to believe it. So the question whether there are limits to belief is independent of the question what are the objects of belief.

114 OBJECTIVITY AND CREDAL ILLUSIONS

Still, one virtue of the modal view is that it allows us to identify very clearly the different sources of those limits. In describing them, I will appeal to a certain logical or metaphysical relation that can obtain among possibilities, one I first mentioned in Chapter 2. It is illustrated by the following.

(1) The possibility that there is someone at the 504 stop.
(2) The possibility that Sarah is at the 504 stop.

If (2) obtains, then so does (1). The obtaining of (2) thus entails or requires the obtaining of (1). Of course, (1) can obtain even if (2) does not. But in that case, some other possibility must obtain, such as (3).

(3) The possibility that Omar is at the 504 stop.

The point here is that (1) cannot obtain unless some other possibility does. It cannot just be the case that *someone* is at the 504 stop; there must be a particular person there. I will say that (2) and (3) are potential "witnesses" for (1).

A person can believe that (1) obtains without believing, of any of its potential witnesses, that it obtains. She can believe there is someone at the stop without believing that Omar is there, or that Sarah is there, or etc. If she is right in believing that someone is there, then one of the potential witnesses for (1) will of course obtain. She can even believe that (1) obtains without any idea at all who it is. Maybe believing (1) requires knowing *something* about the sort of thing—a person—whose presence at the stop is needed for (1) to obtain. But she can, in any event, believe that it obtains without believing, of any of its potential witnesses, that *it* obtains.

Two claims about potential witnesses are controversial but worth noting.

CONTINGENT: It is contingent what potential witnesses there are for a given possibility.

I am inclined to accept this. It is contingent what people there are. Sarah and Omar never had children, but if they had, one of them could have been at the 504 stop. Since they never had children, it is not possible that one of their children is at the stop. But since they could have had children, that could have been possible. (We might say it is possibly possible, but not possible.) In that case, there would have been witnesses for (1) other than those there are.[1]

---

[1] This assumes that it is contingent what is possible. If so, then had things been different, things that are not now possible would have been possible. A parallel point can be made about propositions. If what propositions there are depends on how things are, then had things been different there would have been different propositions. All of this is controversial. But I don't think it matters for the thesis that there are objective limits to believing. If what is possible is not contingent, or if all propositions

OBJECTIVITY AND CREDAL ILLUSIONS 115

The second claim is this:

LACK: There may be no potential witnesses for a given possibility.

To see why we might want to accept this, consider the following.

(4) The possibility that the Earth has a second moon.

Since the Earth has only one moon, (4) does not obtain. But the Earth could have had a second moon. Other planets do. So while (4) does not obtain, it might have. For it to obtain, some other possibility would have to witness it. In this respect, (4) is like (1). The witness for (4) would have to be a possibility, concerning some *particular* thing, that it is a moon of the Earth. Is there such a thing? Is there something that is not a moon of the Earth but could have been? This is a question for astronomers, and I don't know the answer. Maybe one of the moons of Jupiter could have been a moon of the Earth. Or maybe some of the meteors that struck the Earth could have instead joined together to form a second moon. Or maybe there will be, in the future, a second moon formed in some way. These are questions for astronomy to answer, but I take it that the answer might be No. And suppose that is the answer. That is, suppose there is nothing that now exists, or that existed in the past, or that will exist in the future, that could have been but isn't a second moon of the Earth. In that case, there would be no possibility whose obtaining would be a witness for (4). It would have no potential witnesses. It could have had one, but it does not.[2]

Here is the structure of the credal illusions I will discuss in the next sections. They all involve a person's thinking she has got hold of a witness for a possibility that either lacks one or where the witness is beyond belief. The illusion is persistent in part because the person has grasped a genuine possibility. But it is an illusion because there is no witness for it, though the person thinks she has got hold of one. The structure is the same as for visual illusions. The person sees the road and the horizon, and thinks she sees a puddle, but there is no puddle.

---

exist necessarily, then that thesis says that which of the possibilities (propositions) a person can believe depends on which ones obtain (are true) and on that person's relations to them. But I will continue to speak as if it is contingent what is possible.

   [2] What I say here about possibilities follows Stalnaker (2011, 14–19). He uses containment properties to illustrate the idea. An envelope can have the property of containing three sheets of paper only if three particular sheets of paper each have the property of being inside it. The envelope on my desk does not have that property, but it might have had it. And if it had, three pieces of paper would have been inside it. Those papers might actually exist. They might be the three papers now cluttering my desk. The possibility that those three papers are in the envelope is thus a potential witness for the possibility that the envelope contains three pieces of paper. But that envelope might also have contained three pieces of paper that do not actually exist. So some witnesses for the possibility that the envelope contains three pieces of paper do not exist, but might have.

116 OBJECTIVITY AND CREDAL ILLUSIONS

In this section I have introduced the idea of a credal illusion. I have characterized it in terms of the modal view of belief, but I noted that one who accepts the propositional view can agree that credal illusions are possible. I then identified a relation, being a witness of, that can obtain between possibilities. And I noted two controversial claims: that it is contingent what potential witness there are for a given possibility; and that there may be no witnesses for a given possibility. These ideas can help us understand the illusions present in the familiar puzzle cases of belief.

5.2 Unbelievable Possibilities

What a person can believe is limited by her relations to what there is, and specifically by what she knows and believes about those things. I'll consider cases from Russell and Frege that illustrate this. Both drew attention to the possibility of credal illusions, though neither used that term or examined the phenomenon in much detail. The cases concern beliefs about particular objects and properties, and they are meant to show how the limits of belief can be grounded in our cognitive and linguistic limits. But they also nicely illustrate the two features of credal illusions I want to highlight: they are persistent and they are accompanied by genuine belief. And they show one way in which the limits of belief are contingent. Russell's story is a little simpler, so I will start with it.

Russell's case involves believing something about a particular person. He held that we can have such a belief only if we are acquainted with the individual in question, and he famously held that we are not acquainted with other people. On his view, this means that we cannot even *entertain* things that we know other people believe about themselves. Here is how he put it.

> [W]hen we say anything about Bismarck, we should like if we could, to make the judgment which Bismarck alone can make, namely the judgment of which he himself is a constituent. In this we are necessarily defeated, since the actual Bismarck is unknown to us. But we know that there is an object B, called Bismarck, and that B was an astute diplomatist. We can thus *describe* the proposition we should like to affirm....This proposition, which is described and is known to be true, is what interests us; but we are not acquainted with the proposition itself, and do not know it, though we know it is true. (Russell 1912, 31)

I think Russell was wrong about the epistemic requirements on believing things about individuals. We can disagree about what those requirements are while agreeing that there are some. I won't try to settle those debates here. My interest is in how the existence of such requirements, whatever they are precisely, give rise to credal illusions, and so illustrate one ground for the objective limits of belief.

Russell's case illustrates the two central features of credal illusions. First, the illusion is accompanied by genuine belief. Russell says that while we cannot believe (or even entertain) the possibility Bismarck himself believes, we can describe it. We can put Russell's claim in terms of the idea of a witness to a possibility. Russell's case involves something a little more radical.

A. The possibility that Bismarck is an astute diplomat.
B. The possibility that the Chancellor of Germany is an astute diplomat.

A is a potential witness for B. Russell says that only Bismarck himself can entertain or believe A. The rest of us, regrettably, are only able to believe possibilities such as B, whose obtaining we know to require a witness, though it is one we are not able to grasp. In believing B, we believe that some witness for it also obtains. And (if we share Russell's views on acquaintance) we believe that Bismarck is able to entertain and believe that witness. But because we are not acquainted with Bismarck, we cannot believe in the obtaining of the possibility that, as a matter of fact, witnesses B.

But, as Russell notes, we "should like to if we could." And it seems that we are able to: after all, we have a name for the man, and we know he exists, and we know that a possibility obtains that witnesses a possibility that we believe obtains. But, Russell says, though we should like to believe in the obtaining of A, we are "necessarily defeated." The illusion here is that we are able to share Bismarck's belief. The illusion is persistent in that it continues even when we know about it. And its persistence is abetted by the fact that we are able to believe a possibility that is witnessed by the very one we cannot believe.

Again, I am not here defending Russell's views on acquaintance. I want to set aside what the precise limits are, and focus on the fact that there are such limits and on how they give rise to credal illusions.

Frege's case is a little more complicated. It concerns beliefs about properties. He held that there is a deep ontological difference between objects and properties (which he called functions). He held that properties and objects have different logical roles. He characterized the difference by saying that while objects are *saturated*, properties are *un*saturated. The metaphor doesn't matter, but importantly, Frege held that natural languages are not able to express certain truths about properties. For instance, he held that it cannot state the fact that the property of being a horse is a property. To try to say this, we might take the name of the property, "is a horse," and put it in subject position in a sentence that then ascribes to it the property of being a property. But this attempt, Frege says, is necessarily defeated: for in putting the phrase in subject position we either get something ungrammatical (e.g., "Is a horse is a property") or else we get something whose subject term does not refer to a property (e.g., "The property of being a horse is a property").

118 OBJECTIVITY AND CREDAL ILLUSIONS

> A similar thing happens when we say as regards the sentence 'this rose is red':
> The grammatical predicate 'is red' belongs to the subject 'this rose.' Here the
> words 'The grammatical predicate "is red"' are not a grammatical predicate but a
> subject. *By the very act of explicitly calling it a predicate, we deprive it of this
> property.* (Frege 1952, 46; emphasis added)

The difficulty Frege thinks he sees here extends to the deepest parts of logic, he
thought, since logic needs to be able to recognize and make explicit the distinction
between objects and concepts. But this, he said, is not possible in a natural
language. He tries to explain why:

> with the use of my terms ['concept'] and ['object'] I have got hold of a distinction
> of the highest importance. I admit that there is a quite peculiar obstacle in the
> way of an understanding with my reader. By a kind of necessity of language, my
> expressions, taken literally, sometimes miss my thought, in that I mention an
> object, when what I intend is a concept. I fully realize that in such cases I was
> relying upon a reader who would be ready to meet me half-way— who does not
> begrudge a pinch of salt. (Frege 1984, 193)

Frege held that while natural languages are not able to express what we want to
say, an artificially constructed language can. One virtue, as he saw it, of his
begriffschrift was precisely to make it possible for us to say these things.

Here again the details don't matter. Whether Frege was right about the ontological difference between objects and properties is not my interest. Nor does it
matter whether Frege was right that only in an artificial language could we state
this difference. My interest, rather, is in the idea that there are limits to belief and
the way this gives rise to credal illusions. It looks, Frege says, as if we should be
able to believe, of a certain property, that it is a property. But our ordinary way of
formulating this belief fails, and this failure is persistent. Even once we recognize
the failure, we continue to think it must somehow be possible. And here again, the
illusion is accompanied by genuine belief in a possibility (e.g., that the rose is red)
whose obtaining requires a witness (e.g., that being red is a property) that we
cannot believe. Or anyway, cannot express using our natural languages.

These examples of credal illusions concern actual entities. Though Bismarck is
an actual person, and the property of being a horse exists, there are limits to what
we can believe about them. And this gives rise to a credal illusion, where it seems
to us that we are able to believe the thing in question. The illusions have different
grounds. In Russell's case, it is a person's epistemic condition: we can only believe
possibilities about things with which we are acquainted. In Frege's case, the
ground is the expressive limits of natural language: our natural language makes
it seem that we can grasp possibilities in a certain way. The illusions are persistent
in both cases, for we continue to think we can believe (or express) the possibility

even when we know we cannot. The illusions are accompanied by genuine belief in a possibility that is witnessed by the one we cannot believe. And, finally, they are contingent. Bismarck can believe the proposition we cannot, and a formalized language can let us express the belief.

5.3 Future Possibilities

Some limits to belief are grounded in time. Plausibly, what is possible changes over time. This means that what there is for a person to believe changes over time. The case of Sleeping Beauty can help illustrate this. And the modal view can help us understand the dynamics of belief through time.

In the story, Sleeping Beauty is told Sunday evening that she will shortly be put to sleep and that a fair coin will then be flipped. She is told that she will be woken on Monday and then given a potion that will remove her memory of that waking and put her back to sleep. She is told that if the coin lands tails, she will be left to sleep forever. If it lands heads, she will be woken again on Tuesday, given more of the memory potion, and put back to sleep forever. Sunday night, as she reflects on what will happen, Sleeping Beauty knows that the chance the coin lands tails is 1/2. She also knows that she will wake up and not know whether (i) it is Monday and the coin landed tails; (ii) it is Monday and the coin landed heads; or (iii) it is Tuesday and (so) the coin landed heads. She knows, in other words, that she will soon lose track of her location in the week. So far, this description of the case should be uncontroversial.

The puzzle emerges when we consider what it would be reasonable for Sleeping Beauty to believe when she wakes on Monday. In particular, would it be reasonable for her upon waking to change her belief about the likelihood that the coin landed tails? According to some, when she wakes on Monday she won't learn anything she didn't know Sunday night. After all, she knew Sunday night that she would wake up on Monday. If so, then any change of belief on Monday would not be in response to new information. Some, like David Lewis (2001), insist that it is irrational to change one's mind without new information, and so conclude that it would be irrational for Sleeping Beauty to change her mind on Monday about the likelihood that the coin landed tails. The rational thing for her to believe is that it was a 50% chance that it landed tails. But there is a problem here. When Sleeping Beauty wakes, she knows she is in one of three situations though she also knows that she does not know which: one where the coin landed tails and two where it landed heads. Some, like Adam Elga (2000), say that this knowledge makes it reasonable for her to change her mind on Monday and to start believing that it is 1/3 likely the coin landed tails. After all, it landed tails in only one of the three situations she knows she might be in. But here too there is a problem. For if she learns nothing new when she wakes up on Monday, then Sunday night she already

120 OBJECTIVITY AND CREDAL ILLUSIONS

had the knowledge that makes that Monday belief revision reasonable. But surely Sunday night she knew it was a 1/2 chance, not a 1/3 chance, that the fair coin would land tails. Understanding this apparent shift in what it is reasonable for her to believe is the problem.

My proposed solution is not novel, though I think what I have said about credal illusions can help clarify and motivate it. As others have argued, I think that Sleeping Beauty does learn something new when she wakes on Monday.[3] Upon waking, she does, thinks, and feels certain things, and she knows this. She knows she is waking and that she is wondering to herself whether it is Monday or Tuesday. She did not have *this* knowledge Sunday night. Indeed, she could not have had it. For those events of waking and wondering did not exist Sunday night. So in waking on Monday she does learn something new. And this is because the possibilities there are on Monday morning are not the ones there were on Sunday night. (Or, if you prefer: on Monday she can identify possibilities she could not identify Sunday night.) I'll come back in a moment to whether what she learns makes it reasonable for her to change her belief about the likelihood of the coin's landing.

But why might someone think that when she wakes on Monday Sleeping Beauty learns nothing new? After all, everyone would agree that the events of waking and wondering did not exist Sunday night. The idea, I take it, is that on Sunday as Sleeping Beauty reflects on the next few days she knows that she will wake up on Monday and that she will wonder what day it is and how the coin landed. And when she wakes on Monday, she is not surprised to be waking up or to be wondering about that. We need to see how she can learn something new on Monday without being surprised.

The distinction between a general possibility and a witness can help. On Sunday, she knows that on Monday a certain general possibility will obtain, one where she wakes up and wonders what day it is. And she knows on Sunday that on Monday there will be a witness for that general possibility. And she knows on Sunday that on Monday she will know *of that witness* that it obtains. But on Sunday night the witness does not yet exist.[4] There is not yet a possibility that can witness the one she believes Sunday night. There won't be one until Monday when she wakes up and wonders what day it is. When she does wake up on Monday, and grasps the witness, she is not surprised because she remembers knowing that there would be a witness and that she would know it. *She learns something on Monday that she then knows witnesses something that she remembers knowing on Sunday*

---

[3] For this response, see Stalnaker (2008, 2009), Weintraub (2004), and Horgan (2004).

[4] Or, if you prefer, she is not able to identify any witness for it. Only when she wakes and wonders will she be able to grasp and believe the possibility that witnesses the more general one she grasped and believed Sunday night. Since my interest is in the limits of belief, and not the metaphysics of possibility, I will continue to assume that the possibility did not exist Sunday night but will come into existence on Monday. But nothing hangs on this.

she would learn on Monday even though it was something she could not know, or even entertain, on Sunday. Describing these credal dynamics is tricky. On Sunday she suffers a sort of credal illusion: the illusion that she already knows on Sunday the thing that she on Sunday knows she will only know on Monday. The fact that she can on Sunday fully characterize the sort of thing she will on Monday know— "I am waking and wondering what day it is"—only encourages the illusion. And the persistence of the illusion explains, I think, why she is not surprised on Monday. From her point of view, as it were, she learns exactly what she knew she'd learn. But she did not know Sunday night what she learned on Monday. She couldn't have known it, since not until Monday is there anything to know. But on Sunday she feels she already knows it, and this is the illusion, because she is mistaken.

This case is in some ways similar to a puzzling sort of case about plans and intentions. Some intentions about the future are singular. Sarah intends to use the cake plate her mother gave her for the cake she is planning to make. Her intention is, with regards to that very cake plate, to use *it* for the cake. After a day of work she places the cake on the plate. Was her intention all along to make *that* very cake? Was that cake-intention singular like her plate-intention? On the one hand, we want to say she made exactly what she planned to make. We want to point to the cake on the counter and say she had intended to make *it*. It is not as if there is some other cake she intended to make. But the cake on the counter did not exist when she first formed the intention to make a cake. So the intention she had when she started baking could not have been singular with respect to that very cake. There is not really a puzzle here. Sarah's intention to make a cake was general in a certain way. It was to make *a* cake with certain characteristics, and as things developed she brought one cake into existence, one that had those characteristics. As possibilities are realized, more objects and states come into existence, and they can then witness general beliefs and intentions held before those objects and states came into existence, and other beliefs and intentions are abandoned. (Or maybe it makes sense to say the object of the intention shifts through time. I won't take a stand on that here.) The dynamics are complex and tricky to describe, but there is nothing essentially problematic here.

I thus agree with those who say that Sleeping Beauty does learn something new when she wakes on Monday. Whether this knowledge makes it reasonable for her to change her mind is a separate matter. This depends on whether what she learns is relevant to how the coin landed. I don't need to take a stand on this. My interest is in how changes in what is possible affect the limits of belief and on how this gives rise to credal illusions.

For the record, though, I am sympathetic to the idea that when she wakes up it is reasonable for her to start believing that the chance the coin landed tails was 1/3. As Robert Stalnaker argues (2008), in waking on Monday she comes to know more than just that she is waking and wondering what day it is. She also comes to

122 OBJECTIVITY AND CREDAL ILLUSIONS

know that *this* waking and wondering is not occurring in a fourth situation: one where it is Tuesday and the coin landed tails. It is because she knows this that she knows, on Monday, that she is in one of three positions, though she does not know which. Once again, this is not something she knew Sunday night, though she might have known Sunday night that she would on Monday come to know such a thing. Because she knows she is in one of three situations though she does not which and that in only of them did the coin land tails, it is reasonable for her to believe that the chance it landed heads is 1/3.

5.4 Mere Possibilities

The credal illusions I have been considering concern possibilities that a person is not able to believe obtain, either because she is not related to them in the proper way or because they only come to exist later. In those cases, there is or will be a witness for the possibility the person believes, but she is not able to believe that witness. A more puzzling kind of illusion occurs when there is no witness for some possibility. I'll consider two cases that illustrate this. Frege's case involving Hesperus and Phosphorus concerns merely possible individuals. The Twin-Earth cases, originally developed by Hilary Putnam (1975) and Tyler Burge (1979), concern merely possible stuffs. These cases illustrate how a person can think they believe something that they do not, where the illusion is persistent and encouraged by belief in a real possibility.

In Frege's case, we are to imagine an astronomer who would assent to sentence 1, but not to sentence 2.

1. Hesperus is the Evening Star.
2. Phosphorus is the Evening Star.

As the astronomer would put it, she believes that Hesperus is not Phosphorus. On her view, there are two heavenly bodies where, as we now know, there is but one. Hesperus is Phosphorus, and it is Venus, which is a planet, not a star!

Here is what I want to say about this case. It could have been that the last heavenly body seen in the morning sky was not the same as the first one seen in the night sky. Let's call that possibility DISTINCT.

DISTINCT: The possibility that the last heavenly body seen in the morning sky is not the first one seen in the night sky

As a matter of fact, it does not obtain. But it might have. And for it to obtain, two witnesses would be needed, of the following kinds, where X is not identical to Y.

MORNING: X is the last heavenly body seen in the morning.

EVENING: Y is the first heavenly body seen in the evening.

Our astronomer believes that DISTINCT obtains. And she knows that for it to obtain there must be witnesses for it. And she thinks she believes that they do obtain. (And, indeed, she thinks she has sentences in her language that state them, with names for each of the objects. This linguistic mistake further encourages the illusion.) But, I suggest, she is suffering an illusion. For there are no possibilities that would witness DISTINCT, even though the astronomer believes she has got hold of ones that do. The illusion persists partly because she does believe DISTINCT, and partly because of the linguistic mistake she made. That is what I want to say about the case.

Here is reason to think DISTINCT might have no witnesses. What objects could have taken the place of X and Y in MORNING and EVENING? I suppose Venus could have taken the place of X in MORNING. But what object could have then taken the place of Y in EVENING? Not Venus, since X and Y are to be distinct. (And remember: the astronomer thinks she has got hold of possibilities that differ precisely in what objects they concern.) Is there another object that is not the first heavenly body seen in the evening but could have been? This is a question for astronomers. Perhaps some other heavenly body—maybe Mars?—could have been the first one. But I take it that there may not be two things such that one could have been X and the other Y.

That is the case I have in mind when I say that our astronomer is suffering a credal illusion. She thinks she believes something like MORNING and EVENING, but she is mistaken, for there are no possibilities like that. The illusion is accompanied by her genuine belief in DISTINCT, which is a real possibility (though one that does not obtain). And its being a possibility encourages the illusion. For it is easy slide between the following:

There could have been two objects where Venus actually is.

There are two objects that could have been where Venus actually is.

But this inference is not valid. I do not have a younger brother. But I could have. But from the fact that I could have had a younger brother it does not follow that there is a person who could have been my younger brother.

The claim that there are no such possibilities is admittedly controversial. It takes a position in an ongoing debate about merely possible entities. Some in the debate say that though nothing *is* my younger brother, there could have been something that was. But others say that while nothing *actual* is my younger brother, something *non-actual* is. It exists in another possible world where it is my (or my counter-part's) younger brother. Still others say that there *actually is*

124 OBJECTIVITY AND CREDAL ILLUSIONS

something that could have been my younger brother, though it is not actually a person. It could have been a person.[5] I have taken the first of these positions. But I don't need to settle this debate, in order to make my points about credal illusions.

For on the alternative views, our astronomer lacks the sort of acquaintance with the possibilities in question needed for belief. Suppose the second view is correct, and that there are non-actual things that could have been witnesses for DISTINCT. Plausibly, if there are, then there are many of them. Perhaps not infinitely many, but a huge number of them. Which of them has our astronomer got hold of? For remember, she thinks he has got hold of a pair of particular possibilities that witness DISTINCT. It seems to me implausible to think she can have in mind particular non-actual witnesses for it. Likewise, if the third view about merely possible entities is right, then there are surely a large number of actual non-planets each of which could have been the X or Y. It seems equally implausible to suppose that our astronomer has got hold of particular ones. And so implausible to suppose that our astronomer believes in their obtaining.

So if we adopt either of the other two views on merely possible beings, the astronomer case is then just like Russell's case from the previous section. In that case, there is a possibility but the subject lacks the sort of cognitive contact with it needed to entertain and believe it. The illusion persists and is encouraged by the subject's belief in DISTINCT, which is a possibility she does genuinely believe obtains. It is further encouraged by the linguistic mistakes the subject makes. (The three views characterize the linguistic mistakes differently, but I will set that aside.)

A similar sort of credal illusion is illustrated by stories about Twin-Earth. Those stories were introduced by Putnam (1975) and Burge (1979) to show that what a person means and believes does not supervene on her intrinsic physical properties. Putnam argued that facts about a person's physical environment can make a difference to what her words mean without leaving a trace on her intrinsic properties. Burge extended the arguments to show that facts about a person's social and linguistic community can do so as well, and that those facts can also make a difference to a person's psychological states. The stories involve imagining a possible world where something other than water fills the rivers and streams.

In telling these stories about Oscar and his twin, it is very tempting to think that we can entertain the possibility that the twin believes. It is tempting, in other words, to describe the case by saying that Oscar's twin believes that his glass is fully of XYZ, that XYZ runs in local rivers and streams, and that it is a clear and odorless liquid. But if the lessons that Putnam and Burge draw are correct, then this cannot be right. For the lesson is that what a person believes depends on what stuffs they have around them. But we do not have XYZ in our world. So how is it that we can have the very thoughts that Oscar's twin has?

---

[5] I have only roughly sketched these positions, and each has rich resources. The first is based on Stalnaker (2011), the second on Lewis (1986), and the third on Williamson (2002).

There is a possibility that we do grasp and believe obtains.

WATER: A colorless and odorless liquid other than H2O flows in local rivers and streams.

WATER does not obtain, but it might have. Had it obtained, then some witness for it would also have obtained. Oscar's twin, we imagine, inhabits a world where WATER does obtain and where some particular witness for it obtains too. Oscar's twin believes that the witness obtains.

XYZ: XYZ flows in local rivers and streams.

(He does not believe that WATER obtains, even though it does. To believe it he would need to know about water, but by hypothesis he does not.) But we cannot believe that XYZ obtains, nor can we even so much as entertain it. At least not if the lessons that Burge and Putnam draw are correct. And, again, there are countless witnesses for WATER. Oscar's twin has got hold of a particular one. It is implausible to think we could have got hold of the very same one.

5.5 Denying Objectivity

I've suggested that what a person can believe depends on the facts and on how she is related to them. And I've described some of the ways those credal limits are contingent. Had things been different, the limits to what a person can believe would have been different. Some have objected to this on both epistemological and semantical grounds, and have proposed an alternative that is meant to avoid these objections. I don't deny that the objectivity of belief is puzzling. But I am not sure this is itself a reason to reject it. Not all puzzles are problems. I will end this chapter by considering this.

Let's start with what might seem like an epistemological puzzle. It begins from a conception of what is involved in empirical investigation. The conception will prove naïve, but seeing what is naïve about it is not easy. The core idea is that when we engage in rational inquiry it must be possible to know what we do and might believe independently of knowing whether we are right. Our inquiry must begin with some certainty about which possibilities we take to obtain and which ones we think are open without first having to know which possibilities do obtain. Putting it picturesquely: we must be able to know which possible worlds there are without knowing which one we are in fact in. Our inquiry then proceeds by ruling out possibilities as we learn which ones obtain and which ones don't. As we rule out possible worlds, we get closer to knowing which one we are in.

126 OBJECTIVITY AND CREDAL ILLUSIONS

But on the view of objectivity I have been exploring, this conception cannot be right. For that view entails that we can't know what we believe independently of knowing what there is to believe, and we can't know this independently of knowing how things are. It is not just that we cannot rule out possibilities without knowing the facts. No one denies that. It is that, if believing is objective in the ways I have described, then we cannot know what is possible, and so cannot know what we believe, independently of knowing something about what is actual. Picturesquely: what we can believe depends on which world we are in. The credal illusions are precisely cases where we think we believe something but we don't, and we discover this illusion only in discovering how things are. Discovering what there is for us to believe cannot neatly be separated from discovering whether we are right.

I agree that the objectivity of belief that I have tried to describe has this consequence, and I agree that it can seem puzzling. It suggests that, because knowing what there is for us to believe is not independent of knowing what is true, we cannot begin a rational investigation into how things are until we know something about how they are. But how can we get that first bit of knowledge? It is as if a feat of epistemic bootstrapping is needed before we can even start our theoretical investigations. But I think that a little reflection shows that this is not so puzzling after all.

I called that conception of inquiry naïve. Some of the naivety is on the surface. The conception assumes we could engage in rational intentional inquiry without knowing that we are. But rational inquiry is an essentially intentional endeavor. We know we are doing it, though it is contingent that we are. Picturesquely: we know we are in a world where our inquiry is taking place, even while knowing that we need not have conducted the inquiry. What is more, our most sophisticated inquiry employs language, and this requires knowing things about the words and sentences we use. We use words to say how things are and might be, to draw distinctions among the possibilities, and to do this we need to know something about the representational features of these words. And it is contingent that our words mean what they do, and that we make the assertions we do. Picturesquely: we know we are in a world where we are using certain linguistic resources to draw certain distinctions among the worlds. (This is still naïve, as I will explain in a moment.) Any sophisticated view of inquiry will admit that we begin it by knowing *something* about how things are.

But that conception's naivety is deeper than this. Even if we conceded that all rational inquiry presupposes some linguistic knowledge, it remains naïve to think that we can know what there is for us to believe independently of knowing how things are. At least, this is naïve if it is an objective matter what there is to believe. For that objectivity entails that knowing what there is for us to believe cannot be separated from knowing whether we are right. Picturesquely: we can't know what there is for us to believe about which world we are in until we know which world we are in. So long as we are mistaken or ignorant about what is true, we run the risk of credal illusions, and so of being wrong about what there is for us to believe. I think of this as a broadly pragmatic moral. In inquiry we cannot occupy a point of view that is somehow external to the world. Figuring out how things might be, and so figuring out what there is for us to believe, is not independent of figuring out how things are. (Our quest to find our home in a world of possibilities needs to begin at home.)

But Frank Jackson has argued that this notion of objectivity also raises a semantical puzzle. His primary concern is with assertion not belief, but the worry he has is the one I've been describing. He thinks of asserting something as drawing a distinction among a range of possibilities. If which distinction one draws in making some assertion depends on the facts, then we could not know what we are asserting unless we know whether something is true. Here is how he puts the subsequent worry.

> Now suppose that it is impossible to effect a partition among the possibilities independently of how things actually are. No mental state, no linguistic item, no diagram, no system of semaphore. divides the possibilities, except relative to how things actually are. The we can never say, diagram, depict, semaphore, think, ... how things are. All we can do is say (depict, think, etc.) how they are *if*... We are always in the position of one who only ever tells you what to do if you have high blood pressure, never what to do simpliciter. We can say how things are conditional on ...., but can never make an unconditional claim about how things are. We cannot detach. This is a very radical doctrine. It is not that we cannot say with complete precision how things are. We really cannot say how things are at all. (Jackson 1998, 53)[6]

As he sees it, what I have called the objectivity of belief, the idea that it is a contingent matter what there is to believe, would make it impossible to believe anything at all. This is what I called the semantic puzzle.

Jackson claims that to avoid it, we must reject what I have called the modal view of the objects of belief. As I have mentioned, many reject the modal view, insisting that there are *more* belief properties than there are possibilities. But in effect, Jackson's critique is that there are *fewer* belief properties than there are possibilities. On his view, a belief property determines a possibility depending on the facts, and so can determine a different possibility given different facts. Two people can share a belief property and yet, because the facts that obtain are different for one than for the other, the belief property they share determines a different possibility for one than for the other. Because the objects of their belief are

---

[6] See also (Chalmers 2003).

128 OBJECTIVITY AND CREDAL ILLUSIONS

independent of the facts, each of them can know what they believe independently of knowing which possibilities obtain. Knowledge of meaning would, in this way, be independent of knowledge of fact. This is sometimes called the *narrow view* of the objects of belief.

We can illustrate the narrow view with the Twin-Earth case, and this will bring out an objection to it. On the standard view, Oscar and his twin have different belief properties. The object of Oscar's belief is not the object of his twin's. On the modal version of the standard view, the object of Oscar's belief is a possibility about water, while the object of his twin's belief is one about some distinct stuff. But on the narrow view, their beliefs have the very same object. The object is not a possibility or a proposition, but is rather something that determines a possibility or a proposition as a function of the facts. Given the facts in Oscar's world and his relation to them that belief property determines a possibility about water. In his twin's world, it determines a distinct possibility, one about that other stuff. On this narrow view, Oscar and his twin do share a belief property even though that shared belief property determines distinct possibilities. So, in this sense, there are fewer belief properties on the narrow view than there are possibilities.

This narrow view is supposed to avoid a supposed semantical puzzle. But it is not clear that it does. Indeed, it is not clear that anything could. The alleged puzzle starts from the fact that it is contingent that Oscar believes what he does. This means that had things been different, or had his relations to those things been different, he would not have believed it. But this is as true on the narrow view as on the standard view. Even on the narrow view it is contingent that Oscar believes what he does. For even on the narrow view, it must be a contingent matter that Oscar has the narrow beliefs that he does. But this means that had things been different, or had Oscar's relations to those things been different, he would not have had the narrow beliefs he does. In other words, the narrow view must inevitably face the same puzzle as the standard view. (Unless it holds that it is essential to Oscar that he believes what he does!) If the modal view entails that Oscar cannot know what he believes until he knows something about which of his beliefs are true, then so does the narrow view.

5.6 Objectivity and the Inevitability of Credal Illusions

To the extent that there is a puzzle here, it has nothing to do with the *objects* of belief, but concerns the nature of believing itself. To believe something is to have a perspective on how things are, on which possibilities obtain. But it is a fact that a person has the perspective she does, and this fact is the obtaining of one of the possibilities the person must have a perspective on. It is not a fact that obtains independently of all possibilities. What there is for us to believe must depend on what there is. At least this must be so if believing is to be an objective matter.

OBJECTIVITY AND THE INEVITABILITY OF CREDAL ILLUSIONS   129

The modal view says that the objects of belief are possibilities. But it does not deny that people can disagree over what is possible. It insists, though, that such a disagreement is always at the same time a disagreement over what there is to say and believe, and this gives such disagreements a unique rational character. Jones and Sarah can disagree about how to use their words to state some fact they agree on. The disagreement will be a factual one, since it is a factual matter what their words mean, but it need not be a disagreement over what is possible. They can resolve their disagreement if Jones acquiesces in Sarah's linguistic usage. In resolving it, neither need change her mind over what is possible or what there is to say.

But whenever people do disagree about what is possible, they disagree not just about how to use their words to say how things might be, they disagree about what there is to say and believe. If Jones thinks there are fewer possibilities than Sarah does, then Sarah thinks she has grasped a possibility that Jones thinks does not exist. From Jones' point of view, Sarah is suffering a credal illusion. As she sees it, Sarah mistakenly thinks she has got hold of a real possibility, one that witnesses a more general possibility. Jones denies that that general possibility obtains, pre- cisely because she denies there is a witness for it.[7] At the same time, though, the disagreement will be partly about how their language works, and so will be over a contingent matter of fact. For if that more general possibility did obtain, then there would be more to say and believe than Jones currently thinks there is. Her words would draw a different distinction (since there would be more distinctions to be drawn) than she thinks they do. In other words, it is an unavoidable aspect of the case that Jones and Sarah disagree about which distinctions their sentences can be used to draw. Here too the disagreement might get resolved. But the resolution would involve a change in view not just about how to use their words to say how things are or could have been, but about what there *is* to say and believe.

I find this a deeply puzzling sort of resolution.[8] I have trouble seeing how such a disagreement can be resolved through an exchanging of reasons or evidence. But I don't think this puzzle poses a problem that an account of believing needs to somehow settle or show to be merely apparent. No account of the objects of belief is going to solve this puzzle. Such disagreements are inevitable, it seems to me, so long as it is an objective matter what there is to believe. These disagreements emerge whenever we think we have identified the limits of thought, or when we

---

[7] Appeal to impossibilities won't help here. Jones does not think that Sarah thinks that some *im*possibility witnesses that more general possibility. No one thinks an impossibility could witness a general possibility. There is no witness for the general possibility, but there could have been one, and it would have been a possibility not an impossibility. A non-existent possibility is not an impossibility. I don't have a younger brother, but he is not an impossibility, just (as it were) a non-existent possibility.

[8] For more on this, see Hunter (2007). This sort of disagreement is an important topic in Wittgenstein's work, both early and late. And of course it has special relevance for philosophy since philosophical disagreement is characteristically (though not exclusively) over what is possible. For discussion of Wittgenstein's views, see Diamond (2019) and Kremer (2001).

think someone else has crossed them. Any account of belief must allow for these disagreements. One virtue of the modal view, it seems to me, is that it can help us see this inevitability. It can do this because it faces the puzzle head-on.

Our ability to reflect on all of this may be unique to humans. I think that cats and dogs also believe and know things. And I believe they too suffer credal illusions. My cat suffers them when he sees what he thinks is another cat in the mirror. But I don't think cats can reflect on the fact that they suffer these illusions, let alone on how the objectivity of belief makes them possible. This is a significant difference between us and other believers we know about. And it allows us to reflect on possibilities not just for the things in our environment but for ourselves too. We can imagine different ways to be human, and in so doing we can not only discover new possibilities but also maybe even create them. That is, it is not just that by reflecting on the limits of thought we may discover that they are different than we had taken them to be. It might be that such reflection can change the limits. This too would be an exercise of reason. But it is a topic for another book.[9]

This chapter and the next are about what there is to believe, about belief's limits. I have argued in this chapter that some limits are objective or impersonal because they apply to everyone. These, I claim, give rise to what I call credal illusions, where a person thinks she has got hold in belief of a possibility when in fact she has not. The illusions are persistent in part because the believer will have got hold of a general possibility, though it is one that lacks a more specific witness. I then argued that the familiar puzzle cases, often considered counter-examples to the modal view of the objects of belief, involve just such illusions. They illustrate how what a person can believe is limited by her relations to what there is, by her position in time, and by her place in a space of possibilities. The modal view helps us to see these credal illusions, but it is not their source and rejecting it won't save us from the risk of illusion. That risk is inevitable so long as it is an objective matter what there is to believe. All of this is one part of what Anscombe called the logical aspect of belief, as I understand it. In addition to these objective limits, there are also subjective ones, unique to each believer. They mark off her perspective on the world as hers, and they are the topic of the next chapter.

---

[9] Thanks to Charles Travis for encouraging me to think about this. The idea that the space of possibilities—and so the space of thought—is context-dependent and so variable is an important theme in his work, though he would not put it in terms of a space of possibilities. The idea that our capacity to reason itself gives rise to this variability is similar to Cora Diamond's (1982) idea of an "attentive imaginative response" when doing morality. I see it too in Putnam's use of science fiction in Putnam (1962) in order to reveal the role we play in settling what is conceivable.

6

Subjectivity and Credal Necessities

The modal view of the objects of belief implies that what a person can believe is limited to what is possible. This view helps us understand how objective limits to belief give rise to credal illusions. It also helps us understand the essential subjectivity of belief. In this chapter, I will argue that this subjectivity is grounded in what I will call credal necessities. A possibility is a credal necessity for someone if she cannot help but believe that it obtains, and it is a subjective one for her when it is a credal necessity only for her, a possibility that she and she alone cannot help but believe obtains. Because these credal necessities are unique to her, they identify a position among how things are or could have been as *her* position. They mark off a perspective on the world as *her* perspective. As I see it, these subjective credal necessities ground what is essentially personal in believing.

I want to be clear about the sort of necessity at issue. First, it is not that a person's credal necessities are possibilities that must obtain. In fact, the credal necessities that constitute the subjectivity of belief are all contingent ones, possibilities that do but need not have obtained. Second, the necessity is not ethical or normative in any sense. The point is not that a person ought to believe them, but that she has no alternative but to believe that they obtain. I will turn to normative questions about believing and about what a person ought to believe in Chapter 8. But the subjectivity of belief that I want to explore in this chapter concerns what a person cannot help but believe. It is a fact about believing itself that each believer has credal necessities that are unique to her. Because they are unique to her, they ground the subjectivity of belief.

To develop these points, I will argue for the following principle.

BB principle: A person believes that P only if she believes that she believes it.

Two credal necessities follow from BB. First, a believer cannot help but believe in her own existence. The world as she takes it to be must contain her. Second, a believer cannot help but believe that she is right. The world as she takes it to be must be one where she is right about how things are. But none of this is a cognitive achievement. It is not the result of some epistemic procedure nor is it grounded in a special sort of evidence or entitlement. It is part of the very nature of believing itself.

In Section 6.1, I will clarify the BB principle and distinguish it from several closely related ones. In Section 6.2, I will show how it grounds the essential

---

On Believing: Being Right in a World of Possibilities. David Hunter, Oxford University Press. © David Hunter 2022.
DOI: 10.1093/oso/9780192859549.003.0007

132 SUBJECTIVITY AND CREDAL NECESSITIES

subjectivity of believing. In Section 6.3, I will explain why we should accept it. In Section 6.4, I will consider how all of this relates to the so-called transparency of belief. In the final three sections, I will consider whether there is more to the subjectivity of belief than these credal necessities. The standard view is that at least some of a person's belief properties must be ones only she can have, so that no two people could share every (or even any) belief property. Some say this follows from what makes belief essentially self-conscious. Others say it is revealed by puzzling cases of people who seem confused or mistaken about who they are. And some think it is needed to understand how action can be rational. On my view, though, the essential subjectivity of belief is not about *what* a person believes but about what she alone cannot help but believe. Credal subjectivity, as I see it, is about the *limits* of belief.

6.1 The BB Principle

The BB principle says that if a person believes something, then she also believes that she does. According to this principle, if Jones believes that the 504 stops at Garden, then she must also believe that she believes this. The idea is that a person who believes that some possibility obtain must believe that she does.

A natural partner to this is the idea that if a person takes some possibility *not* to obtain, then she believes that she does. Let's call that BD.

BD Principle: If a person disbelieves that P, then she believes that she disbelieves it.

Jones believes that the 504 does not stop at Fern, so she *dis*believes that it does. It strikes me that BD is as plausible as BB. And it also strikes me that BA is plausible too.

BA Principle: If a person is agnostic concerning P, then she believes that she is agnostic about it.

Jones is unsure whether the 504 stops at Howard Park. She neither believes it nor disbelieves it, but knows that it might. BA says that in that case Jones believes that she is agnostic about it. Together these three principles entail that for every possibility a person is aware of, she believes either that she believes it obtains, that she believes that it does not obtain, or that she is uncertain whether it obtains.

We need to distinguish BD from B~B.

B~B Principle: If a person does not believe that P, then she believes that she does not believe it.

THE BB PRINCIPLE   133

I think we should resist B~B. Jones neither believes nor disbelieves that the 504 stops at Howard, though she is aware of that possibility. But there are some possibilities she knows nothing about. She has never heard of Julius Caesar or the day he crossed the Rubicon. So she is wholly unaware of the possibility that he shaved his face the day of the crossing. This possibility is simply not within her perspective. So while it is true that she neither believes nor disbelieves it she is also not agnostic about it. It is not within her perspective one way or the other.[1] So I think we should resist B~B.

The BB principle is close to the KK principle.

KK Principle: A person knows something only if she knows that she knows it.

If the KK principle is true, then Jones must know that she exists and she must know that she knows something, if she knows anything at all. If she knows that the 504 stops at Garden, then she also knows that she knows it. Though I am sympathetic to the KK principle, I won't be defending it here. And it is important to keep in mind how the principles differ.

The KK principle entails the BB principle; at least it does together with certain independently plausible assumptions. One is the standard assumption that if you know something then you believe it. Another is the assumption that if you know that you know something, then you know that you believe it. These assumptions get us from KK to KB:

KB Principle: A person knows that P only if she believes that she believes it.

How can we get from KB to BB? They share a consequent, and their antecedents differ only in that KB concerns knowing something whereas BB concerns believing it. Weakening an antecedent can of course change the truth value of a conditional. But in this case, how could knowing something be sufficient for that consequent if believing it was insufficient? A person can believe without knowing if they are wrong or if they are too lucky to know. But how could either of these block a self-knowledge that comes with knowing? More plausibly, what makes knowing sufficient for the self-knowledge is that it involves a mental state. It is precisely because knowing involves believing that knowing entails that self-knowledge. If so, then believing should entail it too. So I am inclined to think that if KB is true, then so is BB. In this way, we can get from KK to BB.

But there is no way to get from BB to KK. For a person can believe something and be wrong. The following principle might be right.

---

[1] For discussion of the importance of disbelief, see Friedman (2013, 2017).

134 SUBJECTIVITY AND CREDAL NECESSITIES

BK Principle: A person believes that P only if she knows that she believes it.

But it cannot be that if a person believes something then she *knows* that she knows it, for she might not know it at all. Sarah incorrectly believes that the 504 stops at Fern. It might follow that she believes that she knows it. (On some accounts, if a person believes something, then she believes that she knows it.) And it might follow that she knows that she believes it. But it cannot follow that she *knows* that she knows it, since she does not know it. So there is no sound way to get from BB to KK.

My interest is in believing not in knowing. This matters because the subjectivity of believing that I want to consider doesn't concern whether or how a person can be justified in believing that they believe something.[2] BB is wholly silent on justification. It leaves open whether a person who believes something must also know that she believes it. I am inclined to think this is also true, and the argument I give for BB will suggest it, though it will also suggest that this knowledge requires no special basis and is not gained through a special method. But the differences between believing and knowing are a matter of ongoing debate, and I want what I say about the subjectivity of believing to be neutral on those debates. So I want to keep the focus on the idea that believing requires believing that you believe.

It is also worth distinguishing the BB principle from an idea that a Transparency principle like the following aims to capture.

Transparency: A person can answer the question whether she believes that P by answering the question whether it is the case that P.

The idea is that there is a contrast between how a person can know what she herself believes and how she can know what another person believes. To figure out if Sarah believes that the 504 stops at Garden, Jones needs to study Sarah. Whether the 504 does stop there might not matter for this study. But to figure out whether she herself believes that it stops there, Jones does not need to study herself. All that is relevant to her as she tries to figure this out is whether the 504 does stop there. This asymmetry looks like it needs explanation. And so does the method Jones used to gain this self-knowledge.

I think there are connections between the BB principle and the idea underlying this Transparency principle. I will explore them in Section 6.4. But the transparency idea is about self-knowledge, whereas the BB principle is not. Some see the transparency idea as revealing a special form of justification or warrant for a

---

[2] Matt Boyle asks what the rational basis could be for a person's knowledge that she believes something. His answer develops a Sartrean distinction between positional and non-positional consciousness. Boyle (2019) I think he is led to this by assuming that the self-knowledge must be a cognitive achievement needing a rational basis. As I will defend BB, this self-knowledge is no achievement at all, at least none over and above whatever is involved in gaining the original belief.

person's self-knowledge. And some say that it reveals a special method or procedure for acquiring that self-knowledge.[3] But the BB principle is not about justification or epistemic procedures. All it says is that a person believes something only if she believes that she does. It is silent on questions about justification, evidence, and theoretical reflection.

Different ways of defending BB make a difference to its scope. Some have suggested that a person's knowledge of what she believes flows from the operation of a quasi-perceptual faculty of introspection. If so, then BB would apply only to believers who have this additional faculty. The idea that a person's beliefs could be objects of introspection is encouraged by the tendency to hypostasize belief states. If we think of them as things in the same category as neural clusters, hearts, and lungs, then it may seem plausible that a person could have some special way of "looking inside" to identify which beliefs she has. It is probably true, as Shoemaker says, that "[n]o one thinks that one is aware of beliefs and thoughts by having sensations or quasi-sense-experiences of them" (Shoemaker 1994, 255). But the temptation to hypostasize belief states can make such a view seem more natural and on the right track than it deserves. Here again, it is helpful to compare believing something with owning something. No one thinks that a person can inspect her states of ownership, her *possessings*. And this is not because possessings are somehow unobservable or private entities, but because they are not entities at all. Likewise, I think, a person's belief states are not entities, and so are not the right sort of thing to be objects of sensation or introspection.

Other proponents of the BB principle are "constitutivist," in the sense that they think the self-knowledge involves no special rational basis or cognitive procedure. On this sort of view, the self-knowledge of belief follows from the nature of believing itself. But this still allows room for restricting the scope of BB. One might make it dependent on the possession of other capacities. Shoemaker thinks that rational agency would be impossible for a being who did not know what she believes (Shoemaker 1994). One could not form or carry out one's plans if one did not know how one took the world to be. Moran claims that the distinctive abilities that ground a person's epistemic responsibility require such self-knowledge (Moran 2001). One couldn't be answerable or accountable in the ways that humans are for believing what we do if we did not know what we believe. Eric Marcus (2016) offers an argument for BK (and so BB) that starts from a capacity to sincerely assert what one believes. These views restrict the scope of BB to believers who have certain additional capacities.

I want to defend an unrestricted form of BB. As I see it, it is essential to believing that if a being believes something then she believes that she does. If my cats have a perspective on the world, then they and their perspective are

---

[3] For these views, see Peacocke (1998), Byrne (2018), Moran (2001), and (Boyle 2019).

included in the world as seen from their perspective. This will seem implausible if one thinks that believing something is a sort of capacity or disposition, and especially if one thinks that it is or requires having linguistic capacities. But I don't think this. My defense of BB relies on the idea that to believe something is to be in a certain position to exercise the capacities and to manifest the dispositions one has. Being in that position is not itself a capacity or disposition. Some believers have more sophisticated capacities than others, including capacities to reflect on themselves and on their various capacities. While I agree that only a rational agent can be a believer, that is because only a rational agent can act and change in light of ways things are and could have been. The ability to reflect on oneself and on one's nature as a believer is not needed for this.

A related point about idealization is worth making. Defenders of the BB principle have often been viewed as offering highly idealized accounts of belief and knowledge. Kant's idea of the unity of apperception, that at least some of a person's mental states must be "accompanied" by an "I think," is a way of spelling out the BB principle.[4] That principle is also a standard assumption of those working on the logics of belief and knowledge. Indeed, it is a standard axiom that a person who believes something not only believes that she believes it but knows that she does.[5] The formal models developed to understand rational behavior in games and economics have always been highly abstract, and the same is true of Kantian accounts, even though they have relied less on formal models. These accounts are abstract in that they ignore details about how people acquire beliefs and about how their believing what they do interacts with other aspects of their mental lives. Such abstraction is not the same as idealization and does not carry the same risks. A theory idealizes when it assumes to be true things the theorist knows or believes are actually false. The more a theory idealizes the harder it is to see how what the theory says can be relevant to real-life cases. It can be hard to tell when a theory is merely abstracting and when it is idealizing. Any account of believing may do both. It may attribute idealized mental states to the subjects they are about, states that are importantly unlike the belief and knowledge that we have. Or it may concern the conduct of idealized agents, who are in states of belief and knowledge like ours, but who differ from us in their other capacities. I won't claim that my defense of the BB principle involves no abstraction. But I don't mean for it to be an account of an idealized sort of rational agent. I take it to be true cats and dogs as much as of streetcar drivers and chess grandmasters.

---

[4] This idea is central to Rödl (2018). For discussion, see the articles collected in Hennig, Hunter, & Land (2019).
[5] See, for instance, Hintikka (1962) and Von Wright (1957). The connections between these formal approaches and more traditional epistemological projects is helpfully explored in Stalnaker (2006).

6.2 BB and the Center of a Conception

Suppose that BB is true. How would that show that there is something essentially subjective in believing? The answer is that if BB is true, then there are limits to how a person can revise her beliefs, limits that do not apply to anyone else, and that remain even when two people agree on which possibilities obtain. One is that a person must believe that she exists. A second is that she must believe she has the beliefs she does. We might put this first limit by saying that a believer must be the center of her conception of how things are. This section is about this.

It is tempting to characterize this idea of a center in representational or semantic terms. One might say that Jones' conception is *about* Jones in a special sort of way, or that it involves a special mode for representing her. And it may be tempting to say that Jones is not similarly represented in anyone else's conception, even if that other conception is about her. There is something right in this thought, but it is easy to be misled by it. As I argued in Chapter 3, a person's belief states do not have representational properties, they are not true or false and do not make reference to anything. They are not representations of the world, and nor does a person represent the world when she takes it to be some way. The notion of reference has its proper home in speech acts, not in mental states. We can refer to people and things when we say what we believe, and there are more or less special and conventional ways of doing this. But our mental states do not refer to anything. As we saw in Chapter 4, there is a sense in which a possibility is about things. When Jones believes that she exists, the possibility she grasps is about her. But this is not a semantic or representational fact, since possibilities are not representations. And anyway it won't capture the sense in which Jones is the center of her conception of the world, since Sarah can also grasp and believe that very same possibility. I suggest that we not try to understand the sense in which a person is the center of her conception in semantic or representational terms.

It is also tempting to try to characterize this idea of a center in epistemic terms. A person is aware of herself and of what she does, thinks, and feels in a way that others are not. I agree that being the center of one's own conception involves a special self-knowledge. But this needs to be handled carefully. As we will see when we consider Transparency, it is tempting to think of this self-knowledge as a cognitive achievement that needs either a specialized basis or warrant or else a specialized epistemic method or procedure. This is how Matt Boyle frames the task of understanding the knowledge a person has of her own psychological states. "It is this psychological knowledge whose warrant is in question, and the problem of transparency is that nothing in my apparent basis seems to supply a ground for it." (Boyle 2019, 1014). While the subjectivity of believing does make an epistemological difference to a person, because it makes a difference to what she believes, I think it is best not to conceive of it as itself an epistemic achievement.

138 SUBJECTIVITY AND CREDAL NECESSITIES

The BB principle offers a simpler way to understand what it is for a believer to be the center of her conception of things. If BB is true, then there are subjective limits to belief revision. To see this, we need to distinguish possibilities a person can conceive of from ones she can believe obtain. Jones and Sarah can agree about which possibilities obtain, which ones don't, and which ones they remain agnostic about. In particular, they can agree that Jones might not have existed, that such a possibility might have obtained even though it does not. They can even agree that other people might think it does obtain. And they can agree that Sarah may one day come to believe it too. But, if BB is true, then while Jones can conceive of the possibility that she does not exist, she cannot believe that it obtains. This means that she cannot revise her conception of things in such a way that she is not one of those things.

Three facts about this limit are crucial. First, it is a limit that only applies to Jones' conception of things. Jones-less possibilities are believable by you. This limit thus marks a given perspective on the world as Jones' perspective: it is the one from which the possibility that Jones exists must obtain. This is thus a limit that applies only to Jones' perspective on the world. Second, this limit persists even if Jones and Sarah agree not just about what is possible but also about what is so. It is a difference in the *limits* of Jones' belief, a difference that marks one perspective as hers. It is not a sort of disagreement or difference in belief between Jones and Sarah. Third, we can identify and describe this limit on Jones' perspective without appealing to anything more than the resources of the modal view of belief. Understanding this aspect of the essential subjectivity of belief does not require holding that there are more belief properties than there are possibilities.

I have been putting this point about limits in terms of the modal view of the objects of belief, but any account of those objects can accept BB. On the propositional view, the idea would be that Jones must believe that the proposition that she exists is true. Still, the modal view allows for an elegant way to understand how BB gives rise to credal necessities. The modal view says that the objects of belief are possibilities, ways that things are or could have been. What a person believes changes over time, as her view on how things are changes. But there are some possibilities a person must believe obtain, and one is that she exists. That an agent's conception of things must be of a world that includes herself can be put as a constraint on what possibilities can be the objects of her belief. The believer must exist in, putting it picturesquely, every possible world in the set determined by her beliefs. This constraint is meant to capture the idea that a believer must exist in the world as she takes it to be. The image of knowing and believing as like being more or less at home among the facts can help here. A believer can change her mind about the facts, but not about whether she is at home among the facts as she takes them to be.

This credal necessity captures at least some of the semantic and epistemic thoughts I mentioned at the outset. The semantic thought is that my conception of the world seems to be about me in a way that it is not about you, that it represents me in a way that it does not represent anyone or anything else. The fact that my conception must include me but need not include you would seem to amount to some sort of representational difference. My conception is essentially about me, whereas it is only contingently about you. Notice that this does not require any special act or form of self-reference. It is not a semantic achievement of any kind that my conception of the world gets it right that I exist. It is part of what it is for me to have a conception that it be a conception of a world that includes me. This involves no special semantic accomplishments over and above whatever is needed for me to have any conception at all of an objective world.

We get a similar conclusion concerning the epistemic thought. It was the thought that my conception of things seems to involve a special sort of self-awareness. I do seem to be aware of myself in a way that I am not aware of anyone or anything else. The fact that my conception of things must include me captures some of this thought. My conception of the world is sensitive to facts about me in a way that it is not sensitive to facts about you: my conception need not even include you. My conception keeps track of me in a way that is fundamentally different from the way in which your conception keeps track of me. It is an epistemic achievement that your conception is of a world that includes me; but it is part of what it is for me to have a conception at all that it be of a world that includes me. This is not a special epistemic achievement or the result of some special capacity for self-knowledge. The capacity to believe anything at all brings with it a capacity to believe that I exist. At least this is what BB entails.

I have been trying to elaborate the point that my conception of the world must include me in it. As I said, this does not mean that I cannot *conceive* of a world that does not include me. I know perfectly well that I need not have existed, and I can tell a coherent story about a world in which I do not figure. So the limits I am drawing attention to here are limits to what I can believe and not limits to what I can conceive. Nor does this mean that I cannot be mistaken or ignorant about myself. I can be mistaken about my height and weight just as much as I can be mistaken about your height and weight. I can be wrong about what I had for lunch, about episodes in my past, and even about what I am doing right now. And there are surely many facts about myself that I do not and perhaps cannot ever know. There may of course be limits to the error or ignorance that are possible here. Perhaps there are even some false beliefs that I cannot but have about myself. I won't pursue these issues here. I just want to note that the idea that my conception must be of a world that includes me does not mean that I am infallible, incorrigible or all knowing about myself.

I have been developing the image of subjectivity as a center in a person's conception of things. The image of a center goes back to Quine (1968). As he saw it, to specify what a person believes it is not enough to say what possibilities she thinks obtain. For, he thought, there is no fact of the matter as to who anyone

140 SUBJECTIVITY AND CREDAL NECESSITIES

is in any given possibility. Consider one with two women, one walking to Garden Avenue and one walking to Fern. If Quine is right, this possibility leaves open whether one of these women is Jones. If what Jones believes is that she is walking to Garden, then we can't capture what she believes just by saying she takes this possibility to obtain, no matter how completely we describe it. We need to add that for our purposes Jones will be the one in that possibility who is walking to Garden. We need to *center* the possibility on her. This is a stipulation, Quine held, because there is no fact of the matter whether she is or is not that person.

David Lewis (1980) didn't share Quine's doubts about modal determinacy, but he agreed with Quine that we need to center the possibility. A center is needed, Lewis held, not to specify who the believer *is* in a given possibility (or, anyway, about who her counterpart is), but to specify who she *believes* she is. On Lewis' view, a person can be uncertain or mistaken about who she is in some possibility even if there is a fact of the matter about who she is. Jones might take herself to be the woman walking to Garden, even if she is the one walking to Fern. (If in fact she *is* walking to Garden, then she is right in believing that she is walking to Garden, but wrong about who she is.)

Thomas Nagel (1989) agrees with Quine and Lewis that the possibility needs centering. But his reason has nothing to do with Quinean indeterminacy or Lewisian error. Even if Jones knows that in that possibility she is the woman walking to Garden, she might, according to Nagel, find this to be a startling or remarkable fact. Suppose that in that possibility Jones' dreams of being a successful business owner have been realized in surprising ways. Jones might express this surprise at how things could have been by saying, while knowingly thinking of herself in that possibility, "*She* is *me!*" Nagel says that we cannot capture the content of this exclamation merely by describing that possibility. I will return to Lewis and Nagel in Section 6.5,[6] where I will express reservations about their criticisms of the modal view.

But I mention them here to draw attention to something they don't question. While all three doubt that the modal view can fully capture the subjectivity of belief, they agree that a believer must exist in the world as she takes it to be. This is something the modal view can capture, and it is a significant amount of subjectivity. Jones occupies a central place in her conception of the world, a place that no other person or thing does or even could occupy. And it is not just that she is a central *thing* in the world as she conceives of it, one object among many. She is central in it as someone who does, thinks, and feels things. Her practical, cognitive, and emotional life take center stage in her conception of the world. And even though Jones knows that Sarah also does, believes, and feels things, Sarah does not share that central place in Jones' conception of things. Jones alone is its center.

---

[6] For discussion, see Stalnaker (2008).

BEING IN POSITION   141

I have argued that the modal view together with BB captures an essentially subjective element in believing: a believer must believe in her own existence. But BB says more than this. It is not just that a believer must take herself to have a *position* among the ways things are. She must take herself to have a *perspective* on the ways things are. If BB is true, then a believer has to believe that she is right or wrong depending on which possibilities obtain. She needs to believe that she is a believer. This can seem like a substantial cognitive and semantic achievement, involving more than is needed simply for her to believe that she exists. But I think it is not really any achievement at all. And it requires no special cognitive powers or abilities. To see this, it is best to see why we should accept BB in the first place.

6.3 Being in Position

To argue for the BB principle, I will start from the account of believing I defended in Chapter 1. I said that to believe that P is to be in position to do, think, and feel things in light of a possibility whose obtaining would make one right. The key idea in my argument for the BB principle is this. If a person is in a certain position, then she is also in the derivative position of *being in* that original position. In the case of believing, that derivative position just is believing oneself to believe something. Not surprisingly, this iterates. We get a third order belief state, a fourth order belief state, etc. After presenting the argument I will discuss whether this iteration is a problem.

It is helpful to start by developing an analogy between believing something and being in a certain spatial position. This will bring out in a neutral way important points about positions and abilities. The first point is that it need not be an achievement at all for a thing to be in a certain derivative state, or at any rate, no achievement over and above that of being in the related original state. Suppose that Jones is standing on Garden Avenue. She is thus in the following spatial state or position.

G1   Being on Garden Avenue

Now consider the following derivative state.

G2   Being such that Jones is on Garden Avenue

This is a state a thing is in just in case Jones is on Garden Avenue. Jones is in that state. That is, not only is Jones in G1, she is also in G2. But notice that Jones' being in G2 is not a special achievement or the result of something special that she did. She is in G2 simply in virtue of being in G1. As it were, that derivative state comes along for free.

142 SUBJECTIVITY AND CREDAL NECESSITIES

Still, G2 is distinct from G1. G1 is a spatial state or location, whereas G2 is not. If all we know of a thing is that it is in G2, then we still do not know anything about where it is. Moreover, G2 is individuated in terms of Jones whereas G1 is not. If Jones did not exist, neither would G2. And a person can be in G2 without being in G1. Sarah is not on Garden Avenue, she's on Fern. So Sarah is not in G1. But she is in G2. Sarah's being in G2 just comes along for free given that Jones is in G1. Indeed, everything is such that Jones is on Garden Avenue.

It is important to distinguish the capacities and dispositions a thing has from the positions it is in. What a person might do, think, or feel when she in some position depends on what abilities and dispositions she has. What Jones might do and undergo while in G1 depends on what she is able to do and what changes she can undergo. Being a person, she is able to do, think, and feel things. So in virtue of being in G1, Jones is also in G1*.

G1*   being in position to do, think, and feel things while on Garden Avenue

Still, being in a position is not itself an ability or a disposition. So G1 is not a capacity or a disposition. Similarly, a cube of salt will manifest its solubility when it is in warm water, but being in warm water is not itself a disposition or a capacity. So we need in general to distinguish a thing's capacities and dispositions on the one hand from its positions on the other.[7]

Some capacities are specific to a given position, in the sense that a thing will exercise that capacity only if it is in that position. A drop of acetone can melt rubber, but it will exercise that capacity only when it is on a bit of rubber. A thing might also be in a certain position but have no capacities that are specific to that position. That is, there might be nothing that a thing can do or undergo in a given position that it could not also do or undergo in other positions. Suppose the drop of acetone is inside a glass jar. None of its capacities are ones that can be exercised *only* while inside a glass jar. Anything it could do or undergo while in the jar is something it could do or undergo while outside the jar. In effect, there is nothing the drop of acetone could do or undergo that would *manifest* the fact that it is in that position. None of its capacities or dispositions are sensitive to being inside a glass jar. Still, the drop of acetone is inside the glass jar. We might call that an "implicit" position for that thing, intending to capture the idea that none of its capacities or dispositions are specific to that position.

---

[7] A thing might have a capacity where the positions are linked so that it is never in one of them without being in another. This is the situation with believing. When Jones believes that the 504 stops at Garden, she also believes that she believes it. Those positions are linked. So when she exercises a capacity in or from one of them, she also exercises it in or from the other. Whenever she acts on her belief that the 504 stops at Garden she also acts on her belief that she believes that the 504 stops at Garden. For her, acting on the one is acting on the other. But matters are different for Sarah. She does not believe that the 504 stops at Garden, so she won't act on it. But she does believe that Jones believes it, and so can act on that belief.

BEING IN POSITION   143

Let's now turn to believing. On my view, being in a certain belief state is being in a certain sort of position, one relative to ways things might be, and one that makes a difference to the (potential) reasons one has for what one might do, think, and feel. For instance, when Jones believes that the 504 stops at Garden Avenue, she is in the following position.

B1   in position to do, think, and feels things in light of the possibility that the 504 stops at Garden Avenue.

Being in that position makes a difference to what it would be reasonable for her to do, think, and feel. Now consider the following derivative position.

B2   in position to do, think, and feel things in light of Jones' being in B1.

Jones is not only in B1, she is also in B2. She is not only in position to do, think, and feel things in light of a certain possibility. She is in position to do, think, and feel things in light of *being in that position.* But this is not a special achievement or the result of some procedure. She is in B2 simply in virtue of being in B1, just as she is in the position of being such that she is on Garden Avenue simply in virtue of being on Garden Avenue. And B2 is distinct from B1. B2 is a position that essentially involves Jones, whereas B1 is not. B2 would not exist if Jones did not, but B1 could. And a person might be in B2 but not be in B1. Sarah does not believe the 504 stops at Garden, so she is not in B1. But Sarah is in position to do, think, and feel things in light of Jones' being in B1. So Sarah is in B2 though she is not in B1.

What is it for Jones (and Sarah) to be in B2? According to my account of belief, if Jones is in position to do, think, and feel things in light of her being in B1, then Jones believes that she is in B1. And since Sarah is also in B2, she too believes that Jones is in B1. Believing that Jones is in B1 is believing that Jones believes that the 504 stops at Garden. So in virtue of their being in B2, both Jones and Sarah believe that Jones believes that the 504 stops at Garden. We don't know how Sarah came to believe this. But Jones came to believe it simply in virtue of coming to believe that the 504 stops at Garden. She believes that she believes it, simply in virtue of believing it. This is what BB says.

To recap this argument. We started with my view about believing. It says that a person believes something just in case she is in a certain position. I argued that anyone in that position is also in a certain derivative position. According to the view of believing, being in that derivative position is believing oneself to be in the original position. This is how we get from the view of belief to the BB principle.

We can accept the BB principle, as I have defended it, and allow that believing can be implicit in the sense I specified above. The acetone may have no capacities or dispositions that are sensitive only to the fact that it is in a glass jar. In effect, it won't do or undergo anything that would reveal or manifest the fact that it is in a

144 SUBJECTIVITY AND CREDAL NECESSITIES

glass jar. Something similar is true of believing. A person might believe something, and so be in a certain position, without having any capacities or dispositions whose exercise or manifestation are sensitive only to the fact that she is in *that* position. This relates to the iteration that BB generates. If BB is true, then when Jones believes that the 504 stops at Garden, she also believes that she believes that she believes that she believes it. Consider the 76th iteration. Jones need have no capacity whose exercise is sensitive only to her being in that position. But that would not show that she is not in that position, any more than the acetone's lacking a capacity that is sensitive only to being in glass jars would show that it is not in a glass jar. Again, matters are different with Sarah. It would be a cognitive achievement for her to believe that Jones believes that Jones believes that Jones believes....that Jones believes that the 504 stops at Garden, up to the 76th iteration. She can get there if she believes both the BB principle and that Jones believes that the 504 stops at Garden. Still, each of those beliefs is an achievement. My cat has neither belief. But the fact that something is a cognitive achievement for one person does not show it is a cognitive achievement for everyone.

Of course if Jones is a normal adult, then she likely is able to *say* that she believes that she believes that she believes....all the way to the 76th iteration. It'll just take a little patience and concentration. A normal adult has a wide variety of abilities, including the ability to reflect on her own position and perspective and to say what she believes she believes. But, as I argued in Chapter 1, believing something is not itself an ability or disposition. The fact that exercising those reflective and expressive abilities is an achievement does not show that being in a position to exercise them is also an achievement.

This point about implicit believing helps answer a question Matt Boyle raised about whether BB is true of cats and dogs. He notes that standard accounts of knowledge assume some principle like the following.

A subject can know that P only if she possesses the concepts necessary for understanding the proposition that P.

As he says, if this principle is true, then BB entails that cats and dogs have the concept of belief. This, Boyle suggests, is implausible. But if we reject that principle in order to retain BB, then we face a difficult question.

> [I]f we sever the link between ascribing knowledge that one believes that P and ascribing grasp of the concept belief, we make it much less clear what this ascription comes to. Just what does it mean to say that subject 'tacitly knows' this? (Boyle 2019, 1028)

I think that my account suggests an answer to this question. To say that the acetone is tacitly in the glass jar is to say that it has no capacities or dispositions whose exercise or manifestation is sensitive to its being in the glass jar. Likewise, to say that a person's belief is tacit is to say she has no capacities or dispositions whose exercise or manifestation is sensitive to her having that belief. Some story may be needed for how she came by that belief, just as some story may be needed for how the drop of acetone got in the jar. If BB is true, then the story in the belief case concerns the essential subjectivity of believing. But once we distinguish being in a position from having a capacity, and distinguish the special case of believing something from having an ability, the idea that a person might tacitly believe something should seem less puzzling. It is just the idea that a person is in a position to do, think, and feel things in light of a possibility that none of her capacities and dispositions are specifically sensitive to. Given the distinction between positions and capacities, we should expect there to be tacit beliefs. It would be surprising if a believer had, for each possibility, a capacity specially defined for it.

Here is a different worry about whether cats have beliefs about their own beliefs. The worry is that such higher-order beliefs could never make a difference to a cat's behavior, and so never be manifested in their behavior. If it could never be manifested, then what reason is there to think they have it? The worry cannot be that believing something requires actually manifesting the belief, since we can all agree that someone might believe something and never act on it. But one might think that believing something requires being *able* to manifest it. And one might think that cats are not able to manifest such second-order beliefs. That is, one could concede that a cat can manifest the belief that there is food in the bowl, but deny that she could ever manifest the belief that she believes that there is food in the bowl. If not and if being able to manifest it is needed for believing it, then the cat cannot have that second-order belief.

I think this worry misses the mark. For on my view, a cat *can* manifest the higher-order belief. She manifests it whenever she manifests the relevant lower-order one. When the cat runs to the corner believing the food bowl is full, she is manifesting not just her belief that the food bowl is full, but also her belief that she believes that the food bowl is full. For on my view, believing something and believing that you believe it go together. Anything that manifests the one manifests the other. What is more, on my view the fact that the cat has the higher-order belief can even partly explain why she ran to the corner. For (on my view) if she had *not* had it, then she would not have believed that the bowl was full of food, and so would not have had that reason to run to it. In this way, such higher-order beliefs can even make a difference to a cat's actions.

I can imagine the following reply. The connection between belief and action is tighter than this. It is not just that believing something requires being able to *manifest* the belief in action. It is that believing something requires being able to manifest that very belief, all on its own. More precisely, to believe that some possibility obtains you need to have a capacity whose exercise is sensitive to

146 SUBJECTIVITY AND CREDAL NECESSITIES

whether just *that* possibility obtains. So, the cat can believe that she believes the bowl is full of food only if she has a capacity whose exercise is sensitive to just the fact that she has that belief. She would need to be able to act on the fact that she believes that she has that belief without also acting on the belief that the bowl is full of food. But cats don't have such a capacity. And so, this objector might conclude, the cat lacks the second-order belief.

I think this objection also misses the mark. I don't think believing requires the capacity in question. I am inclined to agree that cats do not have a capacity that is sensitive to the fact that they believe things, whereas we do. We can reflect on the fact that we and others believe things, and we can act on the belief that we and others have beliefs. But this difference between cats and us is a difference in the capacities we have, not a difference in what we believe, though our having these additional capacities likely also extends our cognitive reach. Our ability to reflect in this way on ourselves and others makes us able to believe things we otherwise couldn't. But believing, or so argued in Chapter 1, is not itself a capacity. Rather, to believe something is to be in a certain position to exercise the capacities one has. Once we distinguish what a thing believes from the capacities it has to act on what it believes, the possibility that cats might believe things while lacking a specific capacity to act on them should not be so surprising.[8]

The argument I have given for BB shares a strategy with two others in recent literature. Robert Stalnaker (2015) and Daniel Greco (2014b) use this strategy to argue for the KK principle. On their view, for a person to know that P is for her to have an internal state that carries the information that P. This very state, they argue, itself carries the information that the person is in that state. So, they conclude, a person who knows that P knows that they know it. (To avoid possible problems with iteration, Greco suggests that perhaps knowing that P does not entail believing that P.) Eric Marcus (2016) uses this same strategy to argue for the BK principle. (In fact, he argues that believing that P *just is* knowing that you believe that P.) As he sees it, a person believes that P just in case she is able to sincerely assert that P. Anyone with that ability, he argues, is able to act in light of the fact that she believes that P. And having this ability, in turn, is knowing that you believe that P. My argument for BB adapts these argumentative strategies, but is more modest, not only because its conclusion is weaker than either KK or BK but also in starting from a more modest conception of believing, one that requires

---

[8] The scope for implicit belief is wider than I have mentioned. Some credal necessities are universal in that every believer must believe them. I have in mind ways things must be no matter what. If some possibility must obtain no matter what, then any believer is in position to do, think, and feel things in light of it. She is in that position simply in virtue of believing anything at all. Many of those beliefs will be implicit in the sense I have tried to specify. But to say that a person's belief is implicit is not to characterize the believing as such, so much as it is to say that she lacks a capacity that is specific to it, one whose exercise reveals only the fact that she has that belief.

CREDAL NECESSITIES AND TRANSPARENCY 147

no internal information-carrying states and that assumes no special link between believing and language.

6.4 Credal Necessities and Transparency

I have argued that a person must believe not just that she exists but that she has the perspective on the world that she does. The world, according to Jones, must be one where she believes that the 504 stops at Garden. This helps us to understand the so-called transparency of believing.

A person's believing something is transparent in that she can answer questions about whether she believes some possibility by considering whether it obtains. Jones can answer the question whether she believes that the 504 stops at Howard Park by reflecting on the 504 and its route. She would not normally inspect or reflect on her own mental states. It is not just that she might *come* to believe in that possibility by considering the 504's route, but that she can answer a question about her current state of mind by considering it. This is not how she'd answer the same question about Sarah. Indeed, facts about the 504's actual route might be pretty much irrelevant when considering whether Sarah believes that it stops at Howard Park. This asymmetry looks like it needs explaining.

We need to be careful how we understand what Jones did in the story. According to BB, if Jones does believe that the 504 stops at Howard Park, then she also believes that she believes it. If so, then Jones is not, in reflecting on the 504's route, learning something new about her own mental state. She already believed it, if BB is true. (If either KK or BK is true, then she already knew it.) This is important, since some who find BB implausible say that the fact that Jones can, by reflecting on the 504's route, answer questions about her beliefs shows that she has a distinctively first-personal procedure for gaining this self-knowledge. It is first-personal since Jones cannot use that procedure to figure out what Sarah believes. It is a procedure since it yields new belief or knowledge. Since I have already argued for BB, I won't pursue such accounts.[9]

But one who accepts BB might think that the procedure Jones employed made explicit a belief that was until then implicit. The idea is that in reflecting on the 504's route, Jones made explicit something she believed only implicitly, namely that she *believes* that it stops at Howard Park. This would not be a change in what Jones believes, since she already implicitly believed that she believed it. It would, rather, be making it explicit to herself that she believes it. Matt Boyle suggests this sort of view. His example involves Gareth Evans' (1982) case of a person asking herself whether there will be a third world war.

---

[9] The idea of such a procedure is developed by Byrne (2018). For criticism, see Boyle (2019).

148   SUBJECTIVITY AND CREDAL NECESSITIES

If the deliberating subject then goes on to think the reflective thought

> I believe there will be a third world war.

she will be making her attitude on the question explicit, but this awareness was already implicit in her world-directed representation of the likelihood of a third world war. To acquire reflective knowledge of her own doxastic state in this way, she need only understand the relationship between a certain mode of presentation of a worldly state of affairs and her own state of belief. And again, what justifies her reflective step will be, not the sheer thought that there will be a third world war, but her non-positional consciousness of her own stance on this question.   (Boyle 2019, 1035)

Boyle says that the transition from implicitly believing something to explicitly believing it can be a rational one, in the sense that it is epistemically justified. I will set that aside, in order to focus on the idea of a transition between implicit and explicit.

It is helpful, I think, to see Boyle as endorsing something like the following.

$BB_{Implicit}$ If a person believes that P, then she implicitly believes that she believes it.

But notice that the notion of an implicit belief here is not the one I identified in the previous section. I said that a person's believing something is implicit if she has no capacity or disposition whose exercise or manifestation is specifically sensitive to the fact that she believes it. The model was of a drop of acetone whose capacities and dispositions are insensitive to the fact that it is in a glass jar. Nothing the drop would do or undergo would manifest the fact that it is in a glass jar. On this notion of implicit, making an implicit belief explicit would require a change in the believer's capacities or dispositions. But this is not what happens when Jones reflects on the 504's route. It is not that she acquires a capacity or disposition that is sensitive to the fact that she believes that 504 stops at Howard Park. What is more, when Jones acts on her belief that the 504 stops at Howard Park this manifests the fact that she believes it, but it also manifests the fact that she believes that she believes it, and that she believes that . . . . . . So the notion of an implicit belief Boyle has in mind is not the one I identified.

To illuminate the sense of implicit he has in mind, Boyle turns to a Sartrean distinction between two forms or kinds of consciousness. When Jones looks at the 504 streetcar, she is *positionally* conscious of the streetcar, in the sense that the streetcar is the object she is aware of. That state of consciousness *posits* the streetcar. But she is also *non-positionally* conscious of being (positionally) conscious of the streetcar. That is, she is also conscious of being conscious of the streetcar, though that derivative consciousness does not posit the original one in the way that the original one posits the streetcar. Boyle admits that this distinction does not by itself explain the difference, but rather "marks the spot where the clarification is needed" (Boyle 2019, 1030).

I find this Sartrean image highly suggestive. But I worry that it hypostasizes belief states, by suggesting that a belief state is a thing one can be conscious of in something like the way one can be conscious of a streetcar. In the same article, Boyle turns to a slightly different image. He says that a person who believes that P "inhabits" the perspective of the belief that P. There is a nice ambiguity here between two inhabitants. One inhabits the world that is being perceived; the other is doing the perceiving. I want to use this image of inhabiting a perspective to show how the modal view of belief, together with BB, can help us to understand the transparency phenomena.

What needs to be understood, I think, is the fact that, from a believer's point of view, its being the case that P and her believing that P are inseparable. If, from her point of view, the 504 stops at Howard Park, then, from her point of view, she believes that it does. And if, from her point of view, she believes that it stops at Howard Park, then, from her point of view, it does stop there. All of this is just a restatement of what BB entails. But it captures the image of inhabiting a perspective. A person must take herself to be in the world as she believes it to be. In believing that the 504 stops at Howard Park, Jones must see herself as being in a world where it does. In this sense, she must inhabit the world of that perspective. But a believer must also take herself, not just to have a place in the world, but to have a perspective on it. So in taking herself to be in a world where the 504 stops at Howard Park, Jones must also take herself to have a perspective from which it does. In this sense, she must inhabit that perspective on the world. It is this inseparability between inhabiting a perspective on the world and inhabiting the world of a perspective that explains how a person can answer questions about her perspective by answering questions about her world.

I have said that believing is in some respects like owning. A phenomenon very much like transparency is present with ownership. To answer a question about what she owns, a person considers her possessions not her possessions. She considers the things she owns and not her owning of them. Indeed, it is not clear what it would be for her to reflect on or be aware of her state of ownership. It is not the right sort of thing to be an object of awareness. Jones owns many books and has them all on her bookshelf. She can answer a question about her ownership state (e.g., does she own a copy of *Word and Object*?) by answering a question about what books are on the shelf. Whether a copy of *Word and Object* is on the shelf is not a fact about her, but she can settle the question about her ownership state by settling the question about the shelf. Ownership is, to this extent, transparent to what is owned.

Of course, the analogy with believing is imperfect. For one thing, a person can own something without believing that she does. So looking at her shelf can be a way to discover what she owns, whereas (I have argued) if a person believes

150 SUBJECTIVITY AND CREDAL NECESSITIES

something then she believes she does. What is more, a person might not realize she is an owner, whereas (I have argued) if a person is a believer then she believes that she is. Still, the structure of transparency is the same, even if its scope is different. Both an owner and a believer can answer questions about their state by answering questions about the objects of that state. What the dis-analogies reveal, I think, is that at the heart of credal transparency is the fact that a believer must take herself to be a believer. Understanding that is the crux.

6.5 Subjectivity, Force, and Content

I have argued for the BB principle and explained how it gives rise to credal necessities and I have suggested that these necessities ground what is subjective in believing. But many theorists think that the subjectivity of belief involves something else. On standard views, there are essentially subjective belief properties, ones that no two people can share. Some say this is needed to prevent a radical form of uncertainty about oneself, and others that it is needed to understand rational action. I'll consider these views in Sections 6.6 and 6.7. But recently some have argued that the subjectivity of belief requires rejecting the traditional distinction between what a person believes and their believing it, between content and force. If so, then no one can share *any* belief properties. In this section, I will suggest that this rejection stems from what I will call the granular view about belief states, and I will suggest that we reject it.

Sebastian Rödl agrees that a person believes something only if she believes that she does. But he says that this entails that believing something and believing that one believes it are the same state.[10] Rödl puts his point in terms of judgment rather than belief, but this won't matter for our purposes. His focus is on a traditional distinction between the object believed—the content—and the believing—the force.

> If judgment is articulated into force and content, then *I think P* is a content alongside and different from P. It is one thing to think something, it is another to think that one thinks it. That things are so is one object of judgment, inquiry, understanding; one's act of judging that they are so is another object of judgment, inquiry, understanding. One's judging that such-and-such is the case is one bit of reality alongside other bits, among them the bit that consists in such-and-such's being the case.... *This denies the self-consciousness of thought.* (Rödl 2018, 20; final emphasis added)

---

[10] Eric Marcus (2016) argues for the same conclusion.

SUBJECTIVITY, FORCE, AND CONTENT 151

If we are to properly appreciate what he calls the "self-consciousness" of belief, Rödl says we must deny a distinction between force and content, between a person's believing something and the object of her belief. Denying it, Rödl says, requires admitting that "thinking that one thinks P is nothing other than thinking P" (2018, 20).

I have resisted formulating BB as the claim that believing is essentially self-conscious. I feel the attractions of this way of putting it, but also worry that it is misleading. Believing is not a form of consciousness. In believing that the 504 stops at Garden, there is nothing that Jones is aware or conscious of. And in believing that she believes it, she is not conscious or aware of her believing it. At least not in the sense in which she is aware of the streetcar when she sees it, or the sense in which, when she says to herself that it stops at Garden Avenue she is aware that she is saying it to herself. Because I want to mark the fact that believing is not a form of, and does not involve, awareness or consciousness, I want to resist Rödl's way of putting the point. I will stick with saying that what BB says is that believing requires believing that you believe.

If Rödl is right that recognizing this requires denying a distinction between force and content, then people can never share belief properties. Every belief property would be essentially subjective, a property that only one person could have. To see this, suppose Jones believes that the 504 stops at Garden. If Rödl is right, her believing this is her believing that she believes that the 504 stops at Garden. Simon might also believe that the 504 stops at Garden, but he might not believe that Jones believes this. So, if Rödl is right, the belief property Jones has is not the one he has. Peter meanwhile might believe that Jones believes that the 504 stops at Garden without believing himself that it does. Again, the belief property Jones has is not the one Peter has, if Rödl is right. On his view, each of Jones' beliefs is thus essentially about her. Even her beliefs about other people are, if Rödl is right, beliefs about herself.[11] So if Rödl is right, no two people can have the same belief properties. This would be a radical sort of credal subjectivity.

Rödl's view concerns a distinction between force and content. That distinction was originally meant to capture potential similarities and differences between people. When Jones believes and Michael hopes that the 504 stops at Garden, their attitudes are similar in one way but different in another. They are similar in that the possibility whose obtaining would make Jones right in her belief would also fulfill Michael's hope. But they are different because believing and hoping are different attitudes. The contents are the same, but their attitudes are different. As

---

[11] In conversation, Rödl said that the "I" in the "I think" does not refer to the believer, but to something like the capacity of reason itself. If so, then this version of the thought won't cast light on the essential subjectivity of believing, at least not the subjectivity I am trying to focus on. So I will set this aside.

152 SUBJECTIVITY AND CREDAL NECESSITIES

such, this is not a distinction drawn within a theory of the mind. It is just part of the data we start with.

Why does Rödl think it conflicts with the idea that believing requires believing that you believe? I am not entirely sure, but I suspect it has to do with a certain view about the nature of belief states. I'll call it the *granular* view. To see what I have in mind, it is helpful to return to a point I made in Chapter 2. I said that belief properties, such as believing that the 504 stops at Garden, are not sortal properties. We cannot, I said, count believings. We can count the number of things a person believes, or the number of people who share a belief, but we cannot count their believings. In this respect, believing is like owning. If Jones owns ten books, we might say that Jones is in one ownership state, that of owning all ten books, or we might say that she is in ten ownerships states, one for each book. The same two options are available in the belief case. Suppose Jones believes ten things. How many believings by her are there? We might say that she is in ten belief states, one for each thing. This would be the more granular view. Or we might say that she is in one belief state, that of believing all of the objects. This would be the more holistic view. I am not sure that our ordinary ways of thinking about belief decide between these two views. But notice that the propositional view of the objects of belief fits naturally with the granular view, while the modal view fits naturally with the holistic view.

The BB Principle can seem especially puzzling from the granular point of view. It requires a necessary connection between metaphysically independent states. For Jones to believe that the 504 stops at Garden—for her to be in *that* belief state— she must also be in the state of believing that she exists in a world where the 504 stops at Garden. Those states are independent since a person could be in one of them without being in the other. Simon, for instance, believes that the 504 stops at Garden, but might have no beliefs about Jones. So an explanation is needed for why Jones can be in that first state only if she is in the second. Why must there be this necessary connection between these independent states? The fact that believing requires believing that you believe, viewed from the granular point of view, thus seems to require a puzzling inter-connection between independent mental states.

The more holistic view, especially when combined with the modal view of the objects of belief, helps us to see why this is not so puzzling. On the holistic modal view, when a person believes something, the object of her belief is a rich possibility consisting in the sum of the ways she takes things to be. We should think of the object of a person's belief as a single more or less complete possibility. She is in one state of believing a complex possibility, rather than many states of believing comparatively simple ones. Now, since she takes herself to exist, her own existence is among the possibilities she takes to obtain. It is part of how she takes things to be, and in this she has no alternative. So in believing that the 504 stops at Garden, Jones inevitably believes that she is in a world where the 504 stops at Garden. And when she starts believing that the 504 also stops at Galley, then she starts believing that she is in a world where the 504 stops at Galley. There is nothing more puzzling about this than there is in the idea that when a person owns a book she owns every page in it.

Importantly, the holistic modal view avoids the radical conclusion that belief properties are essentially private. For it can also admit the force-content distinction. It allows us to identify similarities and differences in the possibilities different people take to obtain. Simon and Jones might disagree on many things, but they might agree that the 504 stops at Garden. And it can allow that one person can hope what another person fears. And it allows that two people can agree on which possibilities obtain, and so be in the very same belief state. Sarah and Jones both believe that the 504 stops at Garden and, because BB is true, they each believe that they themselves live in a world where they believe that the 504 stops at Garden. The similarity is that each is right in what they believe only if the 504 stops at Garden. This possibility is common to their beliefs. Where they differ is that Sarah must believe that she exists, whereas Jones need not believe that Sarah exists. This difference is traceable, not to a difference in what they believe, for they might agree on how things are. Nor is it traceable to a difference in their attitudes, for it is belief in each case. The difference, rather, is traceable to the fact that Sarah and Jones are different *believers*.

6.6 Subjective Uncertainty

If the BB principle is true, then a person must believe that she exists, if she believes anything at all. But some say that believing *that* one exists is compatible with uncertainty about *who* one is, and that accounting for the subjectivity of belief requires admitting belief properties that can resolve or prevent this uncertainty. The idea is that a person who knows that she exists could be uncertain or wrong, not just about her height or weight or about what she had for lunch, but also about who she is, about *which* person in the world as she takes it to be she herself is. Removing or avoiding such uncertainty, they say, requires a special belief property, one that is essentially subjective. I will argue that this alleged uncertainty is not as coherent as one might think. It is not clear we need to appeal to essentially subjective beliefs to resolve it.

Here is a way to see what the issue is. Suppose we think of our beliefs as like a map, one representing not just places but also people. Think of a map in a shopping mall that represents the stores and their locations but also all of the shoppers and their locations. Presented with such a map I might well be uncertain as to which of the represented shoppers I am. I might even mis-identify myself. To remove or prevent such uncertainty or error I would need a "This is me" tag on the map, to identify myself among all the people I take there to be. If believing is like

154 SUBJECTIVITY AND CREDAL NECESSITIES

having a map of the world, then couldn't something analogous happen with believing? Even if I must believe that I am one of the people in the world as I take it to be, couldn't I be uncertain or mistaken about which of those people I am? To remove or prevent such uncertainty or error, wouldn't I need a special "This is me" belief, one that only I could have? Or so one might worry.

That this sort of uncertainty or error is possible is often taken to be a lesson of now familiar stories about people suffering from radical amnesia or who are lost in libraries.[12] Lewis' story of the two Gods is in many ways the most interesting, but it will pay to start with Perry's story of the shopper pushing the cart through the supermarket following a trail of sugar that, unbeknownst to him, is pouring from his own cart. Our shopper is making a mess, and he doesn't realize this. He is thus mistaken about what is true of him. To this extent the mistake is just like a mistake I might make about my weight or about what I had for lunch. But it has seemed to many theorists that there is more to the shopper's mistake. They want to say, not just that our shopper is mistaken about some property he has, but that he is mistaken about *who* he is, since he is the one making the mess and yet he does not realize this. When he learns the truth, he'll say something like: *I am the one making the mess!* It is, it seems, as if he had failed to identify himself in his own map of the world.

But it is not quite right to say that our shopper does not know who he is. What does our shopper take the world to be like? That is, how should we characterize the world as he takes it to be? This much, I think, is clear. In the world as he takes it to be there are at least two people pushing shopping carts through the supermarket. One is spilling sugar and the other is following the spiller. Our shopper takes himself to be the follower, and he is right about this. He is following the spiller. Of course he does not take himself to be the spiller. And here he is wrong. But it is not as if he is suffering uncertainty about which one he is of the two shoppers he takes there to be. He is quite certain that he is the follower and that he is not the spiller. And given his conception of things, he is right not to take himself to be the spiller. For in that conception it is someone else who is spilling. So this is not a case of someone who is uncertain about who he is.[13]

---

[12] The stories are famously explored in Gottlob Frege (1952). Influential discussions are in John Perry (1979) and David Lewis (1979). Anscombe (1981a) approaches these issues from the point of view of practical knowledge, the distinctive sort of knowledge a person has of her own intentional actions. For helpful essays on this topic, see (Roessler & Eilan 2003). I explore this in (Hunter 2015) and (2017). My views are influenced by the work of Robert Stalnaker; see for instance Stalnaker (2008). A subtle and sustained attempt to make sense of the sort of uncertainty I will argue is impossible is found in Vendler (1984).

[13] What I said in Chapter 5 about credal illusions is relevant here. In the world as the shopper takes it to be someone else is pushing the cart making the mess. Who is that person? There need not be an answer to this question, as the shopper may be suffering a credal illusion. Depending on why we are trying to describe the shopper's conception of things, it may be more or less natural to characterize the merely possible person by reference to an actual person. For discussion of the context-dependence of belief ascription, see my 2011b, and the discussion in Zimmerman (2018).

What about Lewis' story of the omniscient Gods? In the story, two Gods sit atop mountains, one on the coldest and one on the tallest. Each God is omniscient, knowing all there is to know, not just about which God is on which mountain, but about what each God knows about which God is on which mountain. Still, Lewis asks, couldn't we conceive of one of the Gods coming to wonder which of the two Gods he is? Couldn't he wonder whether he is the one on the tallest or the one on the coldest mountain? Part of what makes this story so interesting is that it is supposed to involve no factual ignorance or uncertainty. Perry's shopper has a false belief about himself (about whether sugar is spilling from his cart) whereas Lewis' God is supposed to know everything there is to know about himself. The moral Lewis invites us to draw from this story is that since we do not suffer the imagined God's uncertainty, there must be more in our conception of things than can be represented by a possibility: we need also to represent the fact that each of us identifies ourselves as the center of the world as we take it to be.

I am not convinced the God's imagined uncertainty is coherent. As I said in Chapter 3, I lose my grip on belief and action when I think about omniscient and omnipotent beings. It is easy to over-generalize the uncertainty we imagined our shopper in the mall having, an uncertainty that is coherent. Our shopper in the mall was unsure which of the shoppers he is in the mall's map, even though he is certain that he is one of them. We can make good sense of this uncertainty I think, but only because we assume that our shopper is certain about who he is. He knows that he is staring at a map in the mall, and can use this knowledge to triangulate (as it were) in order to find himself in the world of the map. His uncertainty is conceivable for us partly because we take it to occur against a background of certainty about who he is. But in the case of Lewis' Gods, any such background certainty is supposed to be absent. This is a relevant disanalogy. The fact that we can conceive of the shopper's uncertainty is no reason to think we can just as easily conceive of the Gods' uncertainty.

6.7 Rational Action

I will consider one final reason for thinking there is more to the subjectivity of belief than the credal necessities I have identified. It concerns rational action. The key idea is that when two people act differently, if what each did was rational, there must be some difference in what they believed or wanted. But this difference cannot always be a difference in which possibilities they believe or want to obtain, for two people who agree on all that might nonetheless act differently and rationally so. There must thus be an essentially subjective difference in the people's beliefs (or desires). David Owens (2001) puts this idea by saying that in order to act rationally, a deliberator must "link the point of view of the deliberator with the point of view of the agent by means of the *I* concept"(266), and that this

156 SUBJECTIVITY AND CREDAL NECESSITIES

requires a distinctive first-personal belief.[14] The nature of rational action shows, the thinking concludes, that there is more to the subjectivity of believing than just the credal necessities I identified. In this section I will argue that we should reject that initial key idea. A difference is what it is rational for two people to do does not require a difference in beliefs or desires.

It will help to start with an example. Jones owes Sarah some money, and promised to repay it at a certain time in the coffee shop. They meet in the shop at the appointed time, Jones hands the money to Sarah, and Sarah takes the money from Jones. Jones and Sarah acted differently and rationally so. As I said in Chapter 1, a person's beliefs and desires rationalize their actions, and so one might think that if two people acted differently and rationally so, there must be a difference in what they believe or want. But for all that I have said, Jones and Sarah might agree about which possibilities obtain, and they might agree on which ones they want to obtain. They might agree that Jones owes Sarah money and they might both want Jones to pay it back. So if there must be a difference in their beliefs and desires, but not a difference in *what* they believe or desire, then, or so one might think, their beliefs and desires must differ in some first personal way. Whereas Jones believes, as she would put it, that *I owe Sarah money*, Sarah believes, as she would put it, that *Jones owes me money*. This is not a difference over which possibilities obtain. Jones and Sarah might agree on what their shared world is like. Rather, the difference in their beliefs is a difference in how each of them "centers" themselves in that shared world, how each of them represented herself, and this difference explains why it was rational for them to act differently. Or so one might think.

But we should resist this line of thinking. Indeed, we should reject the key idea about rational action that prompts it. It is not true that if two people act differently and each acted rationally then there must be a difference in their beliefs and desires. For the difference in their actions might be rationalized by a difference in their situations. People in different situations may act differently and rationally so without a difference in their beliefs or desires. This difference in situation can also make for a difference in the reasons each person has, even though they agree on which possibilities obtain.

My point here is just a special case of a general fact about properties and explanations, one I mentioned in Chapter 1. The properties of a thing explain its behavior as a function of the thing's situation. Things with the same properties may behave differently if in different situations. Suppose that two fragile glass vases are on a table, and that one falls and shatters. We can explain the difference

---

[14] This idea that rational action requires a person to link perspectives is also found in (Burge 1998). I suspect that this view about the need for an essentially first personal belief in rational action presuppose the sort of radical uncertainty I discussed in the previous section. I discuss this more in (Hunter 2017).

in behavior without positing a difference in the properties they had prior to the fall. The difference in behavior stems from the fact that they are in different situations—one fell and the other did not. To say that a vase is fragile is to say something about how it would behave in various situations. Likewise, to say what a person believes is to ascribe to them a property, and we should expect that what difference having that property makes to a person will depend on her situation.

So I suggest that we reject the following.

Inter-Personal Explanation: There can be no difference in two people's rational actions without a difference in their beliefs or desires.[15]

We should distinguish this from the following.

Intra-Personal Explanation: There can be no rational change in a person's actions without some change in their beliefs or desires.

I am inclined to think that Intra-Personal Explanation is true. Suppose that Jones suddenly stops handing Sarah the money, and that she does so intentionally. It seems to me that there must have been some change in Jones' beliefs or desires that explains this change in her behavior. Maybe she suddenly remembered that she needed to save the cash to buy medicine for her sick mother. Or maybe he was overcome with a sudden violent resentment against Sarah. It is also possible that something in his situation changed. Maybe Sarah declined the repayment, or maybe Beatrice the barista said something surprising. A change in the situation could explain the change in Jones' behavior only if Jones was aware of the change in the situation, and this would require a change in her beliefs. So, it seems to me, Intra-Personal Explanation is true (or at least plausible). But I think we should reject what I called Inter-Personal Explanation.

But are Jones and Sarah really in different situations? Aren't they both standing in the café, next to a slice of mince pie? This is true, but their situations are still different. For Jones owes Sarah money but Sarah does not owe Jones money. Being confronted with a creditor is very different from being confronted with a debtor. And this difference in their situations is relevant to the difference in their actions. Jones acted reasonably given her beliefs and desires in that situation. Likewise, Sarah acted reasonably given her beliefs and desires in that situation. And notice that each of them is aware of this difference. They both know that Jones owes Sarah money. So not only are they in relevantly different situations, they are aware that they are in relevantly different situations. It thus strikes me that we can

---

[15] For discussion of this, see Setiya (2009).

158 SUBJECTIVITY AND CREDAL NECESSITIES

explain the difference in their actions in terms of a difference in their situations, without needing to posit a difference in their beliefs or desires.

I think that our case also shows that Jones and Sarah had different reasons for action, even though they agreed on which possibilities obtain. That is, I suggest we also reject the following.

Inter-Personal Reasons: There can be no difference in what two people have reason to do without a difference in what they believe or desire.

It is controversial what it is to be a reason for someone to do something, and also controversial what it is for someone to *have* a reason. But let's assume that what reasons a person has depends *only* on her mental states. In other words, let's suppose that the following is true.

Intra-Personal Reasons: There can be no change in what reasons a person has to do things without a change in her beliefs or desires.

Even if Intra-Personal Reasons is true, Inter-Personal Reasons is not.[16] Because Jones believes correctly that she owes Sarah money, Jones has a reason to give someone money. But surely it does not follow from the fact that Sarah also believes that Jones owes her money that she, Sarah, has reason to give someone money. How could it? What reasons for action a person has must in some way depend on their being the person they are. After all, they are the one who will be doing the acting. How could the fact that Jones and Sarah are different people not make a difference to what they each have reason to do? Maybe this is more puzzling than I am allowing, but if it is, then it is a puzzle about how a person's reasons relate to their beliefs and desires, and it would be as much a puzzle for essentially personal ones as for essentially personal ones. Even if we allow essentially subjective belief properties, we still need an account of how they fix a person's reasons.

It is tempting at this point to reintroduce the radical error we discussed in Section 6.6. What if, in our story, Jones mistakenly took herself to be Sarah? Couldn't she nonetheless agree with Sarah about which possibilities obtain and about which they want to obtain. And if she took herself to be Sarah, then wouldn't it be irrational or anyway odd for Jones to hand money to Sarah?

---

[16] Cappelen and Dever consider a close relative: there can be no difference in what two people are rationally motivated to do without a difference in their beliefs or desires (Cappelen & Dever 2013, 52). They accept this doctrine, though they do not argue for it. Applied to my case, their view is that Jones and Sarah are both motivated to perform the action *that Jones gives Sarah the money*. But only Jones can perform it; Sarah cannot. This difference in what each can do explains, on their view, why they act differently. I am not sure I understand what it could be for Sarah to be rationally motivated to do that action. It is not contingent that she cannot do it, and she knows perfectly well that she cannot do it. So how can she take herself to have reason to do it or even be so much as motivated to do it? Far better, it seems to me, simply to deny Inter-Personal Reasons.

Doesn't this show that part of what made it reasonable in the original story for Jones to hand Sarah the money is that Jones identified herself as Jones? And wouldn't this have to be a special essentially first-personal belief?

I am not sure how to make sense of this revised story. It is not clear to me that Sarah and Jones, in the revised story, really could agree on which possibilities obtain. For one thing, they surely would disagree about which person in the coffee shop is named "Sarah." I doubt this story can be turned into a pure case as I defined it in Chapter 3. And if it is meant to be a mundane version of the Lewisian Gods, then I will stick with what I have already said: I lose my grip when we think of divine credal states. I don't deny that Jones can imagine being Sarah. She might imagine seeing the coffee shop from Sarah's point of view and taking the money as she, Jones, hands it to Sarah. But imagining being someone else is not the same as taking oneself to be someone else. And I don't see how Jones could have taken herself to be Sarah without some difference in her beliefs about which possibilities obtain. And this is what matters for the revised story to pose a difficulty for the modal view of the subjectivity of belief.

Let me summarize this chapter. I have been considering what makes a person's belief state subjective or personal. I suggested that it has to do with limits to belief, to personal credal necessities. For each person there are possibilities that she must believe obtain, and these credal necessities mark her perspective as essentially hers. In particular, she must believe that she exists and that she has the beliefs she does. I suggested that this helps understand the so-called transparency of belief, argued that we don't need to deny the force-content distinction, urged that a certain kind of radical uncertainty is not coherent, and ended by arguing that nothing about rational action implies that there is more to the essential subjectivity of belief than these credal necessities. A chief virtue, it seems to me, of the idea that possibilities are the objects of belief is that it helps us understand how the limits of belief ground both the objectivity and subjectivity of belief.

7

Credal Agency

My first four chapters considered the ontology of belief. The next two considered the limits of belief. These final two chapters concern the norms of belief. In this one I will argue that a person is responsible for believing what she does. Through inference she can sustain and change her position on which possibilities obtain. When she does so, she causes herself to keep or to change that position. In a literal sense, she makes up her own mind as to which of them obtain. In the final chapter, I will consider how goodness figures into believing, when believing something is to a person's credit or discredit, and when a person ought to believe something.

Here is my plan for this chapter. In Section 7.1, I will specify the sorts of inferences I have in mind and lay out the core elements of my view. My focus will be on inferences where the person's reasons do not entail her conclusion. The next two sections consider objections to my view. In Section 7.2, I will consider the idea that an inference is not an action at all but rather the onset of a belief state. In Section 7.3, I will consider an objection to the idea that in inference a person acts on herself. We will see once again how the temptation to hypostasize beliefs gets in the way of understanding the nature of believing. In Section 7.4, I consider how inference involves a responsiveness to reasons. I will suggest that this involves the same sort of self-knowledge present when a person acts on a belief. In Section 7.5, I will sketch certain metaphysical ideas about action, causation, and agency that underlie my view. This will extend the account of agency I developed in Chapter 1. In Section 7.6, I will discuss whether inference is intentional. In Section 7.7, I will suggest that the inferences I have in mind are voluntary. In Section 7.8, I look briefly at mathematical inferences, which seem to pose a special problem for the suggestion that they can be voluntary. Section 7.9 argues that the inferences I have in mind, even when voluntary, are not invariably willing. One can be unhappy that one is making up one's mind in some way, even when one is doing so voluntarily. This is one form of credal alienation.

7.1 Inference as a Mental Act

In this section, I will lay out the core elements of my view about inference and illustrate it with examples. The next sections will consider objections to this view and explore its consequences. I will start by identifying the scope of my account.

On Believing: Being Right in a World of Possibilities. David Hunter, Oxford University Press. © David Hunter 2022.
DOI: 10.1093/oso/9780192859549.003.0008

INFERENCE AS A MENTAL ACT 161

My focus will be on inferences where a person's evidence does not entail her conclusion. Here is an example.

> Jones is waiting for the 504 to arrive. She consults the TTC schedule which says the train will arrive at 3:10 pm. She checks her watch and sees that it is 3:09 pm. She looks down the street, hoping to see the train approaching, but it is not in view. She concludes that the 504 will be a bit late.

I have several reasons for this restricted focus. First, I think inferences like this are common in our deliberative lives but often neglected in philosophical accounts of inference and of the agency of belief. Considering them can help expand our diet of examples and, more importantly, reveal otherwise hidden aspects of inference.

My second reason is that cases where the person's evidence does entail the conclusion can be distracting. They raise puzzles about belief and understanding that are independent of the ordinary sorts of inference people make. Everyone agrees we need to distinguish the idea of a valid argument from that of an inference. An argument whose premise and conclusion are the same is valid, but one can't infer the conclusion from the premise. An inference, I take it, involves coming to believe one thing on the basis of something else one believes. If the premise and conclusion are the same, then one already believes the conclusion in believing the premise. That's why one can't infer a truth from itself. Something similar is true whenever an argument's premises entail its conclusion. If its premises are true, its conclusion must be as well. On any view, there would be something odd about someone's believing those premises without believing the conclusion. It would be hard to say how the person takes things to be, since there is no world where the premises are true and the conclusion false or even open. It is natural to think that such a person would fail to understand the words used to formulate the premises or conclusion. All of this is neatly illustrated in Lewis Carroll's (1895) famous story of Achilles and the Tortoise and in the vast literature it spawned. On the view I defended in Chapter 3, in believing the premises of a valid argument one just does believe its conclusion. I think this is right, though I know others disagree. I'll have more to say in Sections 7.7 and 7.8 about inferences where the premises entail the conclusion. But the account of inference I will develop concerns cases where they don't, and I will use "inference" with that restriction in mind.

On my view, in drawing an inference one makes oneself believe (or continue to believe) something. But not every case of making oneself believe is a case of inference. If I paid a hypnotist to make me believe I have quit smoking, then I made myself believe it, but not by inference. Inferring is making oneself believe by attending to reasons, or anyway to the reasons one takes oneself to have. In this respect, inferring is like convincing or persuading. To convince or persuade someone to believe something you need to give them reasons, or things they

162 CREDAL AGENCY

will take to be reasons. Likewise, to infer is to make oneself believe something by attending to reasons.

The core of my view consists of three ideas about inference.

   (i) An act of inference is a causing, and not a cause, of believing.
  (ii) In drawing an inference, the believer is the cause.
 (iii) The believer does not cause the act of inference.

Here is what my view says about the case I gave above, where Jones inferred that the 504 will be a bit late. On my view, her act of inference did not cause her to believe that the 504 will be late. Rather, that inference was a causing by her of that believing. She was agent of that causing. What she caused, in making that inference, is the resulting believing. She also did not cause the inference. An act of inference need not *have* a cause, at least not insofar as it is an inference. A person might make up her mind even though nothing makes her make it up. Together, these elements capture the natural idea that a person can make up her own mind when she reflects on how things are. My goal here is to see how far we can get if we take this idea at face value.

Here are two more examples. The first one is slightly adapted from John Broome (2014).[1] Jones looks out the window and sees that it is raining hard. She knows that a strong rain tends to melt snow quickly. So she concludes that the snow on the ski slopes will melt soon. Here is a second example. Sarah believes that her son is not selling drugs, even though she has known for some time that there are suspicions that he is. But she has found the different bits of evidence she has seen to be inconclusive. She then meets with two police officers who present her with new photos and a signed witness statement. After carefully considering this new evidence, though, Sarah continues to believe that her son is not selling drugs. The view I want to explore is that in cases like this, where a person forms or retains a belief through reasoning, she causes herself to start or to continue believing it.

I'll focus in what follows on cases where a person changes her mind by starting to believe something that she did not already believe. But the picture I develop extends naturally to cases like Sarah's where a person reflects on how things are and continues believing something. We should think of this as *sustaining* belief, in something like the way that a person can hold or maintain a bodily position when standing or sitting. Jones can change her position or she can hold it. Either way,

---

[1] Broome's example is actually a slight variation of one given by Boghossian (2014). Broome agrees that an inference is something a person does. "Some processes of reasoning are 'active', by which I mean they are done by the reasoner. Active reasoning is something we do, like *eating*, rather than something that just happens in us, like *digesting*" (Broome 2014, 622; my emphasis). Broome is concerned with the normativity of inference, but I will wait until Chapter 8 to discuss normative matters.

she is causally responsible for her position. The same, I think, is true when a person upon reflection, continues to hold her position on how things are.

I am not sure whether cats and dogs make up their mind by reflecting on how things are. This is an empirical matter and I won't take a stand on it. But I am going to assume that there is a difference between believing something and making up one's mind about it. I think that cats and dogs know and believe things through perception. And as I said in Chapter 6, I think that when a cat believes something, she believes that she believes it. But knowing that the cat is on the mat by seeing it there is not the same as *concluding* that it is there after attending to others ways things are. This second thing is what I mean by making up one's mind, and I think it carries responsibility that is absent when we come to believe or know things through perception. This chapter is about how to understand this responsibility.

One final preliminary point. I said that inferring is making oneself believe something by attending to reasons. On my view, the person causes herself to believe it. Likewise, if Jones convinces Sarah that the 504 stops at Garden and she convinces her by showing her some evidence, then Jones caused Sarah to believe it. But this is compatible with saying that Sarah was convinced by Jones' presentation of that evidence and that she was convinced by the evidence presented. That is, the following can all be true together.

a. Sarah was caused to believe by a person (Jones).
b. Sarah was caused to believe by an event (Jones' presentation of the evidence)
c. Sarah was caused to believe by some facts (the evidence).

To convince Sarah, Jones had to do something. She convinced her *by* presenting to her some facts. And the facts were themselves convincing, or anyway Sarah took them to be convincing. We get the same trio in the case of an inference. To draw an inference, you need to do something. In particular, you need to attend to some facts (or what you take to be facts). Jones concluded that the 504 would be late by attending to facts about the schedule and what she could see down the street. It was by attending to these that she came to believe that the 504 would be late. These facts convinced her that it would be late. What made it a case of inference is that she made herself believe it by attending to those facts. My interest is in the role the person plays in inference.

My leading idea is that when a person makes up her mind through reasoning she causes herself to believe. I think that this idea is quite natural but that more or less familiar philosophical ideas about action, causation, and inference can make it seem puzzling and hard to accept. Full treatments of these ideas about action and causation are beyond the scope of this book. So my modest aim is to describe in some detail a conception of inference that allows us to take literally the idea that a person can be the sustaining and originating cause of her own beliefs.

164   CREDAL AGENCY

7.2 Inference Is Not an Onset of Believing

In this section and the next I will consider two objections to the idea that an inference is an action. One is that an inference is the onset of a belief, and not an action. The other concerns whether inferring is acting on oneself.

On my view, an inference is an action. Gilbert Ryle argued against this on the grounds that events take time. He suggested instead that an inference is the onset of a state of affairs. But, as we will see, Ryle himself was not completely convinced. Seeing all of this will help clarify my idea that an inference is a causing, and that causings are neither events nor onsets.

Here are two passages from Ryle.

> We saw that there was some sort of incongruity in describing someone as being at a time and for a period engaged in passing from premises to a conclusion. 'Inferring' is not used to denote either a slowish or a quickish process. 'I began to deduce, but had not time to finish' is not the sort of thing that can significantly be said. In recognition of this sort of incongruity, some theorists like to describe inferring as an instantaneous operation, one which, like a glimpse or a flash, is completed as soon as it is begun. But this is the wrong sort of story. *The reason why we cannot describe drawing a conclusion as a slowish or quickish passage is not that it is a 'Hey, presto' passage, but that it is not a passage at all....* [R]eaching a conclusion, like arriving in London, solving an anagram and checkmating the king, is not the sort of thing that can be described as gradual, quick or instantaneous.   (Ryle 1949, 301–2; italics added)

> 'Conclude,' 'deduce,' and 'prove,' like 'checkmate,' 'score,' 'invent,' and 'arrive,' are, in their *primary* uses what I have called 'got it' verbs, and while a person's publications, or other exploitations of what he has got, may take much or little time, his *transition* from not yet having got it to having now got it cannot be qualified by epithets of rapidity.   (Ryle 1949, n. 276; italics added)

Ryle's concern, in that first passage, is with the idea that an inference has a duration. He thinks this cannot be right, since if it were we should be able to sensibly ask how long some inference took, and whether it was slow or quick. But, as he correctly notes, we cannot sensibly ask these questions. Ryle then rejects the suggestion that an inference has an instantaneous duration, completed as soon as it is begun.

On my view, an inference is a causing and I can accept that inferences have no duration, for neither do causings. We need to distinguish how long an exercise of a capacity lasts from how long the exercise takes. The drop of acetone melted the rubber, and it took two minutes for the rubber to melt. Throughout that time, the acetone was exercising its capacity to melt the rubber. It exercised it for two

INFERENCE IS NOT AN ONSET OF BELIEVING   165

minutes, but the exercise itself was neither fast nor slow, for it took no time. Here is another example. A standing person might hold their position for twenty seconds. The holding lasted 20 seconds, but the holding took no time. If it had, we should be able to ask whether it was a quick holding or a slow one, and whether it got faster near the end. These questions make no sense, because holding one's position is causing it not to change, and causings are not events and don't take time.

After Ryle rejects the idea that an inference is an event, he settles on the idea that an inference is the onset of a state of affairs. The idea is that when Jones infers that the snow on the slopes will melt soon, that inferring is the onset or start of her believing that the snow on the slopes will melt soon. It is the onset of a certain mental state of affairs. I agree that onsets have no duration, and so it would make little sense to ask whether the onset was quick or slow. I also agree that onsets are not acts. They seem, rather, to be a possible result of an act.

Judith Jarvis Thomson agrees that an inference is an onset of a state of affairs. She groups inferring with deducing, discovering, remembering, etc.

> Alfred's recalling this and such is an onset of the state of affairs that of his remembering this and such; Bert's recognizing so and so is an onset of the state of affairs this is his being aware of who or what so and so is; Charles's noticing thus and such is an onset of the state of affairs that is his being aware of thus and such; etc. (Thomson 1977, 230)

(She considers onsets to be events, though, and so does not share Ryle's discomfort with the idea of an instantaneous event.) I am inclined to agree that a sentence like "Peter discovered his husband's infidelity" can report the onset of Peter's knowing about the infidelity, and that a sentence like "Simon remembered where he left his key" can report the onset of Simon's awareness of the key's location.

But I don't think that inferring properly belongs in this group. For one thing, the connection to reasons is quite different. One draws an inference in light of certain reasons one already has, but one does not discover or remember something in light of a reason one already has. What is more, one can try or attempt to remember or discover or find something, but one cannot try or attempt to infer something. Here is how Alan White put the point, though he spoke of achievements instead of onsets.

> Inferences are not achievements or arrivals, because, unlike discoveries (and also unlike deductions) they are not something we can try to, promise or resolve to make or can manage to obtain. We can not use means and methods or rely on luck to infer something. We can ask someone what he would infer from the evidence but not how he would infer. An examination paper could ask the

166   CREDAL AGENCY

candidates to solve, prove, find, discover or even deduce so and so, but it could not sensibly ask them to infer.   (White 1971, 291)[2]

So I am not convinced that an inferring is the onset of a state of affairs.

I am also not sure that Ryle was really convinced either. In fact, I think he was somewhat uncertain about the matter. In one place, he suggests that an inference is a *performance*.

> Rules of inference, like the rules of grammar, chess, etiquette and military funerals are performance-rules. Reference to them are references to criteria according to which *performances* are characterised as legitimate or illegitimate, correct or incorrect, suitable or unsuitable.   (Ryle 1946, 22; italics added)

In another he calls it an *operation*.

> So far from being true that 'inference' denotes an operation in which a discovery is made, an operation, therefore, which could not be repeated, we mean by 'inference' an *operation* which the thinker must be able to repeat.
> (Ryle 1949, n. 274; italics added)

And in another he suggests that an inference is the *result* of the operation or performance.

> I hope to show that the words 'judgment', 'deduction', 'abstraction' and the rest belong properly to the classification of the *products* of pondering and are mis-rendered when taken as denoting acts of which pondering consists.
> (Ryle, 1949, n. 260; italics added)

Interestingly, from what I can tell, Ryle did not consider the idea that an inference might be a causing.

A certain linguistic fact might explain what is going on here. Some verbs can be used to report the causing of a state of affairs, to report the onset of that state of affairs, and also to denote that state of affairs. We see this with the verb "to touch."

(1) David touched his nose with his finger.
(2) David's finger touched his nose.
(3) David's finger's touching his nose.

---

[2] White says that "[t]o infer is neither to journey towards, nor to arrive at or to be in a certain position; it is to take up, to accept or to *change to a position*" (291; emphasis added). This seems compatible with my idea that an inference is the causing of the change of mind. For more discussion, see Rumfitt (2012).

The first sentence reports an action of mine, that of my touching my nose. The second does not report an action. Rather, it reports the onset of a state of affairs, that of my finger's being in contact with my nose. And (3) denotes that state of affairs. That is, (3) denotes the state of affairs whose onset is reported in (2). And it also seems plausible that (3) denotes the result of the action reported in (1). The very same verb "to touch" can thus be used to report the causing of a certain state of affairs and the onset of that state of affairs, and also to denote that state of affairs. I suspect that this is also the case for the verb "to infer." At least, it is certainly the case for the verb "to conclude." The conclusion of a play might be the final act; or it might be the result of that act; or it might be the onset of that result. The conclusion of *Hamlet*, for instance, might be the killing of Hamlet (an act), or his being dead (the result of the act), or his death (the onset of that result).

So perhaps there is good reason to find our talk of inferring confusing. In any case, we can now see that even if we want to say that an inference can be an onset of a state of affairs, or even that state of affairs itself, there remains room for the idea that inferring is also a causing.

One final thought about Ryle. Though his views on the nature of inference are, at the end of the day, a bit unclear, we know what sort of view he was opposing. He was opposing what he considered the "para-mechanical idea" of inference as a mental act that causes a mental state.

> Finding premises and conclusions among the elements of published theories, [the Epistemologists] postulate separate, antecedent, 'cognitive acts' of judging; and finding arguments among the elements of published theories, they postulate antecedent *processes of moving to the 'cognising' of conclusions from the 'cognising' of premises*. I hope to show that these separate intellectual processes postulated by epistemologists are para-mechanical dramatisations of the classified elements of achieved and expounded theories.   (Ryle 1949, 291; italics added)

Ryle is opposed to the idea that inferring is a process that is separate from the resulting belief. A good deal depends, of course, on what he meant by "separate." But a natural interpretation is that on the para-mechanical view inferring would be an event or process that causes the resulting belief. This would be a para-mechanical view, with the inferring being a sort of mental process that produces, generates or gives rise to the belief.

Some recent accounts of inference strike me as versions of a para-mechanical view. Robert Audi says that an inference "produces" a belief as a "process of passing from one or more premises to a conclusion" (Audi 1986, 31). According to Broome, "[r]easoning is a mental process through which some attitudes of yours ... give rise to a new attitude of yours" (Broome, 2014, 622). Boghossian says that "[i]t's not sufficient for my judging (1) and (2) to cause me to judge (3) for this to

168   CREDAL AGENCY

be inference. The premises judgments need to have caused the conclusion judgments 'in the right way'" (Boghossian 2014, 3).

I agree with Ryle in opposing such a para-mechanical view. As I argued in Chapter 1, a person's believing something is not the right sort of thing to be a cause, though it can explain that person's doing or causing something. Likewise, what a person believes can be relevant to what inferences she draws. But this does not entail that her believing it caused her to draw the inference. Nor does it entail that the act of inference caused the resulting belief. We can accept that a person's believing something is relevant to her acts of inference while holding that the inference is the causing by her of a resulting believing. Inferring would be like adjusting one's position in space. Crossing one's legs is not an action that causes one's legs to be crossed; it is, rather, an action of causing them to be crossed. Inferring, on the view I have been advancing, is not an action that causes one's position in a space of possibilities to change; it is, rather, an action of causing such a change.

7.3 Inference Is Acting on Oneself

In this section, I want to consider a second objection to the idea that an inference is an action. On my view, in inference a believer causes herself to believe something. She thus acts on herself. This might seem to be the exact opposite of what Stuart Hampshire says in the following.

> The man who changes his mind, in response to evidence of the truth of a proposition, does not act upon himself; nor does he bring about an effect.
>
> (Hampshire 1975, 100)

He says that when a person changes her mind in response to evidence, she does not act on herself. When Jones concluded that the snow on the slopes will melt soon, she did not, Hampshire seems to be saying, *make up her mind*, at least not in a straightforward causal sense of that phrase. But I think Hampshire's view may be more nuanced than this. We need to distinguish two ways of acting on oneself. And we need (once again) to avoid the temptation to hypostasize believing.

One way to act on oneself is to do something that causes or brings about a change in oneself. So, for instance, Jones cuts her nails with a pair of clippers. In doing that, she acted on her nails (and so on herself) by closing the clippers on them. Here she is agent and patient of the action. She is agent since she did the cutting. She is patient since she was cut. A person can cause herself to believe something in this sort of way. Jones can make herself believe that the glass of beer is empty by emptying it. Here she is again both agent and patient. She is agent because she did something that caused her to believe the glass is empty. And she is

INFERENCE IS ACTING ON ONESELF   169

patient since her beliefs were changed. But, I take it, this is not a case of making up one's mind through reasoning.

Another way to act on oneself is to do something that is itself a changing of oneself. So, for instance, Jones can change her bodily position by crossing her legs. Here again she is both agent and patient. She is agent since she crossed her legs. She is patient since her legs were crossed. But I said at the end of the previous section, crossing one's legs is not an action that causes or brings about a change in one's position. Crossing one's legs is changing one's position.

On my view, making an inference is acting on oneself in this second way. It is not an action that causes or brings about a believing. Making an inference is changing (or sustaining) one's state of believing. I suspect that this is what Hampshire had in mind in the passage I quoted. Making up one's mind in inference is not an action that has *as a consequence* that one believes something. It is not acting on oneself in the way that cutting one's nails is acting on oneself. It is acting on oneself in the way that crossing one's legs is acting on oneself.

The tendency to hypostasize believing, to treat belief states as particulars in the same ontological category as lungs and hearts, can make my view difficult to see. For that tendency encourages the idea that if inference is an action it must be like clipping one's nails. Matthew Chrisman seems to have this sort of view in mind.

> What is involved in maintaining a system of beliefs? As the verb phrase suggests, it is dynamic rather than static. Maintaining something (e.g., a flowerbed) can be a reasonable answer to the question "What are you doing?"...More specifically, as I am thinking of it, maintaining a system of beliefs involves *examining* and *adjusting* existing *beliefs* in light of newly acquired beliefs or propositions assumed to be true for various purposes (e.g., by raising or lowering one's credence in the old beliefs, or by *reconceiving* the inferential/evidential relations between beliefs if they seem to be in tension under various suppositions). It can also involve seeking out new beliefs—e.g., by investigation or deliberation—when one's system of beliefs leaves some important question open or some strongly held belief apparently unsupported by other beliefs.
>
> (Chrisman 2016, 16; italics added)

Three ideas about believing that I have critiqued are at work in this passage. First, states of believing are treated as particulars in the same category as plants (hence the plural "beliefs"); they are taken to have semantic properties (for they are taken to bear inferential relations to one another); and they are things a person can, though reasoning, act on and adjust. That is the point of Chrisman's analogy between maintaining one's beliefs and maintaining the geraniums in one's flowerbed. Pictured this way, acting on one's beliefs would be like acting on one's nails.

170 CREDAL AGENCY

Chrisman is responding to Matt Boyle, who has argued that we will have trouble understanding a person's responsibility—their agential control—for believing what they do if we think of believing as a state. As Boyle sees it, on the state view:

> [i]f we exercise agential control over our beliefs, this must consist in our performing occurrent acts of judgment which give rise to new beliefs, or cause extant beliefs to be modified. Beliefs can at most "store" the results of such acts. So a person's agency can get no nearer to her beliefs than to touch them at their edges, so to speak. (Boyle, 2009, 121)

Boyle's thought is that while the state view of belief can allow acts of judging or affirming, their role must be limited to being acts that cause or change states of belief. But this, Boyle charges, distorts our relation to our beliefs.

> [The state view] appears to leave us responsible only for *looking* after our beliefs, in something like the way I may be responsible for looking after my bicycle. I have chosen to acquire this bicycle, and I can take steps to ensure that it is in good condition, that it is not left in a bad spot, etc. I am responsible for it as something I can assess and act upon, something in my care. I am not responsible for it, however, in the way I am responsible for my own intentional actions. My actions stand in a more intimate relation to me: they are not things I control by acting *on* them; they are my doings themselves.
> (Boyle 2009, 121; italics in original)

The image of "beliefs" as stored products of judgment also appears in Pamela Hieronymi's critique of the state view.

> My beliefs do not sit in my mind as last week's lecture sits on my hard drive, recording what I once thought. My beliefs are rather my present, ongoing take on what is so. When I revise a belief, I do not—or, typically I do not—notice that it no longer says what I think and then do something to change it. Rather, as I think about what is so, my beliefs *therein* change. Moreover, the current effect of my beliefs on my thought and behavior is not the indirect consequence of some past activity of mine, via standing dispositions, an effect which I might have once predicted, when I formed the disposition, and might now notice and perhaps do something to change. My beliefs are not like the "out of office reply" feature that I set up for my e-mail account: they are not something I create and then allow to affect things on my behalf. (Hieronymi 2009, 176; italics in original)

Boyle and Hieronymi are, I take it, knowingly offering a caricature of the state view. No one thinks that beliefs are like files on hard drives or recordings on

THE ONTOLOGY OF INFERENCE 171

machines, or that our relation to them is like our relation to our bicycles. Everybody should agree that believing is not like that. The purpose of the caricature is to force us to say how believing is different.

I think we can make a start on seeing the difference if we consider again the analogy between believing and owning from Chapters 1 and 2. Jones can reflect and organize her possessions. But she does this, not by reflecting on and organizing her *possessings*, but by reflecting on and organizing her *possessions*. Her possessings are not things at all, let alone things she can causally interact with. Something similar is true for reflection on how things are. When Jones considers how she takes things to be, her attention is directed at what she believes and not on her believing.

There is of course an important disanalogy between believing and owning. The objects of ownership can be physical things that one can causally interact with. Jones can move and pile up her books. But possibilities (and propositions) are not things one can causally interact with. One cannot move or arrange them. A better analogy is with bodily position. On my view, to believe something is to be in a certain rational position. I have compared this to occupying a position in space. Jones can maintain or adjust her position by moving her legs and arms. This is not a matter of doing something that causes a change in the positions of her arms and legs. It is, rather, doing something that consists in changing her position. This is a better analogy for thinking of reasoning. A person maintains or changes her position on the way things are, not by doing something that sustains or changes that position, but by doing something that is itself a sustaining or changing of it. She is the agent of the action, and its patient, and is causally responsible for the result. To change the image, she is attending to her home among the facts and considering which possibilities obtain in it.

7.4 The Ontology of Inference

In this section I want to sketch some of the ontological ideas underlying my account of inference. On my view, an act of inference does not cause the resulting belief. Rather, it is the *causing* of that belief. The believer herself is the cause or agent. My view is thus a version of agent causation. I hinted at this already in Chapter 1 and while a full treatment of this is beyond the scope of this book it will be helpful to flesh out some elements of the view a bit more. But a reader can skip this section without losing the plot.

The idea that acts are (or involve) causings was defended by Judith Thomson (1977) and Kent Bach (1980), who cited earlier work by Roderick Chisholm (1964b) and Georg von Wright (1963b) and, long before them, Thomas Reid. It has been developed, more recently, by Maria Alvarez and John Hyman (Alvarez & Hyman 1998 and Hyman 2015), following Peter Strawson (1992). The idea is

172 CREDAL AGENCY

simple enough. The act of scratching a table is not an event that causes the resulting scratch. Rather, the act is the causing of the scratch. The cause is whatever did the causing. A nail, perhaps, or little Billy who wielded the nail. But it is not quite right to say that *all* acts are causings. Some acts are defined in terms of a characteristic result. To scratch is to cause a scratch, to melt is to cause something to melt, to bend is to cause something to bend, to push is to cause something to move, etc. But not all actions have a characteristic result. Walking is an action, but there is no characteristic result that walking is in every case the causing of. Likewise, asserting is an action, but it has no characteristic result. Judy Thomson (1977) noted this fact about actions, though she put it in linguistic terms by saying that not all verbs of action are causal verbs. But she also held that every action is either a causing (that is, reportable with a causal verb) or is done by doing something that is a causing. Walking, for instance, is done by moving one's legs and arms, etc., and those acts are causings. Likewise asserting is done by moving one's mouth or one's hands in certain ways, and all of those acts are themselves causings.

In this respect, I think, drawing an inference is not like asserting something. Asserting something is in every case done by doing something else. One cannot simply assert something, one has to do it in a certain way by making certain sounds or hand gestures. But drawing an inference is not like that. Maybe this can be put by calling inference a basic act. John Heil has objected to this idea.

> I am unable to shake the conviction that it is a mistake to regard the adoption of beliefs as actions in any sense, whether basic or non-basic. This conviction is not founded solely on the observation tendered earlier that the forming of beliefs is not something that can be accomplished by a sheer act of will, but on the evident fact that our beliefs seem to come to us rather than issuing from us. Paying a debt is something I can set out to do; believing something is not. (Heil 1983, 358)

Heil is assuming that for an action to be basic it must involve performing an act of will. I have not spoken of acts of will. But I am not convinced that to be an action an assertion would have to be something caused or generated by an act of will. So far as I can see, an inference need not have any cause. The believer does not cause the inference; she is the one inferring. And I am inclined to think we should not tie action so closely to the will. When the acid dissolves the rubber, the acid acts on the rubber, even though the acid has no will. Heil offers as further evidence the contention that our beliefs "come to us rather than issuing from us," but this seems to me to beg the question. And while he is right that we cannot believe or infer intentionally, this does not show that inference is not an action. The acid does not intentionally dissolve the rubber either.

On my view, a person is the cause in an act of inference. The idea that acts are causings is compatible with different views about what sorts of entities can be

THE ONTOLOGY OF INFERENCE 173

agents and about the role of events in causation. Some of these differences might be terminological. John Hyman and Judith Jarvis Thomson, for instance, agree that events can be causes, but seem to disagree on whether events are agents. Hyman says that only individuals and bits of substances can be agents.

> Agents and patients are individual substances, such as a particular cat or man or stone, or else particular quantities of a kind of material, such as a particular vial of poison or a particular ounce of gold. (Hyman 2015, 42)

This suggests that, on his view, events cannot be agents. Judith Jarvis Thomson, by contrast, holds that events can be both agents and causes.

> Consider, for example, Sirhan's shooting of Kennedy. That event killed Kennedy; so there was an event that was a killing of Kennedy by it. Every killing is a causing. Therefore the event that was a killing of Kennedy by Sirhan's shooting of Kennedy is a fusion of causings of things, and therefore . . . Sirhan's shooting of Kennedy is agent of it. (Thomson 1977 252)

On Thomson's view, hurricane Irma was an event and an agent. It tore off rooves, pulled up trees, and killed people. (Indeed, her test for whether a verb is a causal verb is whether it can take an event as its subject. "Walking" and "asserting" cannot; "pushing" and "scratching" can.) So, she would say, hurricane Irma was an event and also agent of those causes. Hyman might reply that when we conceive of hurricanes as agents we are thinking of them as a volume of air, and so as an individual substance, rather than as an event that consists in the movements of those air particles.[3] But, as Thomson notes, this may be little more than a terminological matter. At the end of the day, Hyman and Thomson agree that events can be causes.

Hyman and Thomson also agree that for an agent to cause something the agent must do something. The agent must exercise a power it has. If a rock caused the car to be damaged, then it must have done this in some way, by for instance scratching or denting it. Likewise, if Jones caused the floor to be clean, she must have scrubbed, or swept it, or, etc. The same would hold for inference. Jones caused herself to believe that the snow would melt soon by inferring or concluding that it would. In doing so, she exercised her power of inference.

Thomson adds two further claims. First, she takes what the agent did to be an event. So, on her view, a causing is an event, though one that takes no time. Second, she claims that the event that is the causing also caused the result that the agent caused.

---

[3] He proposed this in correspondence with me.

174   CREDAL AGENCY

> It seems a very plausible idea that a person z causes an event E only if there is
> some event C such that C causes E. Sirhan caused Kennedy's death, but so did the
> event that was Sirhan's shooting of Kennedy cause it; I caused the kitchen floor to
> become clean yesterday, and so did the event that was my scrubbing of the floor
> cause it. Indeed, it seems plausible, more generally, that every caused event is
> caused by an event, so that if anything, of any kind, whether person, event, state
> of affairs—whatever it is that can cause an event—causes an event E, then there is
> an event C that causes it.   (Thomson 1977, 149–50)

Thomson adds that the person z must be "agent of the event" C. Kent Bach, by contrast, seems happy to drop that requirement, in order I think to make room for a reduction of agent causation to event causation (Bach 1980, 114). I am not sure whether Hyman would agree with Thomson. He suggests that causation by agents and causation by events are interdependent, but does not (so far as I can see) endorse Thomson's two claims.

> Events can only acquire the status of causes by participating in action by agents,
> and agents can only exercise causal powers by dint of events....For example,
> we can explain how a man moves his hand by describing the events inside his
> body that cause the motion of his hand: the release of neurotransmitters, the
> contraction of muscles, and so on. But these events are caused by nerve cells and
> muscle fibers, which are agents themselves, with their own distinctive causal
> powers.   (Hyman 2015, 41)

A good deal depends here on what is to be counted as an event. Thomson and Hyman agree that an act can be a causing and that events can be causes. Thomson, though, considers causings to be events and Hyman does not. She might count the exercise of one of a thing's causal powers to be an event that causes the results of that exercise, whereas Hyman would not. I suspect there is little more than a terminological matter here, and I won't try to sort it out.

7.5 Inferring in Light of a Possibility

Inferences are drawn for reasons. When a person draws an inference, she does so in light of reasons, or anyway, in light of what she takes to be reasons. But that she had those reasons did not cause her to draw the inference, and nor did it cause her resulting belief, but her reasons do have a role in my story. They are why she was in position to rationally draw the inference. This is linked to why people are answerable for the inferences they make.

Suppose we ask why Jones concluded that the snow on the slopes would melt soon. I think we might correctly answer with any of the following.

(A) Jones concluded that the snow on the slopes would melt soon because it was raining hard and a hard rain melts snow quickly.

(B) Jones concluded that the snow on the slopes would melt soon because she knew it was raining hard and she knew that a hard rain melts snow quickly.

(C) Jones concluded that the snow on the slopes would melt soon because she believed that it was raining hard and she believed that a hard rain melts snow quickly.

The relations among these are clear. (A) explains the inference by citing certain facts; (B) explains it by citing Jones' knowledge of those facts; (C) explains it by citing the beliefs that Jones had in virtue of knowing those facts.

I am inclined to think that (A) is, conceptually, the more fundamental of the three explanations. For one thing, it better identifies the reasons in light of which Jones drew the inference. She drew it in light of facts about the weather and about the durability of snow. Of course, (A) is a correct explanation only if she did know those facts. So (A) is correct only if (B) is correct. And it seems clear that (B) is correct only if (C) is correct, since Jones knows that it is raining hard only if she believes that it is. But her reasons for drawing that inference were not that she knew or believed in those facts; her reasons were the facts she knew. So (A) better identifies the reasons in light of which Jones drew the conclusion she did. And this makes (A) a more fundamental explanation.

Another reason to consider (A) more fundamental concerns the nature of inference itself. I have said that an act of inference is a causing of a belief. But I am tempted to say that making an inference is exercising a capacity to extend our knowledge. I take this to be Ryle's point when he said that knowing how to infer "is knowing how to move from acknowledging some facts to acknowledging others" (Ryle 1945, 7). It would not be right to say that an inference is a causing of a state of knowledge, since not every inference results in knowledge. A person might reason from false premises; or from true premises they don't quite know to be true; or in a way that does not transmit knowledge from premises to conclusion. In such cases, only an explanation in terms of belief (like (C)) would be correct. So, it is important to see inference as, itself, a causing of a belief.

But this is compatible with seeing inference as an exercise of a capacity for extending our knowledge. I don't mean that inferences that do not yield knowledge are defective. An inference that extends knowledge is not, *qua* inference, better than one that is not knowledge extending. Similarly, a correct believing is not better, *qua* believing, than an incorrect one. (I return to this in the next chapter.) The results of a failed exercise of a fallible capacity need not be defective instances of their kind. My point, rather, is about explanation. In making up our mind we are exercising a capacity that is best understood in terms of extending knowledge. And this is why the most fundamental explanation of an inference is

176   CREDAL AGENCY

in terms of the facts in light of which the inference was made. But, as I say, I am only *tempted* by this view, and, in any case, as I say, sometimes the only correct explanation of an inference will be something like (C).

One last point about (C). It does not entail that Jones' believing what she did caused her to make the inference. I will consider in the next section whether the exercise of a capacity to infer is voluntary or not. But even if something did cause her to make the inference, this would not entail that the beliefs caused her resultant belief.[4] Rather, those beliefs help explain why her drawing that inference was reasonable. Typically, people draw inferences only when they are reasonable.[5] As I said in Chapter 1, I am not sure that this needs to be explained. Someone who draws an unreasonable inference may have explaining to do. And in any particular case we can ask someone why she drew the conclusion she did. But it is not clear to me that we need to explain why, as a general matter, reasonable people ordinarily make only more or less reasonable inferences.

In Chapter 6, I argued that a believer knows that she believes what she does. Plausibly, when she acts on something she believes she knows (something about) what she is doing and why she is doing it. I characterized this by saying that believing and acting on a belief are essentially self-known. This self-knowledge is present also in inference. For when Jones concludes that the snow will melt soon, she knows that she draws this conclusion, and she knows what her reasons are. This knowledge is not based on observation or testimony. In these respects an act of inference is like an intentional action. This self-knowledge explains why people are answerable for their inferences. Jones is responsible for believing that the snow on the slopes will melt soon, since she made up her own mind that it would. And she is answerable for the fact that she drew this inference and for the result of it. We can ask her why she drew it, why she thought it was a reasonable inference to draw, and what her reasons for drawing it were. And we can expect her to have answers to our questions.

I think it is helpful, though, to separate a person's responsibility from her answerability for believing something. As for responsibility, I am inclined to think that an agent is always responsible for the results and consequences of her acts. A beaver is responsible for the dam it built, and for the flood that follows. (If the flood ruined the crop, then the beaver is to blame for the ruined crop.)[6] I am responsible for the movements of my legs as I walk down the hall, and for the subsequent motions of air particles. A drop of acetone is responsible for the

---

[4] Broome's remark that in reasoning certain existing attitudes "give rise" to a new attitude certainly suggests that, on his view, those existing attitudes cause the new one. But if the idea is that the new belief arises out of the existing one, then this image of origins might be helpful.

[5] John Broome holds that an inference like Jones' requires the exercise of a disposition to (i) form a belief and (ii) to acquire a disposition to check. He suggests that this needed disposition is independent of Jones' belief that a hard rain will melt snow quickly. I am inclined to think that having this disposition is just part and parcel of being a believer who is capable of making up their own mind.

[6] This view of responsibility and blame is in White (1973) and Thomson (1989).

melted nail polish. The sort of responsibility here is simply that of being an agent, or being a causer.

Of course, beavers and drops of acetone are not answerable for their acts, whereas Jones is. In the acetone's case, it is not answerable because it does not even know that it melted the nail polish. The beaver, by contrast, does know it is building a dam, and it knows quite a bit about why and how it is doing it. The potential to know all of this is part of the beaver's nature. It is an empirical matter how capable a beaver is at reflecting on and assessing these whys and hows, and I won't take a stand on this. But a beaver is not able to understand or answer our questions, and we do not expect it to. A person, by contrast, is able to reflect on and assess the quality of her reasons when she acts. And a person is normally able to say what she believes and is doing and why. The fact that a person has these reflective, evaluative and expressive capacities explains why we expect people to answer for themselves. This difference in expectations is a matter, not of whether a beaver knows or believes things, but of a difference in the capacities between people and beavers. Recall from Chapter 1 that believing something is not itself a power or disposition, but is rather a matter of being in a certain position to exercise the powers and to manifest the dispositions one has.

And notice that the answerability, in the case of a person, has nothing to do with the act's being known by the person. A person is answerable for all of her acts, whether they are intentional or not. We can always be asked to explain why we are doing something, why we are bringing about certain changes. If we do not realize we are doing it, then we are not doing it intentionally. But we are still liable for what we have done. If we couldn't have known about it, then this can excuse our actions and limit our liability. But this does not mean we are not *answerable* for doing it. Not having an answer is not the same as not being answerable.

7.6 Inference Is Not Intentional

On my view, though inferring is an action, one cannot infer something in order to achieve some further end or purpose. In this sense, an inference cannot be intentional. I am not sure how to argue for this. It just strikes me as obvious. But it would be nice to know why. What is it about an act of inference that explains why it cannot be intentional? This section explores that question, but it does not offer much of an answer.

One might think an inference cannot be intentional because it results in a belief state and one cannot be in any state in order to achieve some further end or purpose. I agree that one cannot believe something in order to please one's mother or as a means to something else. But I doubt this can be the whole story. For one thing, there are some states one can be in on purpose. Jones is vegan in order to help fight climate change. Simon is unemployed in order to focus on his art. What

178 CREDAL AGENCY

is more, we do sometimes call an intended result intentional. The scratch Sarah made on the car with her keys was intentional. In these cases, the state resulted from an intentional action (quitting, scratching) or from an intention (to fight climate change), and this makes them different from inference, which cannot be intentional or done from a prior intention. But what we would like to know is why inference differs in these ways. So I am not sure that the fact that acts of inference result in states of affairs can fully explain why inferences cannot be intentional.

One might think that whatever explains why inference cannot be intentional must be more general than just for believing. For other mental states are like believing in this respect. One cannot hope or admire or expect intentionally, and yet one can make up one's mind to hope, admire or expect. And one cannot start hoping for something or admiring someone or expecting something in order to please one's mother or as a means to something else. I agree with all of this, but it strikes me that hoping, admiring, and expecting all involve believing something, and so it may be that they cannot be intentional because they involve something that cannot be intentional.

Perhaps, instead, it has to do with the fact that inferring requires taking the results of one's inference to be supported by one's reasons. Here is how White put the idea.

> One can wrongly infer, but not infer in the belief that one is wrong, since the position taken up must be one which the person has come to believe to be related in a certain way to a previous position. This is why no question can arise of inferring voluntarily or by decision or resolution or on request.
>
> (White 1971, 291–2)[7]

I agree that we cannot infer in the belief that the result of our inference is a mistake. I also agree that inference requires believing that the result is supported by our reasons, or at least that it requires not believing that the result is not supported by them. But why should we think that inference could be intentional only if an inference *could* result in a belief one took to be false or unsupported by one's reasons? Suppose Jones believes that her reasons do support believing that the snow will melt quickly. Why couldn't she then make the inference in order to please her mom, or in order to win a bet?

I feel a kinship here with Pamela Hieronymi. In a series of important papers, she has drawn our attention to the fact that we cannot believe something for reasons that we think do not show that we are right. But when she considers *why* we cannot do this, she is left saying that

---

[7] Notice that these considerations also explain why inference cannot, as he sees it, be voluntary. I turn to this in the next section.

I do not know how to answer this question, because it seems to me not to make good sense. It seems to me a bit like asking, 'Why can't I subtract two by adding one?' (Hieronymi 2009, 165, n. 27).

Asking why we cannot infer in order to please our mother, even when we know that she will be pleased by the inference, is like asking why we cannot multiply a number by dividing it.

I suspect that part of the problem we have in understanding why inference and believing cannot be intentional is that we find it so natural to think of believing as a form of representing. If one thinks of knowing and believing as ways of representing the world, then it might seem odd that they cannot be intentional given that representing can be done intentionally. For it would be tempting to think of inference as like modifying one's map of the world. Why couldn't one then modify it at will, for any reason at all? I have argued that believing is not a form of representing, the objects of belief are not representations, and belief states are not true or false. I have offered an alternative image. It is that knowing and believing are like being more or less at home among the facts. We can all agree that inquiry—looking for our home—can be done intentionally. But because we cannot choose our home—the facts are whatever they are—settling in at home is not something we can do at will or intentionally. I don't offer this as an explanation, but only as an alternative image to help us think about knowledge and belief, one that might help us resist the allure of the representational one, and can perhaps help us see why believing and inference are not intentional.

One might think that if an inference cannot be intentional, then it cannot be an action. This would be so if the following principle were true.

S's V-ing is an act only if S can V intentionally.

But this principle strikes me as implausible. The tree outside my house scrapes my roof, which is an act, but the tree is not able to do anything intentionally. What about the following, related principle?

V-ing is an act only if it is possible to V intentionally.

Even though trees can't scratch anything intentionally, people can. So, this principle survives the objection I just considered. And if this principle is true, and if it is true that an inference cannot be intentional, then it would follow that inferences are not acts. But is this principle true? A pine tree can produce cones, and I take it that producing cones is an act. But must it then be possible to produce cones intentionally? (I can intentionally make a tree produce cones, but this is different.) I am not so sure.

180   CREDAL AGENCY

And, anyway, what would explain such a principle? In effect, it holds that intentionality is essential to action, that something is an act only if it could be done intentionally. But on the view I have been exploring, it is causation and not intentionality that is fundamental to action. The idea is that to act is to cause or bring about some change. Some acts are intentional, just as some are voluntary and others are reluctant. But there is nothing in the idea of action itself that requires that any act be potentially intentional. And while intentional acts done by people are of interest to ethics, ethics is just as interested in what people do inadvertently and by mistake. Indeed, in considering whether a person ought to have done something, it often matters little whether the person did it intentionally or what their intentions were.[8] So I find it hard to see what considerations could support such a principle.

And notice just how extreme it is. Some of our capacities are ones that, while we cannot exercise them intentionally, we could have been able to. Most people are able to weep, but most of us are not able to weep intentionally. But we can imagine that with training and practice we might become able to weep intentionally, in order to get something we want. Maybe good actors can already do this. So it is plausible to think that *some* of our current powers are ones we could have been able to exercise intentionally even though at present we cannot. But the principle I am considering says that for *every* power we have, we could have been able to exercise it intentionally, and this just in virtue of its being a power. This strikes me as an implausibly strong thesis.

Finally, it seems to me that if we are to take at face value the idea that in inference we are making up our own minds, then we need to reject that principle linking action and intentionality. In effect, insisting on the principle begs the question against my view. But, as I say, I wish I had better arguments for this view.

7.7 Inference Is Voluntary

I have said that an inference cannot be intentional. One cannot draw an inference in order to get or do something one wants to get or do. But it is a separate matter whether an inference can be voluntary. I am inclined to think it can, though getting clear on the relevant sense of "voluntary" is not easy.[9]

I take it that a person did something voluntarily if she did it and she chose to do it.[10] This is just a sufficient condition, and it applies only to what a person does, not to what they may voluntarily undergo or to ways they might voluntarily be. And it leaves open what role the choosing plays. If choosing to do something

---

[8] This is a point that Thomson makes (1977, 253).
[9] Boghossian says it is voluntary (2014, 3), though he does not elaborate.
[10] What follows relies on the discussion of voluntariness in Hyman (2015).

requires that one choose to do it before one does it, then inference is not voluntary in that way, for a person cannot choose to draw an inference. We cannot plan or make up our mind in advance to believe something. I can, of course, make myself believe that some possibility obtains by freely choosing to make it obtain. I can choose to empty the beer glass, drink its content, and thereby make myself believe that it is empty. But even if that choosing made the emptying of the glass voluntary, it would not follow that it made the inference voluntary.

The idea of a choice also suggests that of alternatives. A person who does something by choice was not coerced into doing it. Coercion is itself a nuanced matter, for a person can be coerced into doing something, and so not do it voluntarily, even when they could have refrained from doing it. In one sort of case, if resisting the coercion would have been grossly unreasonable, then the person did not do the thing voluntarily. A person who does something in response to a realistic threat of serious violence, for example, does not do it voluntarily, even if they could have refrained. Still, if a person does something, and they could have reasonably refrained from doing it, and they did not act from ignorance, then they did the thing voluntarily.

Could an inference be voluntary in that way? Some have said that when a person draws an inference their drawing it was determined by the evidence they had. This suggests that the person had no alternative but to draw the inference and so could not have refrained. If so, then an inference would not be voluntary in that way. Here is how David Owens puts the point. His example involves John's being the murderer.

{W]hat directly determines how we think about John are his bloody shirt and absence from work. I do decide to attend to these things, but once that decision is made, the evidence takes over and I lose control. It might be argued that I held off from forming a view on the basis of his pleasant demeanor alone and waited for more evidence. Doesn't this amount to an exercise of control over what I believe? But all that occurred was that his agreeable countenance proved insufficient to close my mind on the matter, to eliminate doubt about his innocence, and so I set off once more in search of evidence. In the end, it is the *world* which determines what (and whether) I believe, not me.   (Owens 2000, 12)

According to Owens, when a person draws an inference in light of the evidence they have, their evidence leaves them no alternative in the matter. This thought also informs the idea that a person has belief forming mechanisms that bring about believing in something like the way the mechanisms that compose their digestive system bring about digestion. John Heil shares this view.

On the one hand, believers seem responsible for what they believe; they seem in this regard doxastic *agents*. On the other hand, believers appear to be passive;

182   CREDAL AGENCY

beliefs are not chosen or rejected, but simply held or not. In this regard, believers seem to be largely *at the mercy* of their belief-forming equipment.

(Heil 1983, 357)[11]

It is, on Heil's view, a person's belief-forming equipment that generates her beliefs. And the operation of that equipment is determined by the evidence she has. There is no room for alternatives.

Before assessing this view, it is worth noting that it is compatible with the idea that an inference is an action by the believer. Think again about the drop of acetone. When it touches the rubber its power to dissolve the rubber is activated, and there is no alternative. (For simplicity I'll set aside those cases where something intervened and blocked or "masked" the capacity.) The conditions that are necessary for the acetone's exercise of its capacity to melt rubber are also (normally) sufficient for that exercise. Still, the acetone melted the rubber, and its melting of the rubber was an exercise of its capacity to melt it. If Owens and Heil are right, a person's having adequate evidence is sufficient for the exercise of her capacity to infer. This would not entail that the person did not make the inference. I can even accept Heil's idea that a person has belief-forming mechanisms. A person's inferring that John is the murder would consist in the operation of those mechanisms. So even if Owens and Heil are right that a person's evidence "determines" what they infer, this would not show that the inference was not something the believer did.

Heil is right that a person does not choose what to believe, for the reasons I gave. And I suspect that Bernard Williams is right that no one can, just like that, bring it about that they believe something.[12] We can only draw an inference in light of what we take to be our evidence. But it seems to me that Owens and Heil overstate the power of a person's evidence. As I see it, we can make inferences when the evidence we have is adequate but not conclusive. In such cases, it seems to me, we are free both to draw the inference and to refrain from drawing it. Drawing it would be reasonable, because the evidence we have is adequate. But refraining from drawing it would also be reasonable, because that evidence is not conclusive. Whether we draw it is up to us and is thus voluntary in the way I specified above.

Others have held this sort of view.[13] Roderick Chisholm suggests it in the following passage. He is especially concerned with the legitimacy of ethical

---

[11] Heil says that the believer is passive. This is right in one sense because the believer is the one acted on in an inference. She is the patient. But, as I explained above, this is compatible with her also being the agent. My thoughts on Heil and Owens and on doxastic agency are influenced by Gary Watson's (2003).

[12] The best response to Williams that I know about is by Trudy Govier (1976). What I say in this section is indebted to that work. See also (Roeber 2019).

[13] Most famously perhaps, James (1896).

appraisal of a person's beliefs, and thinks this presupposes that the believer had alternatives.

> If self-control is what is essential to activity, some of our beliefs would seem to be acts. When a man deliberates and comes finally to a conclusion, his decision is as much within his control as is any other deed we attribute to him. If his conclusion was unreasonable, a conclusion he should not have accepted, we may plead with him: 'But you needn't have supposed that so-and-so was true. Why didn't you take account of these other facts?' We assume that his decision is one he could have avoided and that, had he only chosen to do so, he could have made a more reasonable inference.   (Chisholm 1968, 224)[14]

Trudy Govier also defends this view. She notes that discussions of inference tend to focus on cases where the evidence strongly favors one thing.

> The restriction of decision and choice to this kind of context seems to me to be mistaken. I think that this mistake is a result of concentrating too much on cases where there is no problem about what to believe; – where evidence is taken in and is so straightforward in its import that there is no need for conscious reflection. And of course many (perhaps most) cases in which people come to believe things are like this. But not all are, and this is important. When one has insufficient or ambiguous evidence, or when one has to decide whether to go and seek evidence, and if so, what kind, there is a conscious reflection concerning what to believe.   (Govier 1976, 653–4)

Recently, Philip Nickel defends this view. He too is focused on cases where a person has adequate but not conclusive evidence for something.

> In these cases, it is reasonable but not rationally mandatory to hold that there is adequate evidence for P, and there are not strong non-epistemic reasons to believe P (e.g., that believing P would make one happier). The fact that there is more than one rationally permissible doxastic option, together with the reason-responsiveness of the belief that P, together make it plausible that the formation of the belief that P is voluntary.   (Nickel 2010, 312–13)

There are two elements here. One is that it would be reasonable to believe the thing in light of that evidence, but also reasonable to continue to suspend belief. (Since suspending belief is simply maintaining one's view on which possibilities obtain, we should think of suspending belief as *sustaining* belief.) The second

---

[14] This passage is cited in Pojman (1986) which contains an excellent discussion of voluntarism about belief.

184 CREDAL AGENCY

element is that the belief is formed in response to that evidence, and not in response to something the person wants. We should not think of voluntary inference as requiring that the believing be based on non-epistemic considerations. We should allow that the result of a voluntary inference could be perfectly reasonable.[15]

The examples I gave in Section 7.1 involve these same two elements. Jones has good reason to think the snow will melt quickly, but her evidence is not conclusive. It would be reasonable for her to believe it, but also reasonable for her to suspend judgment. In light of that evidence, she infers that it will melt soon. Making that inference is taking the evidence to be adequate. Sarah has good evidence that her son is dealing drugs, but it is not conclusive. It would be reasonable for her to believe it, but also reasonable for her to sustain her current beliefs. In light of that evidence, she sustains her view rather than changing it. Not concluding that he is dealing drugs is taking the evidence to be inconclusive.[16]

Here is one of Nickel's cases.

Suppose I have lived for three years in an area where I have never heard the sound of a train, although I have observed some seemingly unused train tracks. I do not know whether the train tracks have fallen into disrepair. One morning, as I am working, I hear the sound of a train whistle, and I feel the distinctive vibration of a locomotive. This, I propose, is a situation in which I am in a position voluntarily to adopt the belief that there is a locomotive nearby. I accomplish this by taking the reasons I have to support the belief. But I have more than one reasonable option. I may take the sound of the locomotive to provide adequate reason to believe that there is a locomotive, or I may take not to provide adequate reason for that belief. Both responses are reasonable. On the one hand, since I have never seen trains in the area, how likely is it that there is suddenly a train here now? On the other hand, the sounds and vibration are unmistakable—what else could produce them but a train? I may think, "How remarkable—there is a train nearby!," or I may think, while suspending belief: "How odd—the sounds of a train. This requires investigation."

(Nickel 2010, 313–14)

---

[15] Chisholm (1968) holds that if it is reasonable for a person to believe something given her evidence, then her believing it is either morally permitted or morally required. Miriam McCormick (2015), among others, reject this evidentialist view and argues that a person may be morally permitted or even required to believe something that conflicts with their evidence. In Chapter 8, I will argue for a middle position: what it is reasonable for a person to believe may depend on her evidence, but what she ought to believe never does. I will argue that what a person ought to believe always depends on what she ought to know and this, in turn, depends on what she ought to do, feel, and think and on how she ought to be.

[16] But doesn't a person's epistemic character play a role? Isn't her inference determined by her evidence together with her character? I don't think so. People do have epistemic character traits, such as being hasty or cautious. But these traits are partly the products of repeated acts of inference, and do not cause them. A person's selfishness does not make them act selfishly.

INFERENCE AND DEDUCTION   185

As Nickel stresses, when a person draws an inference voluntarily the resulting belief need not be unreasonable. So the believer need not view it as unreasonable or as somehow arbitrary. Her inference was done in light of evidence, but because the evidence was not conclusive, continuing to suspend judgment was an open and reasonable alternative.

It seems to me that cases of this sort are commonplace.[17] We often have good but not conclusive evidence that some possibility obtains. Believing that it does would be reasonable. Suspending belief would also be reasonable. In such cases, it is up to the believer whether she changes or sustains her belief state. Drawing the inference is taking the evidence to be adequate. Suspending belief is taking it to be inconclusive. Both options are rationally open to the believer, who is free to change or sustain her take on the world. The result, in either case, will be due to the believer's exercise of her inferential power.[18]

I have been suggesting that an inference can be voluntary in a sense I have tried to specify. One might think that an act can be voluntary only if it can be intentional. If so, then either I am wrong to think that inference can be voluntary or else I am wrong to think that it cannot be intentional. But I question this link between the voluntary and the intentional. No doubt many acts that can be voluntary can also be intentional. But why should every act be like that? As Hyman (2015) argues, the concepts of the voluntary and the intentional are keyed to very different aspects of our mental lives. Whether an act is voluntary depends on whether a person was coerced or acted from ignorance. Whether it is intentional depends on whether she did it in order to satisfy a desire. Why couldn't there be an act that a person could voluntarily do, in light of certain reasons, but not ever do it in order to satisfy a desire? It seems to me that inference would be precisely such an act.

7.8 Inference and Deduction

I have argued that inferences can be voluntary. But remember my restriction at the start of this chapter's first section. My account is focused on cases where the premises do not entail the conclusion. In this section I'll discuss cases where they do. In announcing my restriction, I said that cases of valid arguments can be distracting. This comes clear when we consider the voluntariness of inference. For

---

[17] William Alston, who famously argued against a deontological conception of epistemic justification on the grounds that belief is not voluntary, nonetheless allowed that in cases like Sarah's belief might be voluntary (Alston 1988, 265). But, he insisted, such cases are so rare that no plausible conception of epistemic justification should be rested on them. I disagree about their rarity.

[18] Roger White (2005) sees an incoherence in this idea. But, so far as I can tell, it depends on thinking of voluntary inference as involving making a choice, which I deny. For discussion of this, see Nickel (2016).

186 CREDAL AGENCY

some valid arguments make voluntary inference seem suspiciously easy while others make it seem impossibly hard. After discussing these, I'll briefly consider what my account says about formal reasoning in fields like mathematics where inferences seem to be both valid and yet to generate new beliefs.

Some cases of validity can make voluntary inference seem too easy. Disjunction introduction, where the disjuncts are logically independent, is such a case. Suppose Stephanie says the following.

> It is snowing; so either it is snowing or Toronto is in Canada; so either it is snowing or Toronto is in Canada or the 504 will be late; and so on.

If one thinks of this as a case of inference, then one will be tempted to think that it is entirely up to the believer how long to continue drawing the inferences. Stephanie might decide to keep going, drawing more and more consequences from her initial premise. And she might continue until she chooses to stop. She might even do so intentionally, in order to bother her brother, or to win a bet, or just because she finds it amusing. Thinking of this as a case of inference will make it seem all too easy to infer voluntarily. But this is not a case of inference at all. At least, it is not what I take inference to be. I take it that an inference requires changing one's view of which possibilities obtain. But in our story Stephanie is not changing her mind about which possibilities obtain. She is not adding to her map of the world. Nor is she sustaining it. She is simply formulating in new ways what she already believes.

This case of disjunction introduction makes rational voluntary inference look suspiciously easy. Cases of modus ponens can make it look impossibly hard. Suppose Margaret believes that if it is raining, then the snow will melt. And suppose she starts believing that it is raining. She might then report her reasoning by telling us this.

> If it is raining the snow will melt; and it *is* raining; so, the snow will melt.[19]

One might think that any inference would have to be located in between believing the premises and believing the conclusion in her report. That is, one might think that Margaret inferred that the snow will melt after already believing the conditional and its antecedent. But it is hard to see how such an inference could have been rationally voluntary. Once she starts believing the second premise she has no rational option but to believe the conclusion. If it were up to her whether to draw it, then this would be a freedom to be irrational.

---

[19] The example is from Broome (2014). For another paper that takes valid arguments as the model of inference, see Hlobil (2019).

But this description of the case is misleading. I agree that Margaret must believe the conclusion, given that she believes the premises. But this is because *in believing* those premises she already believes the conclusion. She did not form a further belief in addition to the conditional and its antecedent. Given that she believed the conditional, in coming to believe its antecedent she came to believe its consequent. It is misleading to suggest that an additional step is needed in her reasoning, to get from belief in the premises to belief in the conclusion. Think of this in terms of adding information to a novel. Suppose the author has already stated that in the novel's world snow melts whenever it rains. If the author then adds to the story that it is raining, she therein adds that snow is melting. She does not need to add a further sentence saying that the snow is melting. That is already so in the world of the novel.

Margaret may well have drawn an inference in this story. Whether she did depends on how she came to believe that it is raining. Suppose she was listening to the radio while preparing her dinner and heard the announcer say that it is raining. It would be reasonable for her to infer that it is raining, but also reasonable for her to suspend belief. She trusts the weather reporter but also knows the report is sometimes about a distant city. This is exactly like the case Nickel describes. Neither belief nor suspension of belief is rationally mandatory. Suppose she concludes that it is raining. On my view, this was a voluntary inference. And, on my view, she therein also inferred that the snow will melt. And this inference too was voluntary. Indeed, it was the same inference. So the case of modus ponens can make voluntary inference seem impossible, but only by mis-locating the inference.

A slightly different conception of rational inference can also make it seem invariably involuntary. It is sometimes suggested that in theoretical reasoning a person reflects on her attitudes and asks herself whether she ought to believe something else given those attitudes, whether her evidence or reasons for believing it are adequate or, in Heil's terms "epistemically valuable." (Heil 1983, 357) Nishi Shah (2006) holds that this sort of question is definitive of theoretical reasoning. Doxastic deliberation, he says, is governed by a question like "Should I believe that P?" This suggests that in reasoning a person considers various beliefs she has, and asks herself what follows from them or what possibilities they rule out. Their answer to this question then determines what inferences would be rational. Let's apply this picture to my case of Jones. It begins with her already believing that a hard rain will melt snow quickly, and acquiring the belief that it is raining hard. On this conception of reasoning, Jones would ask herself which possibilities these two beliefs imply or rule out. She would then consider the possibility that the snow will melt soon, and ask herself whether she ought to believe that it obtains. Does her information support it? By hypothesis, the evidence she has is adequate but not conclusive. So her answer is that her evidence neither entails nor rules out that possibility. Given this answer, it would be irrational for her to conclude that the

188 CREDAL AGENCY

snow will melt soon. Indeed, it is hard to even conceive of her drawing that conclusion. Doing so would seem entirely arbitrary. On this conception of reasoning, there is no room for rational voluntary inference.

But it strikes me that this conception of reasoning makes the same mistake as in the modus ponens case. It assumes that the inference would have to be a step that occurs in between believing the evidence and believing the conclusion. It pictures Jones as undecided as to whether the snow will melt soon. This indecision is presupposed when we imagine her asking herself whether that possibility is supported by what she already believes. She is asking herself whether she ought to add the belief that it obtains. This question would make no sense if she already believed it. But given that she is undecided whether that possibility obtains, the time for inference is already past. If she is undecided at this point in our story, then in starting to believe that it is raining hard she did *not* start believing that the snow will melt soon. So she did not draw that inference. Not drawing it was reasonable, given the evidence she had. But had she drawn it, that too would have been reasonable. It was up to her whether to draw it, and she did not draw it. Instead, she sustained the view she had.

Notice too how Shah's conception of reasoning hypostasizes believing, by treating beliefs as things one can reflect on and then adopt or abandon. Shah says that "normally when we reflect on our attitudes, we do not merely come to know what we in fact believe or intend; we determine what we shall believe or intend" (Shah 2013, 311). It is hard to understand this passage except as presupposing that theoretical reflection involves reflecting on belief states, and then concluding, with respect to some proposition, that one ought to believe it. John Broome resists the idea that reasoning involves a judgment about what one should or ought to believe. But he holds onto the idea that it involves reflecting and acting on objects. He says that in reasoning "you *operate on* the contents of your premise-belief, following a rule, to construct a conclusion, which is the content of a new belief of yours that you acquire in the process" (Broome 2014, 624; italics added). It is hard to understand this literally, since no one can operate on propositions or possibilities. I think this image of reasoning as involving reflecting or operating on objects, whether belief states or the objects of belief, encourages the idea that any inference would have to occur between the premise beliefs and the conclusion belief. This is especially alluring if one takes modus ponens as a paradigm of inference. All of this, it seems to me, can make voluntary inference seem impossible.[20]

---

[20] The idea that inference involves operating on the objects of belief is also encouraged by the idea that believing involves a cognitive relation to an object. Eric Marcus expresses this idea. He says that "belief is a matter of viewing a proposition as meeting a certain standard of correctness, as being such that one ought to believe it" (Marcus 2016, 376). And he says that inference involves an awareness of the necessity of one proposition's truth given that of other things one believes. (Marcus 2020) and (Marcus 2021). In Chapter 2, I argued that believing is not a cognitive relation to an entity of any kind.

INFERENCE AND DEDUCTION 189

Though Philip Nickel holds that inference can be voluntary, he too seems to make this mistake. It is suggested in his discussion of the scope of voluntary inference.

> My main aim is to establish the intuitive plausibility of the view that there are some instances of doxastic willing, and defend the view against prevalent objections. But for all I have said here, we are often not in voluntary control of our beliefs, for in many cases there may be only one reasonable option. When I see a dog race toward me, I do not feel free to believe that there is no dog (or no animal) racing toward me, no do I feel free to suspend judgment. It seems I come to believe it regardless of my doxastic character traits, because there is, at the end of the day, only one doxastic option. (Nickel 2010, 331)

As he describes the case, there is supposed to be a gap between his seeing the dog race towards him and his believing that the dog is racing towards him, and that during this gap he forms the belief that it is. But this is hard to understand. Normally, if a person *sees* that a dog is racing towards her then she *knows* that it is. Seeing is a way of knowing. And if she knows it, then she believes it, since knowing requires believing. Being presented with a fact, with a way that things are, just is knowing them to be that way. No inference is needed, because none is possible. So there is no room for a gap between seeing that the dog is racing towards him and believing that it is. So Nickel is wrong to think that this is a case of *non-voluntary* inference, for it is not a case of inference at all.

We can easily adjust the case to make it involve an inference. Suppose that Philip does not know that the dog is racing towards him. He sees the dog running but is uncertain about its path. It might be aiming to attack him or it might be aiming to attack something to the side. Given this, it would be reasonable for Philip to believe that the dog is running towards him, but also reasonable for him to suspend belief. Because he does not see *that* the dog is running towards him, he does not yet believe that it is. It is up to him whether to believe it or whether to continue to suspend belief. So when we adjust the case to make it involve an inference, we see that it is, in the sense at issue, voluntary after all.

I will end this section by considering how my accounts of belief and inference can make sense of reasoning in cases where, it seems, the premises do entail the conclusion. Such cases pose two challenges to my views. First, when mathematicians reason they end up believing something they did not believe before, even though their premises seem to entail their conclusions. But I have claimed that in believing the premises of a valid argument one therein believes its conclusion. So how can my account of inference make sense of such reasoning? Second, the conclusions of mathematical reasoning seem to be necessary truths, and mathematical inference seems sometimes to be a valid transition from one set of necessary truths to another. But I claimed, in Chapter 3, that a difference or

190 CREDAL AGENCY

change in belief always involves a difference over which contingent possibilities obtain. So how can my accounts of belief and of inference make sense of what mathematicians believe and do when they reason? This is a complex matter and I can't do much more than gesture at what I think we should say here. I will make two related points.

The first point returns to something I said in Chapter 3. An example of mathematical reasoning would be a counterexample to the modal view of the objects of belief only if it involved no change in which contingent possibilities the mathematician believed to obtain. But the examples we are familiar with do involve such a change. All such reasoning, it seems to me, involves an intentional use of formulas. The mathematician has beliefs about those formulas, and about their semantic properties. Coming to believe that some formula is necessarily true is, in part, learning a contingent fact about its truth conditions and so its meaning. That fact is contingent because the symbolic notations we use, even when doing mathematics, are partly conventional. This doesn't mean that mathematical truths are conventional or contingent, only that the symbolic systems we use when thinking about those truths are. This means, I think, that examples of arithmetical reasoning are not pure cases and so are not counterexamples to the idea that there are no more belief properties than there are possibilities. That is my first point.

My second point is that we can grant this first one without saying that mathematical beliefs are beliefs *about* those symbolic conventions. This would make those beliefs contingent, and would distort what mathematicians see themselves as doing. At the same time, though, it is not easy to say clearly what the contents are of mathematical beliefs. I think what I said in Chapter 5 about credal illusions can be helpful here. Think about Frege's astronomer who changed her mind over whether, as she would have put it, Hesperus is Phosphorus. We shouldn't say that, before she changed her mind, the astronomer merely believed that "Hesperus" and "Phosphorus" do not co-refer. This would leave out important elements in her belief state while also obscuring their essential disorder. Before her change of mind, the astronomer believed that a certain general possibility obtained, roughly that one object appears in a certain position in the morning sky and another object appears in a different position in the evening sky. She was mistaken in thinking it obtained, but that mistake is about a contingent matter, since it might have obtained. After realizing her mistake, the astronomer stopped believing in the obtaining of that more general possibility. So to adequately characterize her change of mind, we need to identify this possibility. And it is not a possibility about language. What is more, we also need to admit, I suggested, that before her change of mind, the astronomer suffered a credal illusion, thinking she had got hold in belief of a specific possibility that witnessed that more general one. There is no such specific possibility, since (I assume) there are no two objects that could have been in those positions. It seems to me that any account needs to acknowledge that the astronomer's state of belief, prior to changing her mind, was not a merely linguistic one but involved a more general contingent possibility as well as a credal illusion. I argued in Chapter 5 that the modal view has the resources to acknowledge this.

Every account of belief, it seems to me, will have to admit that credal illusions with this sort of structure are possible. At least, they will if they take it to be an objective matter what belief properties there are, and so an objective matter what the limits of belief are. As I said in Chapter 5, the modal view might get those limits wrong, but every account of belief has to allow that people can stray beyond those limits without realizing it and that when they do it is hard for us to say what they believe. It seems to me that understanding mathematical practice, and the changing mental states of mathematicians as they reason, requires understanding how the symbolic systems they use make such credal illusions possible and hard to detect. To understand any particular case we need to characterize a more general contingent possibility, one that is not just about the specific symbols the mathematician uses to express her beliefs but about symbolic systems with certain semantic and compositional properties. Such cases may share a basic structure, but the details will likely vary from case to case. I have only gestured here at how my account of belief and inference might flesh this out. And it may be that the modal view ultimately needs to be supplemented to fully account for these cases. But I think it is clear that the difficulties it faces are general ones that face any account of belief. For the puzzle is about how to characterize the limits of belief itself.

7.9 Unwilling Inference

I have argued that when a person draws an inference, their action is voluntary, in a sense I tried to specify. But it does not follow that the person is happy with their inference. A person can do something voluntarily while wishing that they were not doing it, and while preferring that they not be doing it. In this sense, their doing it can be unwilling. Our psychic lives are complex. Sarah might wish she had some better alternative than to report her son to the authorities. When she finally does, she does so intentionally and by choice (and so voluntarily) but against her will. The same psychic complexity is possible in the theoretical realm. A person can draw an inference reluctantly and even unwillingly. There are two sorts of cases.

In one, the person is reluctant because she does not want what she has concluded to be the case. My example of Jones is like that. She spent a considerable amount on the ski trip, and made many personal sacrifices to get there. She will be very disappointed if she is not able to ski. Admitting it would force her to modify her plans, something she did not want to face. And so, she only very reluctantly comes to the conclusion that the snow on the slopes will melt soon. By contrast, others in her group were much less committed to the skiing, and were looking

192   CREDAL AGENCY

forward to spending time with friends. They were much more willing to conclude that the snow on the slopes would melt soon.

In a second sort of case, the person is reluctant to draw the conclusion because they wish they were more able to resist drawing it. A slight alteration of my Sarah case is like this. Sarah feels that a loving mother always gives their children the benefit of the doubt. In her eyes, it would be a sort of failing for her to concede that her son is selling drugs. A more loving mother would not be moved by such evidence. She knows that believing it would make her feel ashamed, and she dreads the look of betrayal in her son's eyes when he confronts her. Still, when she sees the evidence the police provide, she concedes that he is in fact selling drugs. But her concession is reluctant and unwilling. Of course, she would also much prefer that he not be a drug dealer. But what is distinctive in her case is that she also wishes that she were the sort of mother who could continue to believe in her son's innocence even in the face of all that evidence. That's the sort of loving mother she wishes she were. The prospect of failing in her love for her son makes her reluctant to conclude that he is a drug dealer. If she draws this conclusion, she may then feel alienated from her belief, wishing that she didn't believe it, not only because she wishes it were not true, but because she wishes she had been able to resist the evidence. This sort of alienated belief is rare and perhaps the feeling of alienation is always fleeting, but it is not incoherent. In some ways it is like a desire one wishes one did not have or that one wishes would not move one.[21]

In this chapter, I have tried to make room for the idea that a person is causally responsible for her belief state. Through inference, she is able to change or sustain her take on which possibilities obtain. I have suggested we think of this in terms of her being the agent and the inference being a causing by her of the change in her belief. Changing or keeping her mind is not something a person can do intentionally, and while she can do it voluntary, she can also do it reluctantly or unwillingly. Our epistemic agency is thus rich and nuanced. What is more, believing something can be to a person's credit or discredit, and there are things a person ought to believe. This is the topic of my final chapter.

---

[21] For more on this sort of case, see Hunter (2011a).

8
Credal Norms

A full account of the nature of believing needs to combine its logical and psychological aspects with normative ones. This final chapter considers some of these normative aspects. I'll argue that no instance of believing is a good or better instance of believing than any other. In this sense, believing is not inherently normative. Still, as Gideon Rosen put it, facts about the nature of belief "engage with an independent body of cognitive norms" (Rosen 2001, 617). I will argue that believing something can be to a person's credit or discredit, and that there are things a person ought to believe. Credal credit and credal requirements depend, I will argue, on facts about the believer herself and, more specifically, on the sortals she falls under. On my view, this has little to do with what else she believes or knows, and so little to do with what evidence she has. Credal norms, as I see it, are not strictly an epistemic matter.

Here is my plan for this chapter. In Section 8.1, I will argue that belief properties are not goodness-fixing properties. One consequence is that norms of belief cannot be grounded in the goodness of believing itself, since there is no such thing as good believing. To understand the norms of belief, I will suggest, we need to put the believer, and the sortal properties she falls under, at the center of our story. My view contrasts with familiar ones on which truth is or sets an evaluative standard for belief.[1] In Section 8.2 I will try to make these contrasts clear and explain why I resist these views. In Section 8.3, I will argue that a person's believing something is to her credit when it is evidence that she is more or less good in some respect. The fact that Jones believes that the 504 stops at Garden is evidence that she is a good streetcar driver, and so her believing this is to her credit as a streetcar driver. But it does not follow from this that she ought to believe it. In Section 8.4, I will argue that what a person ought to believe depends on what she needs to know in order to do the things she ought to do. That is, it depends on which facts she ought to be in position to act in the light of. This has nothing to do, I will argue in Section 8.5, with what evidence she has. Finally, though a good person believes the things that she ought to believe, sometimes a person is not to blame for not believing what she should. Because she has an excuse, the fact that

---

[1] For discussion of this standard view, see Engel (2007), McHugh & Whiting (2014), and the essays in Chan (2013). For other arguments that believing is not inherently normative, see Thomson (2008), Glüer &Wikforss (2009), and Papineau (2014).

On Believing: Being Right in a World of Possibilities. David Hunter, Oxford University Press. © David Hunter 2022.
DOI: 10.1093/oso/9780192859549.003.0009

194 CREDAL NORMS

she does not believe it is not to her discredit as a person (though it may still be to her discredit in other respects). This is the topic of Section 8.6.

8.1 Believing and Attributive Goodness

In this section, I will argue that believing is not inherently normative. What I mean is that belief properties are not goodness-fixing properties. This means that no instance of believing something is better, *qua* believing, than any other.[2] Belief properties do not set a standard of goodness. The fact that belief properties are qualities and not sortals is central to my argument, and I will argue that no qualities are goodness-fixing properties.

I will start with some remarks about goodness. In Chapter 2, I distinguished among properties between qualities and sortals. Qualities are instantiated *in* individuals and substances while the instantiations of sortals *are* individuals and substances. The property of being tall is a quality, while the property of being a chair is a sortal. Some sortal properties are goodness-fixing properties in the sense that there are better and worse instances of them. Some chairs are better chairs than others, and some rose bushes are healthier than others. The same is true of some of the sortals that people fall under. Jones is a good TTC driver, while Sarah is not. Jones is a good tennis player and so is Sarah. And both Jones are Sarah are fairly good people. Being a TTC driver, being a tennis player, and being a person are thus goodness-fixing sortal properties. They fix or set a standard that a thing must meet to be a good instance of that kind. In knowing each property, one knows something about what it would be for someone to be a good instance of its kind. These standards are gradable. I mean that a thing might meet a standard to a higher or lower degree. One person might be a better TTC driver, or a better tennis player, or a better person than another, just as one chair might be a better chair than another. And there are things a person can do to improve as a tennis player, or a TTC driver, or a person, just as there are ways to make a chair better or a rose bush healthier. In sum, I take it that some sortals are goodness-fixing properties, that these standards are gradable, and that a thing's grade is changeable.

Are belief properties goodness-fixing properties? I think they are not. Jones believes that the 504 stops at Garden, and so does Sarah. Could Jones' believing it be a better instance of believing it than Sarah's? What sort of fact about believing might be relevant to answering this? If Sarah's believing were a little worse than

---

[2] My discussion in this chapter is heavily indebted to the discussion of goodness properties in (Urmson 1950) and, especially, Thomson (2008). Thomson's views, in turn, follow Geach (1956) and von Wright (1963). The idea that there are no norms governing belief is also developed, though in a different way, in (Steglich-Petersen 2006) and Steglich-Petersen (2007).

BELIEVING AND ATTRIBUTIVE GOODNESS 195

Jones', what could be done to improve it, to make it as good a believing as Jones'? It seems to me that these questions do not make much sense. And this, I suggest, is because belief properties are not goodness-fixing properties.

In my example, Jones and Sarah are both right in believing the 504 stops at Garden. But consider a case where one is right and the other is wrong. Jones believes, correctly, that the 504 stops at Garden, while Sarah believes, incorrectly, that it stops at Fern. Is Jones' believing a better instance of believing than Sarah's? If so, could something be done to improve Sarah's believing? I don't see how. Now imagine that the 504 had not stopped at Garden, but that Jones nonetheless believed that it did. Jones would then have been mistaken. But would it follow that Jones' believing in the actual world is a better instance of believing than her believing in that counterfactual world, and this just because she is right in the one and wrong in the other? Could it be a better instance of believing that thing? This does not strike me as plausible.

The same, I think, is true if we consider whether her belief is justified or based on good evidence. Suppose that Jones has much better evidence that the 504 stops at Garden than Sarah has. Jones' belief is in this sense much better justified than Sarah's. Does it follow that Jones' believing that the 504 stops at Garden is a better instance of believing it than is Sarah's or that Sarah's becomes a better believing of it as she collects more evidence for it. It seems to me that whether a person is right or wrong, or even more or less reasonable, in believing something makes no difference to whether her believing is a better or worse instance of believing. Believing something thus contrasts sharply with such properties as being a tennis player, being a TTC driver, and being a person. And this, I suggest, shows that belief properties are not goodness-fixing properties. They do not set a standard that an instance must meet to be a good instance of that property.

In fact, I think this point follows from a more general fact about belief properties. I argued in Chapter 2 that belief properties are qualities. Believing that the 504 stops at Garden is like being tall, being hot, and being red. It is a quality, whereas being human, being a tennis player, and being a pebble are sortals. As we have seen, some sortal properties are goodness-fixing properties. The property of being a person sets a standard, as does the property of being a tennis player. Not all sortal properties are goodness-fixing properties, since there is no such thing as one pebble's being better, *qua* pebble, than another. But, it seems to me, no qualities are goodness-fixing properties. No case of a thing's being tall is a better case of being tall than another. No case of being red is a better case of being red than another. No case of being hot is a better case of being hot than another. And likewise, no instance of believing something is a better case of it than another. This may be explained by the fact that, as J.L. Austin put it, the word "good" is *substantive hungry*. (Austin 1962, 69–70; cited in Thomson 2008) It makes sense only in connection with individual substances and stuffs, not with qualities or their instantiations.

196 CREDAL NORMS

It seems to me that belief properties are not goodness-fixing properties. In this respect, belief states are like pebbles and clouds. No pebble or cloud is a better pebble or cloud than any other. Still, one pebble may be better than another *in some other respect*. One might be a better example of a red pebble than another. One might be better for use as a paperweight than another. Likewise, one cloud might be better as a subject of a painting or photograph than another. The same is true for belief states. Jones' believing that the 504 stops at Garden might be good for her career. It might be good for a high-performance swimmer to believe they are the best in their competition. Believing this might improve their performance. It might be good for a professional poisoner to believe, of some recipe, that it yields a poison that kills quickly and painlessly. But none of this would show that one instance of believing is better, insofar as it is an instance of believing, than another, any more than one pebble's being a better example of a red pebble than another would show that it is a better pebble.

This point about belief properties extends to other mental states. No case of knowing something is a better or worse case of knowing it than another. No case of desiring something is a better or worse case of desiring it than any other. And the same for intending, hoping, anticipating, and so on. The temptation to hypostasize mental states by treating the relevant properties as if they were sortals rather than qualities makes this hard to see. If one takes belief states to be individuals in the same ontological category as chairs and people, then it will seem natural to think that just as with chairs and people there may be such a thing as one belief state's being a better belief state than another. Seeing that belief properties are qualities can help us avoid this.

The fact that belief properties are not goodness-fixing properties means that the norms of belief cannot be grounded in facts about good believing, because there are no such facts. I will argue that they are instead grounded in the sortals a person falls under. For some of those sortals are goodness-fixing. I will suggest that whether believing something is to a person's credit and whether she ought to believe it depends on the sortals she falls under. I'll discuss credal credit in Section 8.3 and credal requirements in Section 8.4. But first I want to consider the role that truth plays in credal norms.

8.2 Truth and Epistemic Value

I have argued that no instance of believing is a better or worse instance of believing than any other and that this is true even if one believer is right and the other is wrong. This might suggest that my account of credal norms will conflict with the familiar view that truth is or sets a standard of evaluation for belief. But I think my view can accommodate what is right in this familiar idea, while helping us to see where this idea can mislead. The aim of this section is to explain this.

TRUTH AND EPISTEMIC VALUE   197

The idea that truth sets a standard for belief is sometimes tied to the idea that belief states are themselves true or false. We see this in the following passage from Anthony Kenny.

> Beliefs, most obviously, may be described as true or false; desires, most obviously may be described as good or evil. Those states and activities which can be evaluated on the true/false scale belong to the cognitive side of the soul; those states and activities which are evaluated on the good/evil scale belong to the affective, volitional side of the soul.   (Kenny 1989, 75)

We also see it in Bermúdez' claim, which I first quoted in Chapter 1, that "almost all cognitive scientists and the vast majority of philosophers hold that brains and *the representations that they contain* are physical entities" (108–9; italics added). The presupposition is that belief states are the right sorts of things to be true or false, to be representations. I have argued that we should resist this. Belief states are not representations. Jones' believing that the 504 stops at Garden is not the right sort of thing to be true or false. The proposition that the 504 stops there is true or false, and so is Jones' assertion that it does. But propositions and assertions are individuals, whereas belief states are not. (Though it is worth noting that being true does not make one proposition better than another. The property of being a proposition is not a goodness-fixing property.) Again, failing to see that belief properties are qualities and not sortals can easily obscure this point.

Still, my view of belief allows truth a central role. Whether a person is right in believing something depends on which propositions are true or which possibilities obtain. That is the logical heart of belief and it distinguishes believing from other mental states. But being right in believing something is not itself a virtue. In saying that a person is right in believing something, we are not invariably praising or commending them. Being right does not by itself make one a better person. As I see it, the connection between being right and creditworthiness is more complex. Whether believing something is to a person's credit depends on the sortals she falls under. It depends on whether her believing it is evidence that she is good in some way, and this is not just a matter of being right. I will return to this in Section 8.3. My point here is simply that being right is not itself an evaluative or normative matter.[3]

I will eventually argue that a person ought to believe something only if in believing it she'd be right. So there is, I will argue, a connection between credal requirements and truth. But here again, the connection is complex and runs through the person's sortals. Whether a person ought to believe something depends on whether she needs to believe it in order to be good in some way. It

---

[3] This point is made in Dretske (2000), Glüer & Wikforss (2009), and Rosen (2001).

198   CREDAL NORMS

is a matter of which facts she ought to be in position to act in the light of. It is not strictly an epistemic matter. I will develop these points in Section 8.4.

Some theorists say that truth plays a normative role in inference and reasoning. Here is how Nishi Shah puts it, in the context of framing a problem for any account of inference.

> Why, when asking oneself *whether to believe that P,* must one immediately recognize that this question is settled by, and only by, answering the question *whether P is true?* Truth is not an optional end for first-personal doxastic deliberation, providing an *instrumental* or *extrinsic* reason that an agent may take or leave at will. Otherwise there would be an inferential step between discovering the truth with respect to P and determining *whether to believe that P*, involving a bridge premise that it is good...to believe the truth with respect to P. (Shah 2003, 447)

The problem, as Shah sees it, is to explain why a person infers that P only when she believes she has sufficient evidence that P is true. His answer is that doxastic deliberation involves deploying a concept of belief that one has only if one is committed to believing that P only if P is true. In asking oneself whether one should believe that P, or whether to believe that P, one immediately sees oneself as committed to believing it only if in believing it one would be right. This commitment is needed, Shah says, to explain why inferring that P requires taking oneself to have sufficient evidence that P.

I am not sure I see the problem Shah's proposal is meant to solve. But I think it may rest on a misconception about the nature of inference, one I tried to identify in Chapter 7. Inference does not involve reflecting on one's belief states. When Jones infers that the snow will melt soon, she is not thinking about her beliefs. Her focus is on the facts, or anyway the facts she takes there to be. She need not deploy any concept of belief. She need not ask herself the question whether to believe that P. This does not mean that truth plays no role. Whether the inference she draws is reasonable depends on whether the evidence she has supports her conclusion, and this is in part a matter of how likely they make its truth.

What is more, thinking of reasoning as Shah does risks mis-locating where an inference would be. The idea is that there can be a gap between finding oneself with sufficient evidence that P and then believing that P, a gap that an act of inference could fill. Shah denies, of course, that closing the gap requires an additional premise. It is hard to see how the gap could be closed just by another belief. But Shah does not deny the gap. His proposed conceptual commitment is meant to explain how the gap closes. It is the closing of the gap, according to Shah, that an account of inference must explain. But so far as I can see there is no such gap. Jones already believed that a hard rain melts snow quickly. In starting to believe that it is raining hard, she infers that the snow will melt soon. She starts believing the second thing in starting to believe the first. The inference, if there is one, is in starting to believe that it is raining hard. I thus have a hard time seeing the problem that Shah's appeal to a commitment to truth is meant to solve.

I think another idea about belief might be at work in Shah's view of inference. It is the idea that believing is a cognitive relation to a representation. Believing that P, on this idea, involves taking a representation to be true, or taking it to be sufficiently justified, or taking it to meet a standard making it fit to be believed. This idea suggests that believing is like having a map of the world that one has understood and determined is accurate. Theoretical reasoning, to extend the analogy, would be a matter of checking and correcting our map, in something like the way one might tend to plants in a garden. (Recall Broome's claim, quoted in Chapter 7, that inference involves operating on propositions.) But we should resist this analogy. The idea that believing is like having a map gets the nature of believing wrong. As David Armstrong noted, "[w]e do not read off our interpretation of reality from the data supplied by our beliefs. Our beliefs *are* our interpretation of reality" (Armstrong 1973, 4). Armstrong's point is that in deliberating about what to believe or feel or do, we do not look to our beliefs for guidance as if they were maps we can interpret and assess. This recalls my argument in Chapter 2 that believing is a state and not a relation. Armstrong took believing to be a dispositional state, while I argued that it is being in a certain rational position. But we agree that while belief states are individuated by a possibility or a proposition, believing is no more a *relation* to a possibility or a proposition than weighing twenty kilograms is a relation to a number.

To end this section I will mention one more way that truth might be thought to figure in credal norms. I argued that no believing is a better believing than any other. And I suggested that the same is true of knowing. Belief properties and knowledge properties are not goodness-fixing properties. One might concede this but insist that there is intrinsic value in being right or in believing with good reason. Richard Feldman puts the idea this way.

> Whatever our goals, it makes sense to suppose that believing truths (or some related state) has epistemic value, that it is a good thing from an epistemic point of view. (Feldman 2000, 683)

Ultimately, Feldman argues that it is being reasonable, not being right, that has this distinctive epistemic value. Feldman's view is a version of the idea that credal norms are grounded in a distinctively epistemic form of value or goodness.[4] This

---

[4] Feldman calls this thesis 'Evidentialism'. In a later article, co-authored with Earl Conee (Feldman & Conee 1985), he suggests that Evidentialism is the thesis that whether a person is reasonable in believing something depends only on the evidence they have. For a discussion of such views, see the introduction in Ahstrom-Vij & Dunn (2018). For a defense of the claim that there is such a thing as intrinsic goodness, see Zimmerman (2001), for critiques see Thomson (2008) and Kraut (2011).

200 CREDAL NORMS

is compatible with my claim that belief properties are not goodness-fixing properties. Even if no instance of believing is better than another *qua* believing, it could still be of intrinsic value for a believer to be right or rational and one might then think that what a person ought to believe could still depend in some way on this value.

But I doubt that the ethics of belief can be grounded in this way. For I doubt that there is any *intrinsic value* in truth or rationality. My doubt is not restricted to epistemology: I doubt there is intrinsic value in anything. This is obviously a controversial matter, and rather than defend this doubt, I want to explore a different route for grounding the norms of belief. I want to argue that some credal norms are grounded in facts about the sortals a person falls under.[5] What a person deserves credit for believing and what she ought to believe depends on what is needed for her to be good in some way.

8.3 Credal Credit

What a person believes can be to her credit or discredit. That is the topic of this section. I have argued that belief properties are not goodness-fixing properties and that this follows from the fact that belief properties are qualities and that no qualities are goodness-fixing properties. But some sortals are goodness-fixing properties. There is, for instance, such a thing as being a good TTC driver, a good parent, a good teacher and, of course, a good parent. Those sortals set a standard a thing must meet to be a good TTC driver, parent, teacher or person. In this section I will argue that what a person believes is to her credit when the fact that she believes it is evidence that she is good with respect to some goodness fixing she falls under.

Some fact about a thing is to its *credit* if it is reason to think that thing is in some respect good. Good knives hold a sharp edge. So the fact that a certain knife holds a sharp edge is to its credit since it is evidence that it is a good knife. Healthy rose bushes have dark green leaves. So the fact that Jane's rose bush has dark green leaves is to its credit since it is evidence that it is healthy. Matters are more complex with people, because people are more complex. Whether some fact about a person is to her credit can depend on what roles and jobs she has. The fact that Jones is usually on time for work is to her credit as it is evidence that she is a conscientious worker, and a good worker is conscientious. The fact that Jones pays careful attention to the nutritional content of the food she prepares for her children is reason to think she is a good parent. That fact about Jones is to her

---

[5] Feldman acknowledges that there are "oughts that result from one's playing a certain role or having a certain position" (Feldman 2000, 676). But he does not consider whether these oughts might include credal ones.

CREDAL CREDIT   201

credit, *qua* parent. Some fact about a thing is to its *discredit*, by contrast, if it is reason to think that it is in some respect bad. Sarah is an employee of the TTC, and the fact that she regularly shows up for work late and hungover is reason to think she is a bad employee. So that fact is to Sarah's discredit. Good employees do not show up late and hungover.[6]

What a person believes can also be to her credit or discredit depending on her roles and jobs. Jones is a streetcar driver for the TTC, and a good driver knows the route. So, the fact that Jones correctly believes that the 504 stops at Garden is reason to think she is a good driver. That fact is thus to her credit, *qua* TTC streetcar driver. It suggests that she is more or less good in that respect. Sarah, in contrast, is also a driver for the 504, and the fact that she mistakenly believes that the 504 stops at Fern is some reason to think she is not such a good driver. That fact is to her discredit, *qua* TTC streetcar driver. It is evidence that she is to some extent not a good TTC driver.

Being right in believing something can thus be to a person's credit. Can being *wrong* ever be to a person's credit? Could a person's being mistaken about something be reason to think she is good at some role or job? I find this hard to imagine. Characteristically, being good at any role or job requires *not* being mistaken with respect to certain things. Typically, for a given role or job there will be certain facts such that being good at that role or in that job requires knowing those facts, and not just believing in them. What facts one needs to know depends on the role or job, and can change over time. A good TTC driver needs to keep track of changes in the route and in the conditions of her vehicle and in the passengers on the streetcar.

Still, I don't think that being wrong is always to a person's discredit. Some mistakes just don't matter. As it happens, there are three leaves on the front porch of my cottage, but Sarah believes that there are five leaves on it.[7] Sarah has never been to my cottage. She first heard about it this morning. She has no role or job such that being mistaken about that fact is reason to think that she is bad at that role or at that job. That Sarah is mistaken about the number of leaves on my porch is not, in itself, to her discredit in any respect. Jones, on the other hand, is right about the number of leaves on my porch. But as with Sarah, this fact is of no relevance to any of Jones' roles or jobs. Jones too only learned this fact this morning. That Jones is right about the number of leaves on my porch is not, in itself, to her credit. There is no role or job such that the fact that she is right about the number of leaves on my porch is reason to think she is good at that role or in that job. (I add the qualification "in itself" because how a person came to believe something can be to her credit or discredit. I will return to this.)

---

[6] It is another matter whether she is to blame for being a bad employee. I discuss blame in Section 8.6.

[7] The example is adapted from Thomson (2008).

202 CREDAL NORMS

But what about being a good believer? Isn't a person's being mistaken in believing something reason to think that she is not a good believer, or anyway not as good a believer as she could be. I don't think so. I don't think there is such a thing as being a good believer, *qua* believer. There would be only if one person could be better than another at believing. But I don't think this is possible. One person can be a better researcher or investigator than another. And one can be a better person than another. But I don't think there is such a thing as one person's being a better or worse believer than another.

It helps to think again about owning books. Some books are better than others. One person can be better than another at preserving or organizing her books. And one person might be more discerning than another at curating her book collection. But what could it be for one person to be better than another at owning books? Could a person become a better owner of books? It seems to me this makes no more sense for believing than for owning. I doubt there is such a thing as one person's being a better believer than another. And this, in turn, makes me doubt that there is such a thing as being a good believer.

In fact, I think this is one more consequence of the fact that belief properties are qualities and not sortals. There is no such thing as a better or worse instantiator of *any* quality, qua instantiator of that quality, because such evaluations apply to sortals and qualities are not sortals. There is no such thing in general as being better or worse at having some quality. A thing either has it or it does not. To be a believer is to have belief properties, just as to be a red thing is to have the property of being red. There is no such thing as one red thing's being a better red thing than another. Likewise, it seems to me, there is no such thing as one person's being a better believer than another.

Of course, one person can be a better *person* than another. And it seems to me that whether someone is a good person depends on what she believes. It depends on whether she believes what she ought to believe, or whether she has an excuse for not believing what she ought to believe. The next two sections consider what a person ought to believe, and the final section of the book considers credal blame.

8.4 Belief Directives and Knowledge

Following Thomson (2008), let's call a claim to the effect that some person ought to believe (or know) something a belief (or knowledge) directive. This section and the next are concerned with when such directives are true.

It strikes me that knowledge directives are far more common in every day discourse than belief directives. I suspect that this is because knowledge directives are more fundamental than belief directives. But whether or not this is so, I think the following is very plausible.

BELIEF DIRECTIVES AND KNOWLEDGE   203

($K_O{\rightarrow}B_O$) If S ought to know that P, then S ought to believe that P.

If, for instance, the following knowledge directive is true, then so is the corresponding belief directive.

Jones should know that the 504 stops at Garden.
Jones should believe that the 504 stops at Garden.

Of course, if she ought to know it then she cannot satisfy that requirement simply by believing it—she must also fulfill any other conditions needed for knowing it. If, for instance, knowledge requires having evidence, then if Jones ought to know that the 504 stops at Garden, then she also ought to have evidence that it does.[8]

($K_O{\rightarrow} E_O$) If S ought to know that P, then S ought to have evidence that P.

So (K_rB_r) doesn't entail that knowledge directives require the person to have hasty or otherwise irrational beliefs. What it rules out is just that a person need not believe something that she ought to know.[9]

The following claim about forbiddings is also part of common sense.

($K_F{\rightarrow} B_F$) If S ought not to know that P, then S ought not to believe that P.

Consider the right to privacy. It is a matter of debate just what this right comes to. But suppose it means that there can be facts about a person that (some) other people ought not to know. Suppose that Susan's right to privacy extends to the fact that she has cancer. And suppose that Jones ought not to know this. In that case, it

---

[8] Knowledge may not always require evidence. Perhaps certain cases of self-knowledge don't. In that case, a requirement that some person have some such knowledge might not entail that she ought to have evidence too. I'll not explore this.

[9] In discussion, Stephanie Leary said that while (1) seems to entail (2), she doubts whether (2) entails (3).
(1) S ought to know that p
(2) S ought to (believe that P and have good evidence that p)
(3) S ought to believe that P.
In support of her doubt, she offered the following apparent counter-example:
(a) S ought to (revise her paper and resubmit it)
(b) S ought to resubmit her paper.
I agree that (a) does not entail (b). In the text, though, I don't rely on an inference from (2) to (3); I get (3) directly from (1). I am also not convinced by her example, since I suspect that unlike the parenthesis in (2) the one in (a) is not a simple conjunction. It seems to me that (a) means something more like (a').
(a') S ought to (*first* revise her paper and *only then* resubmit it).
That would explain why (a) does not entail (b). But I won't pursue the question whether (2) entails (3). As I say, I think (1) entails (3) directly, and that is what I assume in the text.

204   CREDAL NORMS

seems to me, Jones ought not to believe it either.[10] Why would one who agreed that Jones ought not to know about Susan's cancer think that it is nonetheless permitted for her to *believe* that she has cancer? Their view would have to be that it is permitted only so long as her belief does not amount to knowledge, only so long as she lacks sufficient evidence for it. This strikes me as implausible. If there is a right to privacy, it seems to me, it extends to belief and not just to knowledge.

Here is another plausible principle.

If S ought to do X, then S ought to know that S ought to do X.

Here is how Judith Jarvis Thomson puts the point, though in the case of belief.

> I think we take it that if A ought to V_{act}, then he ought to believe that he ought to V_{act}. Moreover, not just any reasons for believing it will do: A ought to believe it for the right reasons. He ought to believe not only that he ought to V_{act}, but also all those propositions such that it is their being true that makes it the case that he ought to V_{act}, and therefore explains why he ought to. In short, when we ought to do a thing, we ought to be clear that and why we ought to.   (Thomson 2008, 226)[11]

It is not just, as Thomson sees it, that people ought to know what they ought to do. They ought also to know *why* they ought to do it. No doubt such a general principle requires careful qualifications. But it strikes me that some such principle is right, at least about what we generally expect from people. We expect people to know more or less what they ought to do and something about why we they ought to do it.[12]

I think a further plausible principle is that people should know *what* they are doing and should pay attention to changes in their surroundings. Consider what we tell little children as they walk through a crowded mall: you should pay

---

[10] It is another matter altogether whether Jones is to blame for believing it. I will return to this in Section 8.6.

[11] What I say about belief directives echoes what Thomson says in that work, though she does not discuss knowledge directives.

[12] Could someone be *incapable* of knowing what she ought to do? It depends on the source of the incapacity. Suppose that Petra is too young to understand the nature of family chores, and so cannot understand what it would be for it to be true that she ought to take out the trash. In that case, I think, it is false that she ought to take out the trash. What a person ought to do cannot outrun what she can understand. Suppose, by contrast, that Martha understands about chores, but misses her only opportunity to find out what her chore is. It might then be true, I think, that she ought to take out the trash even though she is incapable of knowing this. But, it seems to me, it might also then be true that Martha ought to know it. But doesn't this violate the principle that "ought implies can"? It depends on the meaning of the word "can." Sorting this out will have to wait.

attention to where you are going and look out for other people.[13] There are good reasons for this advice. Trudy might get hurt or might hurt someone else, if she is not paying attention to what she is doing. These are prudential and moral reasons, and they apply to adults as much as to children. Joggers should watch where they are going; teachers ought to attend to their students; doctors must pay careful attention during surgery; and so on. The general rule, stated roughly, is that a person ought to know what she is doing and should be on the lookout for how she is changing her surroundings.

Of course, we are never in a position to know every effect we are having or to know about every change in our surroundings. Some are too small to know about, such as the fine motions of air particles around us, and others are too distant in space or time. And some of the things we do are of no importance at all, and so won't be among the things that we ought to know we are doing. An adequate formulation of the principle would have to specify limits. In the case of knowing what one is doing, an adequate formulation might be a version of the following.

S should know that S is doing X if

S is doing X; and

S can easily come to know that S is doing X; and

there is some (moral, prudential, legal, etc.) risk in S's doing X.

This is just a rough first pass at a principle. I won't offer a full development or defense of it. But it seems to me that however the rule is ultimately to be formulated, it is part of common sense that people ought generally to know what they are doing and to keep track of changes in their surroundings.

Let's return now to belief directives. In discussing Jones, I suggested that the following is true.

Jones should know that the 504 stops at Garden.

I have also suggested that the following is true.

$(K_O \rightarrow B_O)$ If S ought to know that P, then S ought to believe that P.

Given this, it follows that:

Jones ought to believe that the 504 stops at Garden.

---

[13] Directives come in different strengths. Roughly, what a person should do is not as strong as what she ought to do, which is not as strong as what she must do. Knowledge and belief directives can differ in strength too. A theory of belief should say something about why directives come in such strengths and about how these strengths relate to one another. I won't say much about that here.

She ought to believe it for the same reason that she ought to know it: discharging her duties as a 504 driver requires that she believe it, and there are no weightier considerations against her believing it.

The fact that Jones has these duties is a reason for her to know that fact. Indeed, it is a good reason. Is it also a reason for her to believe it? That is, can she believe it because she has those duties? I don't think so. On my view, considerations on the basis of which a person *can* believe something are not considerations that make it true that a person *ought* to believe it. Call the fact that Jones has those duties, D. If we ask why Jones *knows* that the 504 stops at Garden, we can correctly answer that she knows it because of D. But if we ask why she *believes* it, then D is not a correct answer. To say why she believes it we need, it seems, to say what evidence she has for it. We need, that is, to say *how* she knows it, not *why* she knows it. If by "a reason" we mean a fact that answers a "why" question, then reasons for knowing are not reasons for believing. This is all more complicated than I can now make out. But notice that it has nothing to do with the fact that belief is not voluntary, since knowledge is not voluntary either.[14]

One might offer the following objection. "It is true that to be a good TTC driver, one needs to know the route. If Jones does not know that the 504 stops at Garden Avenue, then she ought to do some investigations in order to learn this. But the only epistemic directive is to investigate the matter. There are no epistemic directives to know about those matters." I think this objection gets the matter the wrong way around. I agree that if Jones does not know that the 504 stops at Garden, then she ought to investigate the matter. But the reason she ought to investigate is precisely that she ought to know. The matters one should study are surely those matters one should know about. It is because one should know about them that one should investigate them.

We can now see how credit for believing something and directives for belief can diverge. A person's believing something is to her credit if that fact is reason to think she is in some respect good. Consider Terence who has been hired to spy on Susan, and in particular, to discover her private medical condition. He does discover it and comes to believe that she has cancer. The fact that he believes it is thus to his credit, *qua* private investigator, since it is evidence that he is a good private investigator. But it does not follow that he *ought* to believe that she has cancer. Indeed, he ought not to believe it. So whether believing something is to a person's credit is independent of whether she ought to believe.

Still, a good person believes the things she ought to believe, unless she has a good excuse. If she has a good excuse, then she is not to blame for not believing as she should. But before turning to this, we should consider whether facts about the evidence a person has can be relevant to what she ought to believe.

---

[14] Thanks to Ulf Hlobil and Stephanie Leary for helping me see this.

8.5 Belief Directives and Evidence

In Section 8.4, I suggested that we accept the following.

($K_O \rightarrow B_O$) If S ought to know that P, then S ought to believe that P.

What should we say about the following?

($B_O \rightarrow K_O$) S ought to believe that P only if S ought to know that P.

Could it be that Jones ought to believe something even though it is not something she ought to know? It would have to be something that Jones is permitted not to know, and not something that she ought not to know. There are, it seems to me, plenty of topics that many people are permitted to know nothing about. Many people in China don't need to know my height. So they are permitted not to know it. But could it nonetheless be that one of them *ought* to believe that I am six feet tall, even though it is not the case that he ought to know it?

One might think so if one also thought that facts about a person's evidence could make a belief directive true without making the corresponding knowledge directive true. In discussing what Jones ought to know, I said nothing in Section 8.3 about what else she believes. So I said nothing about what evidence she has. Still, I said that she ought to know and so believe that the 504 stops at Garden. But one might think that a person's evidence is always relevant to whether a belief directive about them is true. In particular, one might think that the following is true.

EVIDENCE$_B$:   S ought to believe that P only if S has evidence that P.

It seems to me that we should reject EVIDENCE$_B$. The truth of a belief directive does not always require that the subject has evidence for the belief.[15]

We should first distinguish EVIDENCE$_B$ from EVIDENCE$_K$.

EVIDENCE$_K$:   S ought to know that P only if S has evidence that P.

I also think that we should reject EVIDENCE$_K$. We regularly advise people to learn about things that we know they know nothing at all about. On the first day of classes, I advise my students that they ought to know the rules of academic misconduct.[16] This is good advice even when they have no clue that there is even such a thing as academic misconduct. It may be true, of course, that a person

---

[15] What I say in this section is indebted to discussions with Miriam McCormick and Berislav Marušić. For their views, see (McCormick 2015) and (Marušić 2015).

[16] One might say that my advice is that they ought to study the rules. This is also good advice. But the reason they ought to study the rules is precisely that they ought to know them. Likewise, the reason

208 CREDAL NORMS

cannot know that P without having evidence that P. So it may be true that S cannot satisfy the knowledge directive to know that P without having evidence that P. So S may need to get evidence that P in order to satisfy the knowledge directive. But it is precisely because S ought to know that P that S ought to have (and so get if she does not have) evidence that P.

If $EVIDENCE_K$ is false but $EVIDENCE_B$ is true, then the following principle that I have said is part of common sense must also be false.

$(K_O \rightarrow B_O)$ If S ought to know that P, then S ought to believe that P.

For if $EVIDENCE_K$ is false but $EVIDENCE_B$ is true, then there is a condition on belief directives that is not a condition on knowledge directives. What could that be? One might think that the following principle about rational belief provides such a condition.

RATIONALITY: It is irrational for S to believe that P without evidence.

Let's assume that RATIONALITY is true. Does accepting it really require that we abandon $(K_O \rightarrow B_O)$?

Let's consider Jones. Suppose that she is a new employee and has not yet had time to study the route. She has no reason to believe that the 504 stops at Garden. Wouldn't it be irrational for Jones to believe without evidence that the 504 stops at Garden? Let's assume that it would. I don't see how that shows that we need to deny $(K_O \rightarrow B_O)$. For that principle does not say that if a person ought to know that P, then she ought to believe *without evidence* that P. For one who accepts it can also accept the following:

$(K_O \rightarrow E_O)$ If S ought to know that P, then S ought to have evidence that P.

And this seems to me enormously plausible (at least for those cases where knowing requires evidence). If Jones ought to know that the 504 stops at Garden, then she ought *both* to believe that it does *and* have good evidence that it does. A true knowledge directive does not require that one have an irrational belief. In fact, it does not even permit one to. So we are free to accept both $(K_O \rightarrow B_O)$ and RATIONALITY.

I have been formulating belief and knowledge directives without specifying time. If we do, then we need to distinguish a synchronic from a diachronic reading of our principle.

---

why people should eat moderately and exercise regularly is that they should be healthy. Directives to do something, including directives to study or learn about or examine certain subject matters, can follow, it seems to me, from directives to be a certain way.

$(K_O \rightarrow B_O)^S$ If, at t, S ought to know that P, then, at t, S ought to believe that P.

$(K_O \rightarrow B_O)^D$ If, at t, S ought to know that P, then, after collecting sufficient evidence for P, S ought to believe that P.

I have been assuming the synchronic version: that if a knowledge directive is true of a person at some time, then the corresponding belief directive is true of that person at that same time. But one might think that the diachronic version coheres better with RATIONALITY. For the diachronic version allows the subject time to get the evidence for P. And one who accepted all of this might then say, about Jones, that while it is true at the time she is assigned the route that she ought to know that the 504 stops at Garden, it is false at that time that she ought to believe that the 504 stops at Garden. That belief directive would be true, on this line of thinking, only once Jones had enough evidence.

I think we should reject $(K_O \rightarrow B_O)^D$. For it leads to a conflict in what a person ought to do. I take it that the following is very plausible.

(K) If, at t, S ought to know that P, and if, at t, S does not know that P, then, at t, S ought to collect evidence that P.

This captures the idea that people ought to investigate matters they ought to but don't yet know about. I also take the following to be highly plausible.

(B) If, at t, S is permitted not to believe that P, and if, at t, S does not believe that P, then, at t, S is permitted not to collect evidence that P.

This captures the idea that people are permitted not to investigate matters they are permitted not to have beliefs about. The problem with $(K_O \rightarrow B_O)^D$ is that it forces us to deny one of these two principles. Suppose, as a proponent of $(K_O \rightarrow B_O)^D$ might hold, that (i) Jones ought to know that the 504 stops at Garden but (ii) is permitted not to believe it. (K) and (i) entail that Jones ought to collect evidence for it. But (B) and (ii) entail that she is permitted not to collect evidence for it. This is a contradiction. Accepting $(K_O \rightarrow B_O)^D$ thus requires abandoning or qualifying one of (K) or (B). Rather than face this problem, I suggest we simply stick with the synchronic version of $(K_O \rightarrow B_O)$, especially since we can accept it together with RATIONALITY.[17]

---

[17] There is much more to say about the relevance of times in directives. A knowledge directive might concern future-knowledge: S ought, at t, to know, at t + n, that P. Or past-knowledge: S ought, at t, to have known, at t − n, that P. And like any directive, a knowledge directive can expire. So while it was true, at t, that S ought to know that P, it might not be true by t + n. All of this gives rise to complications. For discussion of some of these issues, see Zimmerman (2018) and Kiesewetter (2017).

210 CREDAL NORMS

I argued that it might be true that Jones ought to believe that the 504 stops at Garden even if she has no evidence for it. If so, then facts about what evidence a person has do not always outweigh other considerations relevant to the truth of belief directive. But are evidential facts, as I will call them, *ever* relevant? It seems to me that they are not. I mean this in a strong sense: facts about the evidence a person has have no bearing at all on what she ought to believe. What a person ought to believe is fixed by what she ought to know and this, in turn, has nothing to do with what evidence she has. Seeing this will help us to answer a question we raised above, namely whether the following is true.

($B_O \to K_O$) S ought to believe that P only if S ought to know that P.

But first a quick word about how I have been formulating directives. I have used "ought" instead of "ought, all things considered." I am happy to make the replacement, so long as we mean "all *relevant* things considered" or "considering all the things that *need* considering." On my view, in deciding whether Jones ought to know that the 504 stops at Garden, we need to consider lots of things, including facts about what she ought to do and about how she ought to be. Such facts are relevant. But other facts are not relevant and don't need to be considered. For instance, facts about the number of leaves on my cottage porch. Those facts are not relevant and don't need to be considered. I think that evidential facts are like those leaves facts. They are of course, along with facts about the number of leaves on my porch, included among *all the facts*. But they are not among the *relevant* ones. So we don't need to consider them. At least not when considering whether Jones ought to believe that the 504 stops at Garden.[18]

Consider Beatrice, a barista at a local coffee shop. Nothing in her duties as a barista requires her to know that the 504 stops at Garden. Suppose further that no other duties or personal obligations are relevant. Now suppose that Simon tells her that it does stop at Garden and she knows him to be extremely reliable and trustworthy on such topics. Does the fact that she has this evidence support a belief directive?

Consider first the following permission directive.

Beatrice is permitted to believe that the 504 stops at Garden.

I am inclined to think that this directive is true. But I also think this has nothing to do with the fact that she has evidence for it. I think that everyone is permitted to believe it. And I think this general permission follows from the more general truth that everyone is permitted to *know* it. It is not a state secret or subject to anyone's

---

[18] Thanks to Stephanie Leary for helping me here.

BELIEF DIRECTIVES AND EVIDENCE   211

privacy rights. So the fact that Beatrice is permitted to believe that the 504 stops at Garden does not, it seems to me, show that evidential facts are relevant to the truth of a belief directive. She would be permitted to believe it even if she had no evidence for it.

What about the following directive?

Beatrice ought to believe that the 504 stops at Garden.

Does the fact that she has Simon's testimony show that it is true? It might, but for a reason that does not generalize to all evidence. I am inclined to think that we have a personal obligation to our friends to trust them.[19] It is a failing not to believe what our friends tell us, when we have no reason to doubt their sincerity or expertise. So it would be a failing for Jones not to believe what Simon tells her about the 504. It would be disrespectful towards him. This, it seems to me, lends some support to the claim that she ought to believe that the 504 stops at Garden. She ought to believe it because she ought to believe him.

But this result has more to do with the fact that her evidence came from Simon, than with the fact that she has that evidence. Suppose instead that she simply saw a sign on the street saying that the 504 stops at Garden. I take it we have no duty or personal obligation to trust such signs. It is not a sort of failing not to trust street signs. In that case while she is surely permitted to believe it (for the reasons given above) I do not think that she positively ought to believe it, even though she has evidence for it and no other considerations weighs against her believing it.

In that case, though, wouldn't it be irrational for her not to believe it, given that she has seen the sign and has no counter evidence and no reason to doubt the reliability of the sign? Let's suppose it would be irrational. It would follow that she ought to believe it only if the following were true:

IRRATIONALITY: If it would be irrational for S not to believe that P, then S ought to believe that P.

But we should reject IRRATIONALITY. Consider again Terence who believes that Susan has cancer, violating her right to privacy. Suppose that Terence came to believe this by reading her confidential medical files. He has excellent evidence that she has cancer (and he knows he does). Given this, it would be irrational for him not to believe that she has cancer. Still, it is not the case that he ought to believe it. In fact, he positively ought *not* to believe it. The right to privacy would not amount to much if we could override it simply by learning the private fact! So from the fact that it would be irrational for someone not to believe something it

---

[19] For discussion of this see Stroud (2006) and (Marušić 2017).

212 CREDAL NORMS

does not follow that she ought to believe it. Whether it would be irrational for someone not to believe something is one thing, whether she ought to believe it is another.

The same is true, it seems to me, in the case of action directives. The following is false, I think.

IRRATIONALITY$_A$:   If it would be irrational for S not to do X, then S ought to do X.

Consider Tom, an assassin hired to shoot the Prime Minister. Suppose that Tom believes that he ought to pull the trigger now, and desires more than anything else that he pull it now. It might then be irrational for him not to pull the trigger. Not pulling it might manifest weakness in his will. And this might reveal a defect in Tom's practical faculties. Still, it might also be true that he ought not to pull the trigger. (What is more: he perhaps ought not to want to! The fact that he does may reveal yet another defect in his practical faculties.) Likewise, if after reading the medical report Terence does not believe that Susan has cancer, this might manifest an intellectual or cognitive weakness on his part, revealing a defect in his intellectual faculties. But it would not follow from this that he ought to believe it or even that he is permitted to believe it.[20]

I have been considering whether the fact that Beatrice has evidence for the proposition that the 504 stops at Garden lends weight to a belief directive concerning that proposition. But perhaps the fact that the proposition is true is distorting our discussion. Maybe the relevance of evidence to belief directives is clearer when the person would be mistaken in believing the thing. So suppose that Beatrice saw a sign, placed without her knowledge by vandals, saying that the 504 stops at Fern, which it does not. Does the fact that she has this misleading evidence lend support to a belief directive?

Consider the following.

Beatrice is permitted to believe that the 504 stops at Fern.

Is it true? It would be false if the following general directive were true.

FALSE: No one is ever permitted to believe mistakenly.

But I am doubtful about this. It seems to me that one would be permitted to believe mistakenly if the mistake carried no risk at all, if there were no chance that

---

[20] I do not deny that there are intellectual virtues and defects. All I am denying is that there is a direct route from facts about them to belief directives. For further discussion, see Zagzebski (1996) and (Cassam 2019).

by believing it one would be led to do (or not do) something that one ought not to do (or ought to do). Now, perhaps there are no such mistakes. Or perhaps no one could ever believe such an unimportant thing, one so disconnected from anything of any importance to her life. But this would not show that believing mistakenly is *in itself* impermissible. And perhaps there *could* be an entirely unimportant mistake that some possible person *could* make. And in that case, it might be permissible for that person to believe it whether she had evidence for it or not. This general permission to believe the wholly unimportant but false might be the flip side of a general permission to believe any old unimportant truth. And both permissions might then be independent of any evidential facts. So even if FALSE were incorrect, this would not yet show that evidential facts are relevant to belief directives.

But, to return to Beatrice, is *she* permitted to believe that the 504 stops at Fern? I think not. After all, this is not a case where there is no risk at all in her believing that it does. She might, for instance, tell her elderly customers that the 504 stops at Fern, and thereby delay their needed trip to the hospital, a possibility that could end very badly. And even if this bad end is unlikely, the possibility of it seems to me to outweigh the fact that she has misleading evidence that the 504 stops at Fern. It seems to me that she should not believe that the 504 stops at Fern. In fact, she ought not to believe it, even if her husband Mike, who she surely has a very strong obligation to believe, told her that the 504 stops at Fern, and even if she knew him to be highly trustworthy and reliable on such matters. And this because it is a mistake that might lead her to do (or not do) something that she ought not to do (or ought to do). It would perhaps be irrational for her not to believe it, given what else she believes. And, in the case where Mike tells her it stops at Fern, it might be very disrespectful for her not to believe it. But this, it seems to me, is not decisive.

We can return now to the following thesis.

($B_O \rightarrow K_O$) S ought to believe that P only if S ought to know that P.

I started by asking what could make a belief directive true without making the corresponding knowledge directive true. I have now considered, but rejected, two possibilities. First, I considered whether having evidence in favor of it might have this result. I suggested that permission to believe something does not require having evidence for it and that having evidence for something is compatible with being forbidden from believing it. Second, I considered whether having evidence in favor of a *false* proposition could have this result. I suggested that people are generally not permitted to believe mistakenly unless the mistake is wholly unimportant, in which case they may be permitted to believe it whether they have evidence or not. It seems, then, that whether a person has evidence for something has little relevance to whether a corresponding belief directive is true.

214 CREDAL NORMS

The cases I have discussed also help us to see that the following is false.

($B \to E_O$) If S believes that P, then S ought to have evidence that P.

Terence believes that Susan has cancer. But it does not follow that he should have evidence that she does. For in fact, he should *not* have evidence that she does. Again, the right to privacy would not amount to much if we could override it simply by collecting evidence for the private fact. Still, I think something like the following may be true.

($B_O \to E_O$) If S ought to believe that P, then S ought to have evidence that P.

Indeed, this follows from the following doctrines, each of which I have suggested is quite plausible.

($B_O \to K_O$) S ought to believe that P only if S ought to know that P.

($K_O \to E_O$) If S ought to know that P, then S ought to have evidence that P.

Together, these doctrines capture the idea that belief directives flow from knowledge directives.

8.6 Credal Blame

Sometimes, a person who does not believe something she ought to believe, or who believes something that she ought not to believe, has a good excuse. In that case, she is not to blame for believing it or for failing to believe it. And this means that her believing it or not believing it is not to her discredit, at least not *qua* person. The aim of this section is to develop this idea.

I'll start by stepping back and considering three related notions. One is that of being *responsible* for believing something. A second is that of being *appraisable*, either positively or negatively, for believing something. The third is that of being *to blame* or *blameworthy* for believing something. Rik Peels thinks these notions all go together very tightly. Here is how he summarizes his view.

> [T]o believe responsibly is to believe blamelessly, that is, to be the proper object of either neutral appraisal or praise for one's belief. Responsible belief excludes blameworthy belief, but one can believe responsibly even if one does not believe praiseworthily. (Peels 2016 51)

The idea is that for a person's believing something to be a case of responsible believing is for it to be a case where it is proper to praise (or at least neutrally appraise) the believer and this, in turn, is for it to be a case where the believer is not blameworthy for believing it. Anne Meylan offers a similar view. She says that "we praise or blame people for...the doxastic states, in which they are as a result of their investigative behavior" (Meylan 2015, 2).[21] Like Peels, she links together the notions of credal praise, blame, and responsibility.

I think we should keep the notions apart, or at any rate, that the links connecting them are different than Peels and Meylan suggest, but I concede that there is room here for terminological regimentation.[22] In Chapter 7, I argued that a person is responsible for what she believes in the sense that she is the originating or sustaining cause of her beliefs. This applies to everything she believes, not just to those beliefs that are to her credit or discredit. In this sense, responsibility is not an ethical notion. I think it is helpful to separate when a person is responsible for believing something from when believing it is to her credit or discredit.

I also think we should separate praise and praiseworthiness from blame and blameworthiness. Praise is a speech act. To praise someone is to say that she is in some respect good. To say of Terence that he is a good investigator is to praise him. To say of Jones that she is a good TTC driver is to praise her. Praise is correct if the person is indeed good in that respect. If the person is good in that respect, then she is, in that sense, worthy of that praise.

But notice two things. First, this way of thinking of praise entails that saying, of Simon, that he is a good assassin is praising him. (I assume that there is such a thing as being a good assassin.) That might seem to jar a little. But we can quickly add that Simon ought not to be an assassin, not even a good one, and the fact that he is a good assassin is to his discredit as a person. We can say that only a bad person is a good assassin. Since I think it is helpful to keep the notions of praise and blame separate, I am happy to stick with this way of thinking of praise.

The second point to notice is this. It is one thing whether a person is praise-worthy and another matter whether that person ought to be praised. It can't be true that if a person is praiseworthy then each of us ought to praise her. We'd never stop praising, since each of us is in multiple respects worthy of praise. So whether a person ought to be praised, and whether someone in particular ought to do that praising, must depend on something more than just whether the person is praiseworthy. And might it not happen that someone ought to praise a person who is not, in that respect, praiseworthy? Suppose a bit of false praise would prevent a terrible crime. In that case, a bit of (even false) praise might be just the thing to do.

Let's connect this to believing. In Section 8.1, I argued that no instance of believing something is better than another. So it is never correct, it seems to me, to

---

[21] See also Meylan (2019).
[22] What follows is influenced by the discussion of credit, praise and blame in Thomson (1989). For an alternative way of thinking of blame, see Wolf (2011).

praise someone's belief state. It is not correct, for instance, to say of Jones' believing that the 504 stops at Garden that it is a good believing. And this is so even if she is right that it stops there. Being right does not make one's belief state a good or better belief state. So I don't think belief states are worthy of praise.

But a believer can be worthy of praise. I claimed that there is no such thing as one person's being a better believer than another. So there is no such thing as correctly praising someone for being a good believer. Still, a person might be praiseworthy because of what she believes. It is, for instance, to Jones' credit as a TTC driver that she believes that the 504 stops at Garden. Her believing that is evidence that she is a good TTC driver, and one might on that basis praise her by calling her a good driver. But notice that saying of Jones that she believes that the 504 stops at Garden is not itself to praise her, even though her believing it is to her credit as a TTC driver. (Special conversational contexts might make it the case that in saying that one is praising her; but set this aside.) The praise is in saying of her that she is a good TTC driver. Likewise, it can be to a person's discredit that she believes something. Sarah believes, incorrectly, that the 504 stops at Fern and this is evidence that she is not an especially good streetcar driver, since a good streetcar driver would know that it does not stop there. We might, on that basis, dispraise her by saying that she is not a very good streetcar driver. The dispraise is in saying that she is not a good streetcar driver, not in saying that she is incorrect in believing that the 504 stops at Fern.

Let's turn now to blame and blameworthiness. Blame differs from praise in one key respect. Blaming is not a speech act. Rather, it seems to me to be a sort of belief. To blame someone for something is to believe that she is to blame for it. A person can be to blame both for what she does and for the results of what she does. Here is a rough formulation of when a person is to blame for something.

BLAME: S is to blame for X when

X is in some way bad; and

S caused X by doing (or not doing) something that she ought not to have (or ought to have) done; and

S has no excuse for causing X.[23]

Suppose Ella broke the bowl. The bowl's being broken is a bad thing; Ella was being careless when she lifted it; and she has no excuse, since she knew the risks and could have taken her time. So she is to blame for breaking the bowl. And given this, she is blameworthy for it: it is correct to blame her for breaking it. Whether anyone should dispraise her by saying she was careless and is to blame for the

---

[23] This comes from Thomson (1989). Her account also includes clauses for when a person is to blame for doing something, but this won't be relevant for us.

broken bowl is another matter. Such dispraise would be correct, since she was being careless. But it does not follow that she ought to be called out for it.

When might a person be to blame for believing something? I have argued that a person is the originating or sustaining cause of what she believes. So the causal condition is easily satisfied. We can therefore focus on the badness condition and the excuse condition.

I am not sure that being mistaken is always a bad thing.[24] Sarah is mistaken in believing that there are three leaves on my cottage front porch, but is that really a bad thing? It is an unimportant mistake on which nothing hangs. If it is not a bad thing, then even if she has no excuse for being mistaken, she would not be to blame for it. But as it happens, she does have an excuse for being mistaken: she believed me when I lied to her about the number of leaves on my porch. (And let's add that she had no reason not to trust me.) So she is mistaken but through no fault of her own. She is thus not to blame for being mistaken, even if being mistaken is a bad thing.

It is a bad thing when a person does not believe something she ought to believe or believes something she ought not to believe. Think of Terence. He ought not to believe that Susan has cancer. It is a bad thing that he believes this, for it violates her right to privacy. He came to believe it by reading her medical file, which he ought not to have done. But to know whether he is to blame for believing it we need to know whether he has an excuse.

Suppose, first, that Terence was paid a lot of money to discover Susan's private medical condition. He knew it was a violation of her privacy, that it would be wrong for him to read the file, but he did it anyway for the money. It seems to me he has no excuse for believing it. So he *is*, in this case, to blame for believing that Susan has cancer. But here is a second version of the story. Suppose that he was threatened with severe violence if he did not read her medical file and report its contents. The threat was real and he was right to take it seriously. He read the file, knowing it was a violation of her privacy and that he should not be reading it. It seems to me he has an excuse for reading the file and for believing that she has cancer. The reading and the believing are both bad things, since he ought not to have read the file and he ought not to believe that Susan has cancer. (The excuse does not make what he did right, it just makes him blameless for doing it.) But he has a sufficient excuse. So, he is not blame for believing that she has cancer. Or so it seems to me.

Why does it matter whether Terence is to blame for believing that Susan has cancer? It matters because his being to blame for believing it would be to his

---

[24] I think that believing something without what one takes to be good evidence would be a bad thing. It would be a more or less serious failure of rationality. But I also think it is hard to imagine a clear case of it. So I won't pursue it. It is a bad thing to be hasty or stubborn, since a good person is neither. But this a matter of one's critical thinking skills and dispositions, not so much a matter of what a person believes.

discredit. It would be evidence that he is not a good person. In the first version of the story, he is selfish and greedy. But nothing in the second version is reason to think poorly of Terence. Though he violated her privacy, and ended up believing something that he (knew he) ought not to believe, he had a sufficient excuse, and this means that even though he believes something he should not believe, which is a bad thing, it is not to his discredit that he believes it.

But isn't it really Terence's action of reading the file that is to his discredit as opposed to his believing that she has cancer? Isn't the thing he is really to blame for his reading without a good excuse, as opposed to his believing without a good excuse? I am not sure we need to choose here. Ella is to blame for carelessly dropping the bowl and for the bowl's being broken. She is to blame for something she did and for a result of something she did. I think we should say the same about Terence. In the first version of the story, he is to blame for reading the file and for a result of reading it, namely that he believes that Susan has cancer. Both were bad things, because he ought not to have read the file and he ought not to have believed what he read.

One final example will help tie some things together.[25] It is a third version of the Terence story. In it, he is threatened with severe violence to his entire family if he does not take a pill that will cause him to believe that Susan has cancer. Let's add that he has no evidence one way or the other whether she does. (I will leave it as an exercise to explain how the pill works.) Here is what I want to say about this case.

Terence has excellent reason to take the pill, but he has no reason to believe that Susan has cancer. He has excellent reason to *make himself* believe that Susan has cancer, but no reason to believe that she does. This links back to what I argued in Sections 8.3 and 8.4. I said that what a person ought to believe does not depend on the evidence she has. Whether a person ought to believe of some possibility that it obtains depends on whether she ought to be in position to do, think, and feel things in light of that possibility. But this does not entail that the considerations that determine what a person ought to believe are also reasons on the basis of which the person can believe what she ought to believe. I don't think they are.

Terence ought to take the pill. It would be an awful thing, given what would happen to his entire family, if he did not take it. And this is so even though by taking the pill he will end up believing something where that believing violates Susan's right to privacy. Suppose that the harm to his family if he does not take the pill overrides Susan's right to privacy. In the second version of the story, while Terence should not read Susan's medical file, the threat of violence excuses his conduct but does not override Susan's right to privacy. In this third version, the

---

[25] Thanks to David Horst for making me think about this sort of case.

threat of violence is so great that it overrides the violation of Susan's privacy. (I am assuming that this sort of pair is possible. If you think that my examples are not such pairs, create ones that are.)

But in this third story, ought Terence to believe that Susan has cancer? Suppose I am right that he ought to take the pill. It does not follow that he ought to believe that Susan has cancer. If it were true that he ought to believe it, then this would be a reason to take the pill. But from the fact that he ought to take the pill it does not follow that he ought to believe that Susan has cancer. Whether he ought to believe it depends, *inter alia*, on whether there is something that he ought to do that he would not do if he did not believe it. But for all I have said in the story so far, there is nothing like that. For all I have said, it might be that he ought not to believe that Susan has cancer, even though he ought to take a pill to make himself believe that she does.

If Terence takes the pill, he won't be to blame for taking it, as taking it was not wrong or bad. And nor would he be to blame for believing that Susan has cancer, even though believing this violates her right to privacy. This violation is a bad thing, but he has a good excuse for it. It would thus not reflect badly on him that he believes that Susan has cancer. It is compatible with all of this, it seems to me, that it is also not true that he ought to believe that she has cancer.

In this chapter, I have touched on some of the ethical aspects of believing. I argued that belief properties are not goodness-fixing properties. That means that no instance of believing something is a good or better instance of believing than any other. Still, what a person believes can be to her credit or discredit. It can be reason to think that she is in one or another respect more or less good. And there are things a person ought to believe. What a person ought to believe, I argued, has nothing to do with what evidence she has but depends on what she ought to know and this, in turn, depends on what she should do and on how she should be. I ended the chapter by discussing when a person is praiseworthy or blameworthy for believing something. Both are connected to credit and discredit. A person is praiseworthy for believing something when her believing it is to her credit. And she is blameworthy for believing something when her believing it is to her discredit. But I also suggested that praise and blame do not track what a person ought to believe. What I mean is that a person can be praiseworthy in a certain respect for believing something she ought not to believe and blameless for believing something she ought not to believe.

Let me end by linking the topics of this chapter to the broader themes of the book. I have argued that to believe something is to be in position to do, think, and feel things in light of a possibility whose obtaining would make one right. The logical aspect of believing is that whether one is right or wrong depends only on whether that possibility obtains. The psychological aspect is that what one does, thinks, or feels can be rationalized by that possibility. The normative aspect is that there are some possibilities one ought to be positioned to do, think, and feel things in the light of. These are the possibilities one ought to believe. Indeed, they are the facts one ought to know, since we ought to believe only what we ought to know. To return to the image I offered in my introduction, knowing is like being at home among the facts, and what a person ought to know is a matter of where among those facts should ought to make her home. This is how the normative aspects of believing link up with the logical and psychological ones.

APPENDIX

Fragmented Believing

People sometimes don't act on something they seem to believe. These cases are puzzling and some have said their disorder shows that a person's belief state can be *fragmented*. Either the information the person believes is fragmented or else their access to it is. The account of belief I have developed suggests a simpler strategy for understanding these cases. On my view, the disorder resides, not in the person's belief, but in how they exercise their capacities in light of what they believe. Like all capacities, the ones we exercise in light of what we believe are fallible, gradable, and often exercised in tandem. The puzzling cases arise because in exercising our capacities we can fail in ways that are perfectly familiar and have nothing to do with belief. The aim of this appendix is to illustrate this strategy for explaining these puzzling cases.

I'll start by sketching the puzzles and describing the fragmentationist response. That response tends to assume that beliefs are representational states containing information the believer can access. I argued in Chapter 4 that belief states are not representations, and I think this representational picture makes it hard to understand the puzzles. I will offer a different way to understand the sense in which believing is an informational state. The fragmentationist response also tends to assume that believing is itself a disposition, and this naturally suggests that the puzzles involve a failure in the exercise or manifestation of belief. I have argued that while believing is not a disposition, what a person believes can make a difference to what capacities she is likely to exercise. I'll end by sketching how this suggests we locate the disorder in the exercise of those additional capacities.

Here are some puzzle cases. Sometimes, people lose track of what they are knowingly doing. David Velleman's pedestrian who suddenly stops his purposeful striding on Fifth Avenue and asks himself, "Wait! Where am I going?" is like this (Velleman 2007, 15). And people sometimes seem not to put two and two together. David Lewis' commuter who in the morning acts as if two streets are parallel but then in the evening treats them as not parallel is like this (Lewis 1982). Sometimes people seem able to act on a belief or knowledge for some purposes but not for others. Rayo and Elga's student who can correctly spell the word "dreamt" without any effort but who cannot think of a word ending in "mt" is like this (Rayo and Elga, manuscript).[1] And people sometimes sincerely say one thing but then do another. Eric Schwitzgebel's implicit sexist is like this (Schwitzgebel 2002). The sexist says that gender differences don't matter for intelligence or competence, but then he treats women as if they were less intelligent and competent than men. In each case, a person seems not to act on something it also seems they know or believe.

Two methodological points are worth keeping in mind. First, understanding a puzzle does not always require resolving it. An account of a puzzling case can be satisfying if it sheds light on how the case's puzzling features arise. It can do this without showing that there is no disorder. I discussed this methodological point in Chapters 3 and 4 in connection with puzzles about the limits of belief. I think the same is true when we consider puzzles about acting on belief. Second, we should not assume that every puzzling case will

---

[1] Their case is based on one in (Powers 1978, 340–1).

222 APPENDIX

have the same explanation. Each may be disordered in its own way. Though I'll offer a general strategy for understanding these cases, it won't yield a neat story in every case.

Some say the puzzling cases show that a person's beliefs can be *fragmented*. These fragmentationist responses tend to describe beliefs as informational states in the sense that they contain information that the believer must access before she can act on them, and they often invoke the image that having a belief is like having a map. This image in turn suggests two forms of *fragmentation* that can lead to our puzzle cases. The fragmentation might reside in *the information* the believer is trying to access or it might reside in her *access* to it. Here is how Andy Egan describes the first form of fragmentation.

> Our beliefs are *fragmented*, meaning that we've got, each of us, more than one corpus of beliefs, and different ones run different bits of our behavioral show in different contexts. One way to think of this is in terms of the image of calling up files ... We each have in our heads (or it's as if we each had in our heads) a bunch of distinct representational items, each storing some part of all of our beliefs about the world. Only some proper subset of these representational items is accessed at any given time, by any given behavior-guiding mechanism. And so my behavior-guiding mechanisms only have access to some fragments of the total body of information that I've got in my total system of mental files at a given time. (Egan 2008, 51)

The image here is of a body of information that is fragmented like a map torn into pieces, with some fragments accessible for some purposes but not others.[2] The second form of disorder involves fragmentation, not in what the believer is trying to access, but in her access to it. Here is how Daniel Greco describes it.

> The fragmentationist will hold that the concept of belief is too crude a tool to use to capture the implicit sexist's mental state. Instead, the fragmentationist will distinguish various different belief-like attitudes, and hold that [the sexist] bears some of them but not others to the claim that the sexes are equal in intelligence. One version of this strategy involves distinguishing between explicit and implicit belief ...
> (Greco 2014a, 659)[3]

The idea is that a person who believes something may have a cluster of different belief-like attitudes to it, each of which can be acted on for some purposes but not others. The image here is of a person whose map is not torn, but whose access to it is fragmented into different streams or modes.[4]

These two broad forms of fragmentation—fragmented information and fragmented access—differ in important ways, and they suggest different explanations of the puzzle

---

[2] This also seems to be what Aaron Norby, who is critical of the fragmentation strategy, has in mind when he writes:

> Fragmentationalism attempts to account for [our cases] by thinking of some subject's total set of beliefs as "divided up" into fragments or compartments, where on any particular occasion only some of these fragments will be available for utilization in reasoning and behavior. (Norby 2014, 31)

[3] Along similar lines, other authors have responded to our puzzle cases by distinguishing alief from belief (Gendler 2008), or full belief from in-between belief (Schwitzgebel 2001), but common to them all is the idea, as Greco puts it, that our puzzle cases reveal that "belief and knowledge are not unitary attitudes, but instead ... fragment into different but related sub-attitudes" (Greco 2014a, 659).

[4] Seth Yalcin proposes a slightly different form of this strategy. He says that we need to distinguish "accessible and inaccessible content" in what a person believes (Yalcin 2016, 8). His proposal is to individuate beliefs using sets of possible worlds with different "resolutions", to capture what he calls the "information about the richness, or lack thereof, of the possible alternatives that an agent's state of belief

cases, but they agree that our cases involve a disorder that is specific to belief and knowledge and that stems from the fact that beliefs are informational because they have or contain information that can be accessed. That is why the map or document metaphor is meant to be illuminating. I think these images distort what it is to believe something. They suggest that belief states are things a believer can access. And they encourage, and are encouraged by, the idea we saw Bermúdez voice that belief states are internal representations (Bermúdez2020, 108). In Chapter 4, I argued that belief states are not true or false, and so do not contain information. When a person believes something, whether she is right or wrong depends on whether a certain possibility obtains, or a certain proposition is true. This link is the logical heart of belief and it is missing with states like imagining, supposing, and hoping, where the obtaining or a possibility or the truth of proposition has nothing to do with whether one is right or wrong. Acknowledging a special link between belief and truth does not require holding that a person's beliefs contain accessible information in anything like the way maps and documents do.

My view of belief suggests a different way of understanding how belief states are informational. On my view, to believe that P is to be in a certain position. To know that P is to be positioned to do, think, or feel things in light of the fact that P, and to merely believe that P is to be positioned to do, think, or feel things in light of the possibility that P. Facts and possibilities are reasons or potential reasons, and I have characterized this position as a rational one. But we can also think of it as an informational position, as a position in an informational space. The space is defined by the facts and possibilities that can inform the believer's actions. Belief states are informational in the sense that they are individuated by a piece of information, by a possibility. But they are not informational in a richer sense, for they do not carry or contain information, they are not representations and they cannot be accessed.

The fragmentation strategy may also seem plausible if one takes believing and knowing to be dispositions or capacities. If one thinks that to know that "dreamt" ends in "mt" is to have a capacity to, say, make one's actions depend on its truth then it will seem that the puzzle case involves a failure in the exercise of that capacity. Likewise, if one thinks that believing is a disposition to act in the ways one would if one knew, then the puzzle cases will look like they involve a failure of that disposition to manifest itself. The disorder in the cases will look like they arise from a failure in the exercise of the knowledge or the manifestation of the belief. They will look like defects in the knowing or believing.

In Chapter 1, I argued that believing and knowing are not capacities or dispositions. A person's beliefs are revealed or made manifest in the reasons why she does, thinks, and feels what she does. Ryle's skater reveals her belief that the ice is thin, not in her skating by the edge of the pond, but in her skating there *because (as she sees it) the ice is thin*. It is the fact that her skating is a response to the fact (or possibility) that the ice is thin that reveals her knowledge (or belief). To believe or know something is not to have a capacity or disposition one can exercise or manifest. It is, rather, to be in a certain position to exercise and manifest one's capacities and dispositions in the light of certain facts and possibilities. What a person believes and knows is revealed, not in *what* they do, think or feel, but in *why* they do, think or feel it.

A certain view about how belief guides action will make the cases I sketched seem especially puzzling. The view starts with the plausible idea that a fact or reason can guide

---

distinguishes, about what questions these alternatives speak to and fail to speak to" (Yalcin 2016, 8). Differences in such richness, he suggests, can explain some cases where a person fails to put two and two together, that is, where they fail to be logically omniscient.

224   APPENDIX

choice or action only if it can persuade or excite. The fact that the ice is thin can guide the skater only if her knowing or believing it can excite or move her to avoid the thin ice. One might next think that knowing a fact can move or excite only if it does move or excite. If one could know the fact without being moved by it, then in what sense (one might think) could it guide one? Knowing and believing *can* guide, the thought is, only if they *do* guide.[5] (I suspect this thought explains why the dispositional and causal views I discussed in Chapter 1 are so attractive.) But if we take this next step, then our cases will seem especially puzzling, for they seem to involve knowing or believing that does not guide. Our characters know or believe something but are not moved or excited by it. What this view of acting on a fact leaves out, I think, is that a fact can guide one's actions only if one *attends* to it and then takes it to *heart*. It is not the knowing or believing that can move us, it is attending to what we know or believe that can. Knowledge and belief are not enough. One has to *consider* the facts (as one takes them to be) and even this activity won't be enough if one then fails to take them seriously. It is not enough to know the reasons; you also need to listen to them. This is not the place to develop an account of the springs of action. My point here is just that an overly simple view of what it is to act on a belief can distort what is puzzling in our cases.

I suggest that to understand the puzzle cases we need to understand the exercise of those additional capacities, the ones the characters exercise in the stories, including the capacities to consider and take to heart the facts as one takes them to be. In particular, we need to understand how their exercise can fail. This explanation will appeal to features common to all capacities—such as their fallibility, their complexity, the fact that they can be masked and are gradable, often are exercised in tandem, and so on—features that are anyway needed to understand failures of capacities of any sort in any domain. On this strategy, these puzzling cases do not reveal something special about knowledge or belief. Indeed, the cases will cease to be surprising: it would be surprising if knowledge and belief did not exhibit them.[6]

We can start by noting that all capacities are *fallible*. An exercise of a capacity is not guaranteed to succeed. A failure may have an explanation in a particular case. A liquid that is capable of melting a piece of rubber may be prevented from doing so by an intervening liquid. In that case, the acid's ability is masked. A capacity may instead be impeded. Though Sarah can play the piano, the bees stinging her nose are an obstacle she cannot overcome. It is not that they mask her capacity; they simply interfere with its normal exercise. In such cases, the capacity fails and there is an explanation for the failure.

The Sexist may be a case like this. Perhaps he does know that gender differences make no difference to intelligence or competence, but has strong feelings of insecurity about his own intelligence and competence. Perhaps these feelings don't interfere when he is asked his opinion, especially given the importance he places on being viewed as likable and thoughtful, but do interfere when he interacts with his female colleagues. The feelings are so powerful that he cannot act on what he knows. They mask his knowledge. Eric Marcus has recently offered this sort of account (Marcus 2016). Think too of students who are not able to do well on multiple choice tests or who need quiet and private rooms to do well. They are not able to demonstrate their knowledge, not because they lack the knowledge, but because they face special impediments to performing actions in whose performance they could reveal their knowledge.

---

[5] W.D. Falk calls this the "jukebox model" for how knowing and belief guide action, and what I say in this paragraph develops his criticisms; see (Falk 1963).

[6] What I say in this section is indebted to the discussion in Small (2017) and Marcus (2014).

APPENDIX 225

But it may also be that nothing explains a capacity's failure. A thing's capacity might misfire even though the opportunity was perfect and there were no impediments or obstacles of any kind. At least, this is what J.L. Austin held. He describes a golfer who is more than able to sink the short putt, and is perfectly placed to do it, and is free of all impediments and distractions and obstacles, and yet who misses anyway. Austin said that "a human ability or power or capacity is inherently liable not to produce success on occasion and that for no reason (or are bad luck and bad form sometimes reasons?)" (Austin 1961, 166). If Austin is right about this then it may be that in some cases when a person does not act on information they have there is nothing to explain this failure.

The pedestrian might be a case like this. He seems to know where he is going—after all, he is walking quite purposefully in a certain direction—though cannot say where he is going. But this case is actually somewhat complex. For maybe he forgot where he was going—and so no longer knows where he was going. When you forget something, you don't know it. And maybe nothing explains why he forgot; he just did. Bad luck. Happily, his destination is the sort of thing he can very easily remember, and so come once again to know. Capacities, after all, can come and go. But maybe, instead, he did know all along where he was going and nothing explains why he couldn't express that knowledge in words. This would be like a case where I momentarily lose track of a friend's first name. I don't exactly forget it; but I can't seem to recall it either. So, I cannot say what her name is, even though I know it.

Capacities are also *gradable* and this is relevant in our cases. Hydrochloric acid is better than vinegar at melting rubber. Cedars are better than birches at surviving the cold, but birches are better than maples. This gradeability can take different dimensions. Some acids are better at melting rubber because they work faster. Some are less fallible than others. But, as Will Small notes, a person can be an excellent batter even though he strikes out most of the time (Small forthcoming). Small also notes that one piano player might be better than another, not because he can play faster or more reliably than the other, but because he can play with less effort or with more imagination. Some piano players are better than others because they are immune to certain impediments: they can play even when the audience is coughing and sneezing. So, capacities can be graded along many different dimensions.

All of this is so for cognitive capacities too. Some children know their times tables better than others. They may be faster than the others at answering questions about them. Or they may make fewer mistakes. Or they may do it with less effort. It is not that one of them knows something the other doesn't. They both know the times table. But one knows it better than the other. And this is reflected in their different exercises of their shared capacity. The commuter may be a case like this. Some people know their city's layouts better than others. This may be because they know more about the layout. One person may know streets and neighborhoods that another doesn't. But it may be that they know the same information, but one is better able to exercise that knowledge in action. They are faster at finding their way, make fewer mistakes, expend less effort, and are faster at giving directions.

Something else may also be going on in the commuter case. A capacity that is relevant for a certain task may not be needed for completing it. Cedars and birches are able to secrete a sort of anti-freeze into their leaves and shoots so their cells won't burst and die in the winter. But birches rarely do this because they are also able to expel most of the water from inside the cells in their leaves and shoots, which has the same effect. The same is true for cognitive capacities. A piece of information may be relevant for a certain complex action but not needed for it. Maybe the commuter knows that the streets are parallel, but doesn't

226 APPENDIX

need to act on this to find his way home. He has found a route home that is good enough, even though he could find a better route if he did a bit of planning.

Our stories all involve people engaged in activities that are *polygenic*, that involve the combined exercise of many capacities, and this matters too. If a person tries and fails to do something that requires the exercise of many capacities, it may be difficult to identify which of the capacities failed. Think about photosynthesis in the leaves of a birch. This is a complex process requiring the exercise of many capacities. When a leaf fails to photosynthesize, it may be difficult to know which of the capacities failed or performed poorly.

All of our cases may exhibit this. Start with the student. Trying to think of words that end in "mt" requires the exercise of lots of capacities. The student needs to be able to imagine or recite or somehow visualize the endings of words. Most of us don't do this very often, and so are not very good at it. It may also be that the student's attempt to exercise those capacities is easily impeded, by the pressure of the situation, etc. Maybe he could more easily picture the endings of words if he were in a quiet, private space. The fact that the student cannot think of "dreamt" as an example of a word ending in "mt" may be best explained as a failure or an impeding of certain other capacities.

Now think about the commuter. Planning a route is a complex task, involving many capacities, including a capacity to visualize spatial relations. And making one's way to and from work is also a pretty complex task, requiring the exercise of many capacities. And, as I noted earlier, not every relevant capacity needs to be exercised. On the way to work he takes the route he does because the roads are parallel. Doing it this way reveals that knowledge. But the fact that he acts on that knowledge on the way to work does not entail that he must act on it on the way home too. On the way home, he takes the route he does because it will get him home without his having to think about it, which is also true and he knows it. This is like the birch tree that though it can secrete anti-freeze to ward off winter freezing, doesn't because it instead expels the water from within the cells.

One final point is worth making. It concerns the context-dependence of capacity ascriptions. It is often noted that such ascriptions are context dependent, and what we have seen in this section helps to explain why this is so. Capacities are fallible and gradable, and much of what people do is polygenic, requiring the exercise of many capacities all at once. In saying what a person is able to do, we are sometimes interested in how reliably they can do it, how well they can do it, what form their doing it can take, and what means they can employ. When we consider whether someone knows some fact all of these considerations may be relevant. It might matter whether they can manifest their knowledge in an assertion or in a drawing, and whether they can overcome certain obstacles and impediments, such as nerves and anxiety.

Let me take stock. My strategy for understanding the puzzle cases is to locate the disorder, not in the person's knowledge or belief, but in her exercise of her capacities, ones she is exercising in the light of what she knows or believes. In acting on something she knows or believes a person always exercises capacities she has. Like all capacities, these are fallible, gradable and often are exercised in tandem. And there is something plausible about this strategy. For the puzzle cases are not about knowing or believing itself, they are about putting what is known or believed to use in action. Acting on knowledge and belief requires exercising capacities and it is not surprising that their exercise exhibits these features. Indeed, it would be surprising if they didn't.

Bibliography

Ahstrom-Vij, K. and Dunn, J. 2018. *Epistemic Consequentialism*. Oxford: Oxford University Press.

Alvarez, M. 2010. *Kinds of Reasons: An Essay in the Philosophy of Action*. Oxford: Oxford University Press.

Alvarez, M. and Hyman, J. 1998. Agents and their acts. *Philosophy*, 73, 219–45.

Alston, W. 1988. The deontological conception of epistemic justification. *Philosophical Perspectives*, 2, 257–99.

Anderson, J. 1962. *Studies in Empirical Philosophy*. Sydney: Angus and Robertson.

Andrews, K. 2015. *The Animal Mind: An Introduction to the Philosophy of Animal Cognition*. Milton Park: Routledge.

Anscombe, G. E. M. 1959. *An Introduction to Wittgenstein's Tractatus*. Second Edition. New York: Harper and Row.

Anscombe, G. E. M. 1981a. The first person. In G. E. M. Anscombe (ed.), *Metaphysics and the Philosophy of Mind* (21–36). Minneapolis: University of Minnesota Press.

Anscombe, G. E. M. 1981b. Causality and Determination.In *Metaphysics and the Philosophy of Mind*, The Collected Philosophy Papers of G.E.M. Anscombe, Volume 2. Minneapolis: University of Minnesota Press, 133–147.

Anscombe, G. E. M. 1995. Practical inference. In *Virtues and Reasons*, edited by R. Hursthouse, G. Lawrence, and W. Quinn (1–34). Oxford: Clarendon Press.

Armstrong, D. 1973. *Belief, Truth and Knowledge*. Cambridge: Cambridge University Press.

Armstrong, D. 1981. *The Nature of Mind*. Sussex: The Harvester Press, Ltd.

Audi, R. 1986. Belief, reason, and inference. *Philosophical Topics*, 14(1), 27–65.

Austin, J. L. 1950. "Truth." *Proceedings of the Aristotelian Society*, 24, 111–28.

Austin, J. L. 1961 Ifs and cans. *Proceedings of the British* Academy, 42, 109–32. Cited as reprinted in his *Philosophical Papers* (1961).

Austin, J. L. 1962. *Sense and Sensibilia*. Oxford: Oxford University Press.

Austin, J. L. 1961. *Philosophical Papers*. Oxford: Oxford University Press.

Bach, K. 1980. Actions are not events. *Mind*, 89(353), 114–20.

Baker, L. R. 1995. *Explaining Attitudes: A Practical Approach to the Mind*. Cambridge: Cambridge University Press.

Barwise, J. and Perry, J. 1999. *Situations and Attitudes*. Palo Alto: CSLI.

Bennett, J. 1988. *Events and their Names*. Indianapolis: Hackett.

Bennett, J. 1991. Folk-psychological explanations. In J. Greenwood (ed.), *The Future of Folk Psychology*. Cambridge: Cambridge University Press.

Bennett, J. 2003. *A Philosophical Guide to Conditionals*. New York: Oxford University Press.

Bermúdez, J. L. 2020. *Cognitive Science: An Introduction to the Science of the Mind*. 3rd. ed. Cambridge: Cambridge University Press.

Boghossian, P. 2014. What is inference? *Philosophical Studies*, 169, 1–18.

Boyle, M. 2009. Active belief. *Canadian Journal of Philosophy*, Supplementary volume 35, 119–47.

Boyle, M. 2019. Transparency and reflection. *Canadian Journal of Philosophy*, 49(7), 1012–39.

228 BIBLIOGRAPHY

Braddon-Mitchell, D. and Jackson, F. 1996. *Philosophy of Mind and Cognition*. Malden: Blackwell Publishers.

Brandom, R. 2000. *Articulating Reasons: An Introduction to Inferentialism*. Cambridge, MA: Harvard University Press.

Broome, J. 2014. Normativity in reasoning. *Pacfic Philosophical Quarterly*, 95, 622–33.

Burge, T. 1978. Belief and synonymy. *Journal of Philosophy*, 75(3), 119–38.

Burge, T. 1979. Individualism and the mental. *Midwest Studies in Philosophy*, 4(1), 73–121.

Burge, T. 1998. Reason and the first person. In C. Wright, B, Smith, and C. MacDonald (eds.), *Knowing Our Own Minds* (243–71). Oxford: Oxford University Press.

Byrne, A. 2018. *Transparency and Self-Knowledge*. Oxford: Oxford University Press.

Cappelen, H. and Dever, J. 2013. *The Inessential Indexical*. New York: Oxford University Press.

Carnap, R. 1947. *Meaning and Necessity: a Study in Semantics and Modal Logic*. Chicago: University of Chicago Press.

Carroll, L. 1895. What the Tortoise said to Achilles. *Mind*, 104 (416), 691–3.

Cassam.Q. 2019. *Vices of the Mind*. Oxford: Oxford University Press.

Chalmers, D. 2003. The nature of narrow content. *Philosophical Issues*, 13, 46–66.

Chan, T. 2013. (ed.) *The Aim of Belief*. Oxford: Oxford University Press.

Chisholm, R. 1964. Human freedom and the self. *The Lindley Lecture*.

Chisholm, R. 1968. Lewis' ethics of belief. In P. A. Schlipp (ed.), *The Philosophy of C.I. Lewis*, Open Court.

Chomsky, N. 1975. Remarks on Nominalizations. In D. Davidson and G. Harman (eds), *The Logic of Grammar*. Encino, CA.: Dickinson Publishing Company.

Chrisman, M. 2016. Epistemic normativity and cognitive agency. *Noûs*, 52(3), 504–29.

Churchland, P. 1979. *Scientific Realism and the Plasticity of Mind*. Cambridge: Cambridge University Press.

Clark, P. 2001. The action as conclusion. *Canadian Journal of Philosophy*, 31(4), 481–506.

Collins, A. 1988. *The Nature of Mental Things*. Notre Dame, IN: Notre Dame University Press.

Dancy, J. 2000. *Practical Reality*. Oxford: Oxford University Press.

Davidson, D. 1984. *Essays on Actions and Events*. New York: Oxford University Press.

Davidson, D. 1991. What is present to the mind. *Philosophical Issues*, 1, 197–213.

Dennett, D. 1987a. Beyond belief. In his *The Intentional Stance*, Cambridge: MIT Press.

Dennett, D. 1987b. *The Intentional Stance*. Cambridge, MA: MIT Press.

Diamond, C. 1982. Anything but argument? *Philosophical Investigations*, 5(1), 23–41.

Diamond, C. 2019. *Reading Wittgenstein with Anscombe, Going on to Ethics*. Cambridge: Harvard University Press.

Divers, J. 2002. *Possible Worlds*. London: Routledge.

Dretske, F. 2000. *Perception, Knowledge and Belief*. Cambridge: Cambridge University Press.

Edgington, D. 1986. Do conditionals have truth conditions? *Critica*, 18, 3–20.

Edgington, D. 1995. Conditionals. *Mind*, 104, 235–329.

Egan, A. 2008. Seeing and believing: perception, belief formation and the divided mind. *Philosophical Studies*, 140, 47–63.

Egan, A. and Weatherson, B. 2011. *Epistemic Modality*. Oxford: Oxford University Press.

Elga, A. 2000. Self-locating belief and the sleeping beauty problem. *Analysis*, 60, 143–7.

Engel, P. 2007. Belief and normativity. *Disputatio*, 2(23), 179–203.

Evans, G. 1982. *The Varieties of Reference*. Oxford: Oxford University Press.

BIBLIOGRAPHY 229

Falk, D.W. 1963. Action-guiding reasons. *The Journal of Philosophy*, 60, 702–18.

Falvey, K. 2000. Knowledge in intention. *Philosophical Studies*, 99, 21–44.

Feldman, F. 1973. Sortal predicates. *Noûs*, 7(3), 268–82.

Feldman, R. 2000. The ethics of belief. *Philosophy and Phenomenological Research*, 60(3), 667–95.

Feldman, R. and Conee, E. 1985. Evidentialism. *Philosophical Studies*, 48, 15–34.

Field, H. 2001. Attributions of meaning and content. In his *Truth and the Absence of Fact*. New York: Oxford University Press.

Fine, K. 1982. First-order modal theories III: facts. *Synthese*, 53, 43–122.

Floyd, R. 2017. *The Non-Reificatory Approach to Belief.* Cham, Switzerland: Palgrave Macmillan.

Fodor, J. 1978. Propositional attitudes. *The Monist*, 61, 501–23.

Fodor, J. 1987. *Psychosemantics.* Cambridge: MIT Press.

Frankfurt, H. 1978. The problem of action. *American Philosophical Quarterly*, 15(2), 157–62.

Frege, G. 1984. *Collected Papers on Mathematics, Logic, and Philosophy.* B. McGuiness (ed.), Oxford: Basil Blackwell.

Frege, G. 1918. The thought. In B. McGuiness (ed.), *Collected Papers on Mathematics, Logic, and Philosophy* (351–72). Oxford: Basil Blackwell, 1984.

Frege, G. 1952. *Translations from the Philosophical Writings of Gottlob Frege.* Edited by Geach, P. and Black, M. Third edition. Oxford: Basil Blackwell.

Fricker, M. 2009. *Epistemic Injustice: Power and the Ethics of Knowing.* Oxford: Oxford University Press.

Friedman, J. 2013. Suspended judgment. *Philosophical Studies*, 162, 165–81.

Friedman, J. 2017. Why suspend judgment. *Noûs*, 51(2), 302–26.

Geach, P. 1956. Good and evil. *Analysis*, 17(2), 33–42.

Gendler, T. 2008. Alief and belief. *The Journal of Philosophy*, 105(10), 634–63.

Glüer, K. and Wikforss, Å. 2009. Against content normativity. *Mind*, 118, 31–70.

Govier, T. 1976. Belief, values, and the will. *Dialogue*, 15, 642–63.

Greco, D. 2014a. Iteration and fragmentation. *Philosophy and Phenomenological Research*, 41(3), 656–73.

Greco, D. 2014b. Could KK be OK? *The Journal of Philosophy*, 61(4), 169–97.

Hacker, P. 2004. On the ontology of belief. In Siebel, M. and Textor, M.(eds.), *Semantik und Ontologie* (185–222). Heusenstamm: Frankfurt Ontos Verlagg.

Hacker, P. 2013. *The Intellectual Powers: A Study of Human Nature.* Oxford: Wiley-Blackwell.

Hanks, P. 2013. What are the primary bearers of truth? *Canadian Journal of Philosophy*, 43 (5–6), 558–74.

Hampshire, S. 1975. *Freedom of the Individual.* London: Chatto and Windus.

Heil, J. 1983. Doxastic agency. *Philosophical Studies*, 43(3), 355–64.

Hennig, T., Hunter, D., and Land, T. 2019. Transparency and apperception, special issue of *The Canadian Journal of Philosophy*.

Hieronymi, P. 2009. Believing at will. *Canadian Journal of Philosophy*, supplementary volume 35, 135–87.

Hintikka, J. 1962. *Knowledge and Belief.* Ithaca: Cornell University Press.

Hlobil, U. 2019. Inferring by attaching force. *Australasian Journal of Philosophy.* 97(4), 701–714.

Horgan, T. 2004. Sleeping Beauty awakened: New odds at the dawn of the new day. *Analysis*, 64, 10–21.

230 BIBLIOGRAPHY

Hornsby, J. 1995. Agency and causal explanation. In Heil, J. and Mele, A. (eds.), *Mental Causation*. Oxford: Oxford University Press.

Hornsby. 2004. Agency and actions. In H. Steward and J. Hyman (eds.), *Agency and Action* (1–23). Cambridge: Cambridge University Press.

Huber, F. and C. Schmidt-Petri. 2009. *Degrees of Belief: An Anthology*. Oxford: Oxford University Press.

Hunter, D. 2001. Mind-brain identity and the nature of states. *Australasian Journal of Philosophy*, 79(3), 366–76.

Hunter, D. (2007). Common ground and modal disagreement. In H.V. Hansen, *et. al.* (Eds.), *Dissensus and the Search for Common Ground*, CD-ROM (pp. 1–7). Windsor, ON: OSSA.

Hunter, D. 2008. Belief and self-consciousness. *International Journal of Philosophical Studies*, 16(5), 673–93.

Hunter, D. 2009a.Guidance and belief. *Canadian Journal of Philosophy*, 35, 63–90.

Hunter, D. 2009b. Contextualism, skepticism and objectivity. In R. Stainton and C. Viger (eds.), *Compositionality, Context and Semantic Values* (105–28). Springer.

Hunter, D. 2011a. Alienated belief. *dialectica*, 65(2), 221–40.

Hunter, D. 2011b. Belief ascription and context dependence. *Philosophy Compass*, 6(12), 902–11.

Hunter, D. 2015. Davidson on practical knowledge. *Journal for the History of Analytical Philosophy*, 3(9), 1–19.

Hunter, D. 2017. Practical reasoning and the first person. *Philosophia*, 45(2), 677–700.

Hunter, D. 2018a. The metaphysics of responsible believing. *Manuscrito*, 41(4), 255–85.

Hunter, D. 2018b. Manifesting emotions. *Philosophy and Phenomenological Research*, 47 (2), 507–11.

Hunter, D. 2018c. Directives for knowledge and belief. In Daniel Whiting et al. (eds.), *Normativity: Epistemic and Practical*. Oxford: Oxford University Press.

Hunter, D. 2021. Lacking, needing, wanting. *Analytic Philosophy*, DOI: 10.1111/phib.122.

Hyman, J. 1999. How knowledge works. *The Philosophical Quarterly*, 49(7), 433–51.

Hyman, J. 2006. Knowledge and evidence. *Mind*, 115, 891–916.

Hyman, J. 2015. *Action, Knowledge and Will*. Oxford: Oxford University Press.

Hyman, J. 2017. Knowledge and belief. Manuscript.

Jackson, F. 1998. From Metaphysics to Ethics: A defense of Conceptual Analysis. Oxford: Clarendon Press...

Jackson, L. 2018. Belief and credence: Why the attitude-type matters. *Philosophical Studies*.176(9), 2477–2496.

James, W. 1896. The will to be. *The New World*, Volume 5, 327–47.

Kenny, A. 1963/2003. *Action, Emotion and Will*. London: Routledge & Kegan Paul. Second edition with a new preface, 2003.

Kenny, A. 1989. *The Metaphysics of Mind*. Oxford: Oxford University Press.

Kiesewetter, B. 2017. *The normativity of rationality*. Oxford: Oxford University Press.

Kim, J. 1996. *Philosophy of mind*. Boulder: Westview.

Kimhi, I. 2018. *Thinking and Being*. Cambridge, MA: Harvard University Press.

King, J., Soames, S., and Speaks, J. 2014. *New Thinking about Propositions*. Oxford: Oxford University Press.

Kraut, R. 2011. *Against Absolute Goodness*. Oxford: Oxford University Press.

Kremer, M. 2001. The purpose of tractarian nonsense. *Noûs*, 35(1), 39–73.

Lewis, D. 1979. Attitudes *de dicto* and *de se*. *Philosophical Review*, 88, 513–43.

Lewis, D. 1982. Logic for equivocators. *Noûs*, 16, 431–41.

BIBLIOGRAPHY   231

Lewis, D. 1986. *The Plurality of Worlds*. Oxford: Oxford University Press.
Lewis, D. 2001. Sleeping beauty: reply to Elga. *Analysis*, 60: 171–6.
Marcus, E. 2006. Events, sortals, and the mind-body problem. *Synthese*, 150, 99–129.
Marcus, E. 2009. Why there are no token states. *Journal of Philosophical Research*, 34, 215–41.
Marcus, E. 2012. *Rational Causation*. Cambridge, MA: Harvard University Press.
Marcus, E. 2016. To believe is to know that you believe. *dialectica*, 70(3), 375–405.
Marcus, E. 2020. Inference as consciousness of necessity. *Analytic Philosophy*, 61(4), 304–322.
Marcus, E. 2021. *Belief, Inference, and the Self-Conscious Mind*. Oxford: Oxford University Press.
Marcus, R.B. 1993. *Modalities: Philosophical Essays*. Oxford: Oxford University Press.
Marušić, B. 2015 *Evidence and Agency: Norms of Belief for Promising and Resolving*. Oxford: Oxford University Press.
Marušić, B. 2017. Trust, reliance, and the participant stance. *Philosopher's Imprint*. 17(17), 1–10.
Mates, B. 1952. Synonymity. In L. Linsky (ed.), *Semantics and the Philosophy of Language*. Urbana: University of Illinois Press.
Matthews, R. 2007. *The Measure of Mind*. Oxford: Oxford University Press.
McCormick, M. 2015. *Believing against the Evidence*. New York: Routledge.
McDowell, J. 2013. Acting in the light of a fact. In D. Bakhurst, B. Hooker, and M. Little, (eds.), *Thinking about Reasons*. Oxford: Oxford University Press, 13–28.
McHugh, C. and Whiting, D. 2014. The normativity of belief. *Analysis*, 74(4), 698–713.
Melden, A. 1961. *Free Action*. London: Routledge, Kegan, & Paul.
Melden, A. 1966. Desires as causes of action. In F. C. Dommeyer and C. J. Ducasse (eds.), *Current Philosophical Issues: Essays in Honor of Curt John Ducasse*. Springfield, IL: Charles C. Thomas.
Mele, A. 2017. *Aspects of Agency: Decisions, Abilities, Explanations, and Free Will*. New York: Oxford University Press.
Merricks, T. 2012. *Propositions*. New York: Oxford University Press.
Meylan, A. 2015. The legitimacy of intellectual praise and blame. *Journal of Philosophical Research*, 40, 189–203.
Meylan, A. 2019. The reasons-responsiveness account of doxastic responsibility and the basing relation. *Erkenntnis*, 84, 877–93.
Moltmann, F. 2003. Propositional attitudes without propositions. *Synthese*, 135, 77–118.
Moltmann, F. and Textor, M. 2017. *Act-based Conceptions of Propositional Content: Contemporary and Historical Perspectives*. Oxford: Oxford University Press.
Moon, A. 2017. Beliefs do not come in degrees. *Canadian Journal of Philosophy*, 47(6), 1–19.
Moore, G. E. 1953. *Some Main Problems in Philosophy*. London: George, Allen and Unwin.
Moore, G. E. 1954. Wittgenstein's lectures in 1930–33, Part I. *Mind*, 43(249), 1–15.
Moran, R. 2001. *Authority and Estrangement*. Princeton, NJ: Princeton University Press.
Moss, S. 2018. *Probabilistic Knowledge*. Oxford: Oxford University Press.
Mourelatos, A. 1978. Events, Processes, and States. *Linguistics and Philosophy*, 2, 415–34.
Nagel, T. 1989. *The View from Nowhere*. New York: Oxford University Press.
Nickel, P. 2010. Voluntary belief on a reasonable basis. *Philosophy and Phenomenological Research*, 81(2), 312–34.
Nickel, P. 2016. Virjheid door scepticisme. *Algemeen Nederlands Tijdschrift voor Wijsbegeerte*, 108(1), 19–36. English translation is "Freedom through Skepticism".

232 BIBLIOGRAPHY

Norby, A. 2014. Against fragmentation. *Thought*, 3, 30–8.

O'Connor, T. 2000. *Persons and Causes: The Metaphysics of Free Will*. Oxford: Oxford University Press.

Owens, D. 2000. *Reason without Freedom*. London: Routledge.

Owens, D. 2011. Deliberation and the first person. In A. Hatzimoyis (ed.), *Self-knowledge* (261–77). Oxford: Oxford University Press.

Papineau, D. 2014. There are no norms of belief. In Chan, 2013 64–79.

Peacocke, C. 1998. Conscious attitudes, attention, and self-knowledge. In C. Wright, B. Smith, and C. MacDonald (eds.), *Knowing Our Own Minds*, Oxford: Oxford University Press.

Peels, R. 2016. *Responsible Belief: a theory in ethics and epistemology*. Oxford: Oxford University Press.

Perry, J. 1979. The essential indexical. *Noûs*, 13(1), 3–21.

Pojman, L. 1986. *Religious Belief and the Will*. London: Routledge, Kegan, and Paul.

Powers, L. 1978. Knowledge by deduction. *The Philosophical Review*, 87(3), 337–71.

Price, H. H. 1969. *Belief*. London: George Allen & Unwin.

Putnam, H. 1962. It ain't necessarily so. *Journal of Philosophy*, 59(22), 658–71.

Putnam, H. 1975. The meaning of "meaning." *Philosophical Papers, Volume 2*. London: Cambridge University Press.

Quine, W.V.O. 1960. *Word and Object*. Cambridge, MA.: MIT Press.

Rattan, G. 2016. Are propositions mere measures of mind? *Philosophy and Phenomenological Research*, 94(2), 433–452.

Rattan, G. and Hunter, D. 2013. *New Essays on the Nature of Propositions*. Oxford: Routledge.

Ravenscroft, I. 2005. *Philosophy of Mind: A Beginner's Guide*. Oxford: Oxford University Press.

Rayo, A. and Elga, A. Fragmented decision theory. Manuscript.

Reid, T. 1991. *Essays on the Active Powers*. In D. D. Raphael (ed.), *British Moralists: 1650–1800, vol. 2*. Oxford: Clarendon Press.

Richard, M. 2013. What are propositions? *Canadian Journal of Philosophy*, 43(5–6), 702–19.

Rödl, S. 2018. *Self-consciousness and Objectivity*. Cambridge: Harvard University Press.

Roeber, B. 2019. Evidence, judgment, and belief at will. *Mind*, 128(511), 837–859.

Roessler, J. and Eilan, E. (eds.). 2003. *Agency and Self-Awareness*. Oxford: Oxford University Press.

Rosen, G. 2001. Brandom on modality, normativity and intentionality. *Philosophy and Phenomenological Research*, 63, 611–23.

Rumfitt, I. 2012. Inference, deduction, and logic. In J. Bengson and M. Moffett (eds.), *Knowing How: Essays on Knowledge, Mind, and Action*. Oxford: Oxford University Press.

Rundle, B. 2001. Objects and attitudes. *Language and Communication*, 21, 143–56.

Russell, B. 1912. *The Problems of Philosophy*. Oxford: Oxford University Press.

Russell, B. 1918. *The Philosophy of Logical Atomism*. Reprinted in his *Logic and Knowledge*, ed. R. Marsh. London: George, Allen & Unwin, 1968.

Russell, B. 1919. On propositions: what they are and how they mean. *Proceedings of the Aristotelian Society, Supplementary Volumes, volume 2*, 1–43.

Ryle, G. 1946. Why are the Calculuses of Logic and Arithmetic applicable to Reality? *Proceedings of the Aristotelian Society*. Volume 20, pages 20–60.

Ryle, G. 1949. *The Concept of Mind*. New York: Barnes & Noble.

BIBLIOGRAPHY   233

Sandis, C. 2009. *New Essays on the Explanation of Action*. London: Palgrave Macmillan.

Scanlon, T. 2014. *Being Realistic about Reasons*. New York: Oxford University Press.

Schueler, G. F. 2003. *Reasons and Purposes: Human Rationality and the Teleological Explanation of Action*. Oxford: Oxford University Press.

Schwitzgebel, E. 2001. In-between believing. *The Philosophical Quarterly*, 51(202), 76–82.

Schwitzgebel, E. 2002. A phenomenal, dispositional account of belief. *Noûs*, 36(2), 249–75.

Sehon, S. 2005. *Teleological Realism: Mind, Agency, and Explanation*. Cambridge, MA: MIT Press.

Setiya, K. 2009. *Reasons without Rationalism*. Princeton: Princeton University Press.

Setiya, K. 2013. Causality in action. *Analysis*, 73, 501–12.

Shah, N. 2003. How truth governs belief. *Philosophical Review*, 112, 447–82.

Shah, N. 2013. Why we reason the way we do. *Philosophical Issues*, 23, 311–25.

Shoemaker, S. 1994. Self-knowledge and "inner sense." *Philosophy and Phenomenological Research*, 54, 249–314.

Shoemaker, S. 1989. Self-intimation and second order belief. *Erkentnnis*, 71, 35–51.

Slote, M. 1974. *Metaphysics and Essence*. Oxford: Blackwell.

Small, W. 2017. Agency and practical abilities. *Royal Institute of Philosophy, Supplements. Volume 80: Philosophy of Action*, 235–64.

Soames, S. 2010. *What is Meaning?* Princeton: Princeton University Press.

Soames, S. 2013. Cognitive propositions. *Philosophical Perspectives*, 27, 479–501.

Soames, S. 2015. *Rethinking Language, Mind, and Meaning*. Princeton: Princeton University Press.

Sosa, E. 2011. *Knowing Full Well*. Princeton: Princeton University Press.

Speaks, J. 2014. Representational entities and representational acts. In J. King, S. Soames, and J. Speaks, *New Thinking about Propositions* (144–65). Oxford: Oxford University Press.

Stalnaker, R. 1976. Propositions. In A. F. MacKay and D. D. Merrill (eds.), *Issues in the Philosophy of Language*, New Haven: Yale University Press, pp. 79–91.

Stalnaker, R. 1984. *Inquiry*. Cambridge, MA: MIT Press.

Stalnaker, R. 1991. The problem of logical omniscience I. *Synthese*, 89, 425–40.

Stalnaker, R. 1996. Impossibilities. *Philosophical Topics*, 24(1), 193–204.

Stalnaker, R. 2006. On logics of knowledge and belief. *Philosophical Studies*, 128, 169–99.

Stalnaker, R. 2008. *Our Knowledge of the Internal World*. New York: Oxford University Press.

Stalnaker, R. 2009. Another attempt to put sleeping beauty to rest. *Canadian Journal of Philosophy*. Supplementary volume 35, 25–40.

Stalnaker, 2011. *Mere Possibilities*. Princeton: Princeton University Press.

Stalnaker, R. 2015. Luminosity and the KK thesis. In S. Goldberg (ed.), *Externalism, Self-Knowledge, and Skepticism*. Cambridge: Cambridge University Press.

Stalnaker, R. 2019. *Knowledge and Conditionals*. New York: Oxford University Press.

Steglich-Petersen, A. 2006. No norm needed: on the aim of belief. *The Philosophical Quarterly*, 56(225), 499–516.

Steglich-Petersen, A. 2007. Against essential normativity of the mental. *Philosophical Studies*, 140, 263–83.

Steward, H. 1997. *The Ontology of Mind*. Oxford: Oxford University Press.

Steward, H. 2014. *A Metaphysics for Freedom*. Oxford: Oxford University Press.

Stich, S. 1985. *From Folk Psychology to Cognitive Science: The Case against Belief*. Cambridge, MA: MIT Press.

Strawson, P. 1959. *Individuals*. London: Methuen.

234 BIBLIOGRAPHY

Strawson, P. 1992. Causation and explanation. In *Analysis and Metaphysics: An Introduction to Philosophy* (109–31). Oxford: Oxford University Press.

Strawson, P. 1998. "Reply to John Searle." In L. E. Hahn, *The Philosophy of P. F. Strawson*. La Salle, IL: Open Court.

Stroud, S. 2006. Epistemic partiality in friendship. *Ethics*, 116(3), 498–524.

Thompson, M. 2008. *Life and Action*. Cambridge, MA: Harvard University Press.

Thomson, J. 1977. *Acts and Other Events*. Ithaca, NY: Cornell University Press.

Thomson, J. 1987. Verbs of action. *Synthese*, 72, 103–22.

Thomson, J. 1989. Morality and bad luck. *Metaphilosophy*, 20(3&4), 203–21.

Thomson, J. 2008. *Normativity*. Peru, IL: Open Court.

Travis, C. 2014. The preserve of thinkers. In B. Gertler (ed.), *Does Perception Have Content?* New York: Oxford University Press.

Turner, D. 2006. *This Is Not a Peace Pipe: Towards a Critical Indigenous Philosophy*. Toronto: University of Toronto Press.

Urmson, J.O. 1950. On Grading. *Mind*, 59(234), 145–169.

Velleman, J. 2007. *Practical Reflection*. Stanford, CA: CSLI Publications.

Vendler, Z. 1972. *Res Cogitans*. Ithaca: Cornell University Press.

Vendler, Z. 1984. *The Matter of Minds*. Oxford: Clarendon Press.

Von Wright, G. H. 1957. *Logical Studies*. New York: The Humanities Press.

Von Wright, G. H. 1963. *The Varieties of Goodness*. London: Routledge & Kegan Paul.

Williams, B. 1973. Deciding to believe. In *Problems of the Self* (136–51). Cambridge: Cambridge University Press.

Watson, G. 2003. The work of the will. In S. Stroud and C. Tappolet.(eds.), *Weakness of Will and Practical Irrationality* (172–200). New York: Oxford University Press.

Weintraub, R. 2004. Sleeping Beauty: a simple solution. *Analysis*, 64, 8–10.

White, A. 1971. Inference. *Philosophical Quarterly*, 21(85), 289–302.

White, A. 1972. What we believe. *American Philosophical Quarterly*, Monograph Series, No. 6, 69–84.

White, A. 1973. Responsibility, liability, excuse and blame. *Studi Internazionale die Philosofia*. 5, 63–70.

White, A. 1975. *Modal Thinking*. Ithaca: Cornell University Press.

White, R. 2005. Epistemic permissiveness. *Philosophical Perspectives*, 19, 445–59.

Williamson, T. 2000. *Knowledge and Its Limits*. Oxford: Oxford University Press.

Williamson, T. 2002. Necessary existents. In A. O'Hear (ed.), *Logic, Thought and Language* (233–51). Cambridge: Cambridge University Press.

Wittgenstein, L. 1958. *The Blue and the Brown Books*. Oxford: Basil Blackwell.

Wolf, S. 1980. Asymmetrical freedom. *The Journal of Philosophy*, 77(3), 151–66.

Wolf, S. 2011. Blame, Italian style. In R. J. Wallace, R. Kuma, and S. Freeman (eds.), *Reasons and Recognitions: Essays on the Philosophy of T. M. Scanlon*. New York: Oxford University Press.

Wolf, S. 2015. Character and responsibility. *The Journal of Philosophy*, 112, 356–72.

Yablo, S. 2016. *Aboutness*. New York: Oxford University Press.

Yalcin, S. 2016. Belief as question-sensitive. *Philosophy and Phenomenological Research*, 97(1) 23–47. doi: 10.1111/phpr.12330.

Zagzebski, L. 1996. *Virtues of the Mind*, Cambridge: Cambridge University Press.

Zimmerman, A. 2018. *Belief: A Pragmatic Picture*. Oxford: Oxford University Press.

Zimmerman, M. 2001. *The Nature of Intrinsic Value*. Lanham: Rowman & Littlefield Publishers, Inc.

Index

For the benefit of digital users, indexed terms that span two pages (e.g., 52–53) may, on occasion, appear on only one of those pages.

ability view
  Hacker 31n.15
  Setiya 31n.15
achievements
  and actions 48–9
  and the BB Principle 131, 134n.2, 137–9, 141, 143–4
  and being in a position 141, 143–4
  cognitive 131, 134n.2, 137, 143–4
  epistemic 137, 139
  inference is not 165–6
  semantic 138–9, 141
  White 165–6
actions. *See also* rational action
  and accomplishments 48–9
  and achievements 48–9
  are affected by knowing 14–16
  and assigning good or evil 97
  and believing 16–19, 21, 26–32
  and believing a possibility sheds light on an 33
  as bodily movements 110
  and capacities 29–30
  and the Capacities view 18–19, 21
  and causal explanations 21
  and causalism 22, 25–7
  and dispositionalism 18, 21
  and events 20, 25
  falsity applies to 51–2
  and inference 170–2, 177
  and knowledge 31–2
  in the light of possibility 14–18
  and linguistics 171–2
  and the modal view of objects of belief 83, 85
  and rationalization 7–8
  as responses 10–11
  and the speech act 71
  and subjective limits 145, 156–8
  truth applies to 51–2
action theory 110
activity
  compared to believing 49–51
  and fact consideration 224
  and inference 183
  is not a consequence of believing 170

and linguistics 48
as polygenic 226
representing is an 65
and true/false evaluation 97, 108, 197
agents. *See also* doxastic agency; epistemology; rational agency
  acting on reasons 1–2, 7–8, 11, 13–16, 33
  being in a position 7–8, 11
  belief states do not cause action by 8
  and capacities 8–9, 11
  and causation 9, 24–6, 162, 171–4
  deliberation and 11
  and dispositions 8–9, 11
  as liable to change 9
  as non-living things 9–10
  and responses 10–11, 13–14
  and responsibility 10–11, 176–7
agnosticism 80, 95
Alvarez, Maria 171–2
Anscombe, G. E. M.
  on belief as a topic 1
  believing without representing 110
  on cause 27
  center of a conception 137
  logical aspects of belief 4, 130
  on sentences that express necessities 71–2
  uncertainty 154n.12
Armstrong, David
  beliefs are interpretation of reality 199
  beliefs are not true or false 106n.7
  belief states are causes 20–1, 27, 45
  belief states are internal states 44–5
  believing is a state 48
  reporting on Anderson 83n.19
Austin, J. L.
  on a fact as a true proposition 87
  facts as true possibilities 37–8
  'good' is substantive hungry 195
  nothing explains a capacity's failure 225
  only propositions are true or false 106
  state of affairs in-the-world 88–9, 94

Bach, Kent 171–2, 174
the BA Principle 132

236 INDEX

the BB Principle 132–41
  the BA Principle 132
  the BD Principle 132
  the BK Principle 134–5, 146–7
  Boyle 144
  and cognitive achievements 131, 134n.2, 137, 143–4
  constitutivism 135
  credal necessities 131–2, 138
  and epistemology 134–5, 137–9
  the KB Principle 133
  the KK Principle 133–4, 146–7
  and linguistics 135–6
  mental states 133, 136–7, 147, 152, 158
  self-consciousness of believing 150–1
  and self-knowledge 133–5, 137, 139, 147
  and semantic achievements 138–9, 141
  and subjective uncertainty 153
  and transparency 134–5, 137, 147–9
  and truth 133
the BD Principle 132
being in a position
  defined 2, 8–11
  and ability 31n.15, 142, 144–5
  and achievements 141, 143–4
  agents 7–8, 11
  and believing 1–2, 4, 141–7
  and capacities 144–5
  and credal norms 205
  and dispositions 15–16, 76, 142–5
  and individuation 142
  and reasons 2–3, 8, 29–30, 32, 143
  and subjective limits 141–7
  and voluntarily adopting beliefs 184
belief properties
  are not causal qualities 27–33
  are not sortals 2, 41–3, 152
  Burge 43
  as capacities 8, 18–19
  compared to belief states 38–9
  as dispositions 8, 18, 27, 33
  and ethics of belief 36
  and goodness-fixing properties 5, 194–6, 199
  individuation of 2–3, 53–4, 63, 64n.2, 65–8, 74–5, 101
  as instantiated in objects/substances 2
  ownership properties as analogous to 42–4
  propositional attitudes 66
  as qualities 2, 5, 7, 22–3, 39, 44, 195–6
  truth as a standard for belief 193–4
belief states
  are not causes 2, 8, 19–27
  Armstrong 27, 44–5, 48
  Bermúdez, José Luis 23–4, 27

Boyle 46–8, 134n.2
Burge 46
as causes 8, 18, 20, 44
compared to facts 38, 44
compared to properties 38–9
Cromwell's sense of humor 44–5
Davidson, Donald 27
and deliberation 2
and fragmented believing 221–3
Hieronymi on the act view 46–8
as individuated 7, 33–4, 56–7, 223
as instantiation of a quality 23–4
Kenny 45
Mele 27
Mourelatos 48
Putnam 46
and realizers 44–6
Shoemaker 47–8
belief tokens 44–5, 51, 101–2
believers, in general
  as agents 9, 11
  credal credit of 5–6
  limits on 4
  as living things 9, 46
  positioning 2, 26–7, 33
  and subjectivity 4
believing in general. *See also* actions; belief
    properties; belief states; ethics of belief;
    fragmented believing; mental representations;
    possibilities
  essence of 7
  and agency 8–9, 14, 22–3, 46–7
  agential aspects of 2, 7–8
  ambiguity of 2, 23–4, 42
  Armstrong on 20–1
  Austin 37–8
  being correct 17–18
  being mistaken 11, 17, 43–4
  belief properties are not causal qualities 27–33
  the Capacities view 18–19, 21, 29
  the Causalist view 18, 21–7
  causation 20–1
  Chisholm on 21
  Chrisman 48n.11
  Davidson 56
  and desire 20–4, 26–7
  the Dispositionalist view 18
  Floyd 20n.6, 22n.9, 39n.8
  Fodor 52n.13, 54–7
  Hanks 51–2
  hypostasizing of 36, 44
  is a relation 54–5
  is a relational property 61
  is not a linguistic matter 37n.2

INDEX 237

is not an action or activity 23, 46–52
is not a relation 52–60
is to be in a position 2, 7–11
Kenny 57
and knowing 2–3, 6
and knowledge 16, 31, 43–4
logical aspects of 1–2, 7, 33
Marcus, E. 27
Measurement Theory of Mind 56–7, 60n.18
non-human belief 34–5, 163
as not normative 193
and possibilities 2–4, 11–13
of a possibility sheds light on an action 14–18, 33
propositional attitudes 54–6, 59
and propositions 37–9, 42, 47, 51
psychological aspects of 1–2, 7, 33
and rationalization 1–2, 7–8, 14–15, 17–18, 21, 32
Rattan 60–1
and reasons 13–14, 27
Reid on 20–1
as a relation 52–4
as a representation believed 24
Richard 50–1
Russell 36
Ryle 31–2
sortals 5–6
and truth 4, 64
and understanding 60–3
believing without representing
action theory 110
Anscombe 110, 154n.12
arithmetical properties 100–1
Armstrong 106n.7
Austin 106
belief properties are neither true nor false 100–1
beliefs as true or false 108
belief states are neither true nor false 100–1
Braddon-Mitchell 99
and desire 97–8, 108–10
Hornsby 110
Jackson 99
Kenny 108
Kim 99, 104–5
and nominals 102–3
physicalism 97, 104
propositional attitudes 97
Quine 102
Ravenscroft 99, 104
and realizers 104–5
Soames 106
speech act 104
Stich 100, 102

and tokens 101–2
and truth 96–100, 105–8
Williams 98, 107
Bermúdez, José Luis 23–4, 27, 197
Bismarck 116–19
the BK Principle 134–5, 146–7
Boghossian, P. 162n.1, 167–8
Boyle, Matt
BB Principle and cats and dogs 144
and the center of a conception 137
implicit belief 147–9
on the responsibility characteristic of believing 46–8
self-knowledge 134n.2
on the state view of belief 170–1
Braddon-Mitchell, D. 99
Broome, John 162, 167–8, 176nn.4, 5, 188
Burge, Tyler 43, 46, 122, 124–5

capacities
and actions 29–30
and agents 8–9, 11
are fallible 222, 226
are gradable 225–6
and being in a position 144–5
causal 28–9
and dispositions 1–2, 29–31, 110
and fragmented believing 221, 223–6
Hyman 29
inference as 30–1
knowing as 28–33
perception as 30–1
and reasons 8, 110
Stalnaker 28–9
the Capacities view 18–19, 21, 29
Carnap, R. 92
Carroll, Lewis 161
causal capacities 28–9
causalism
and action 22, 25–7
causal dispositions 28
and deliberation 26–7
no states are causes 26–7
view of belief 18, 21–7
causal powers
and agents 9
and beliefs 1–2, 24–5
and belief states 8, 19–20, 22–5
instantiations of sortals 22–3
and mental states 22–3
causal qualities
belief properties are not 27–33
Kenny 28–9
Stalnaker 28–9

238 INDEX

causation
  defined 20
  and agents 24–6, 171–4
  Anscombe, G. E. M. on 27
  defined 20
  mental states as 27
  state causation modeled on event
    causation 24–5
  as transitive 20, 27
certainty. *See also* subjective limits
  the modal view 75–9
  the omniscient Gods 73, 155
  and strength 77, 80
Chisholm, Roderick 21, 171–2, 182–3, 184n.15
Chrisman, Matthew 48n.11, 169–70
cognitive psychology 26–7
constitutivism 107, 135
credal alienation 160, 192
credal illusions
  Anscombe 130
  and the astronomer 190–1
  Burge 122, 124–5
  and confusing sentences 72, 73n.9
  Elga 119–20
  Frege 116, 122–3
  Lewis 119–20
  and limits of belief 1–2, 4, 74, 111, 116, 121, 191
  and linguistics 123–4, 126–7, 129, 190–1
  the modal view 116, 127–30
  and objective limits 4, 111, 113–22, 128–30
  as persistent 113, 115
  and plans and intentions 121
  and the propositional view 116
  Putnam 122, 124–5, 129n.8
  Russell 111–12, 115–19, 124
  sentences that express necessities 71–2
  Sleeping Beauty puzzle 111–12, 119–22
  Stalnaker 121–2
  and visual illusions 113, 115
credal necessities
  the BB principle 131–2, 138
  and dispositions 148
  Greco 146–7
  Lewis 140
  Marcus, E. 146–7
  and the modal view 131, 140
  Nagel 140
  Quine, W. 139–40
  Stalnaker 146–7
  and subjective limits 4, 72, 81, 111, 132–7
  and subjectivity 4, 72, 111, 132–7, 150–2, 155–6
  and transparency 147–50, 159
  and universality 146n.8

credal norms
  appraisability 214–15
  Armstrong 199
  and attributive goodness 194–6
  Austin 195
  being a good believer 202
  and being in a position 205
  being wrong to one's credit 201
  and belief directives 202–7, 210–11
  believing is not inherently normative 194–6
  Bermúdez, José Luis 197
  capacities are fallible 222, 226
  capacities are gradable 225–6
  credal blame 214–20
  credal credit 5–6, 193–4, 200–2
  and desire 197
  and discredit 200–1, 214–19
  and doxastic deliberation 187–8, 198
  and doxastic state 148
  ethics of belief 200
  and evidence 1–2, 5–6, 207–14
  Feldman 199–200
  Kenny 197
  and knowledge 202–7
  and knowledge directives 202–3, 207–8, 207n.16, 208–9, 213–14
  Meylan 214–15
  Peels 214–15
  Rosen 193
  Shah 198–9
  sortals 194
  Thomson 202, 204
  and truth 196–200
credal subjectivity 131–2, 151
Cromwell, Oliver 41, 44–5

Davidson, Donald 21–3, 27, 56
desire
  and believing 20–4, 26–7, 156
  and believing without representing 97–8, 108–10
  and credal norms 197
  and subjective limits 156–8
determinism 12, 77–80
the Dispositionalist view 18, 21
dispositions
  and agents 8–9, 11
  and the BB Principle 135–6, 142
  and being in a position 15–16, 76, 142–5
  belief properties as 8, 18, 27
  and believing 75n.11
  believing as 32–4
  and capacities 1–2, 29–31, 110
  causal dispositions 28

The Concept of Mind (Ryle) 36
and credal necessities 148
and fragmented believing 221, 223
and inference 170, 176n.5
as liability to undergo change 10
manifesting a 30–1
and the modal view of objects of belief 15–16, 76, 80
and non-humans 34
and reasons 8, 110
and truth 98
doxastic agency 148, 181–2
doxastic deliberations 187–8, 198
doxastic options when inferring 183, 189
doxastic state 148

Egan, Andy 222
Elga, Adam 119–20, 221, 223, 226
epistemology
  agency 182n.11, 183, 192
  and the BB Principle 134–5, 137–9
  being mistaken 43–4
  and believing 116, 118–19
  and credal credits 5–6
  and credal limits 125–6
  and credal necessities 131, 148
  and credal norms 192–3
  directives 206
  epistemically valuable 187–8
  epistemic responsibility 47
  and inference 167, 182n.11, 184n.16, 187–8, 192
  and the modal view 75, 90
  and possibilities 12–13
  state of mind and believing 56
  truth and value 196–200
ethics of belief
  and belief properties 36
  credal norms 200
  and intentionality 180
  the modal view 74–5, 112–13
  and responsibility 215
  and voluntariness 183
Evans, Gareth 147
event causation. *See* causation
externalism 36, 45–6

Feldman, Richard 199–200
Floyd, Richard 20n.6, 22n.9, 39n.8, 98n.1
Fodor, Jerry 52n.13, 54–7
fragmented believing
  Austin 225
  and belief states 221–3
  and capacities 221, 223–6

and dispositions 221, 223
Egan on 222
fragmented access 221–3
fragmented information 222–3
Greco on 222
Lewis's commuter story 221, 225–6
map metaphor 222–3
and mental states 222
Norby on 222n.2
and possibilities 222–3
Rayo and Elga's student 221, 223, 226
Ryle 223
Schwitzgebel's implicit sexist 221, 224
Velleman's pedestrian 221
Yalcin on accessible and inaccessible content 222n.4
Frege, Gottlob
  astronomer case 69–71, 73–4, 122–3, 187
  credal illusions 111–12, 116
  modal notions are not metaphysical 90
  objective limits 111–12
  properties and objects have different logical roles 117–19
  saturated and unsaturated objects 117
Fricker, Miranda 43–4
Friedman, Jane 80

Govier, Trudy 183
Greco, Daniel 146–7, 222

Hacker, Peter 31n.15
Hampshire, Stuart 168–9
Hanks, Peter 51–2
Heil, John 172, 181–2, 187–8
Hieronymi, Pamela 46–8, 170–1, 178–9
Hornsby, Jennifer 110
Hyman, John 29, 89, 171–4

individuation
  and being in position 142
  of belief properties 2–3, 53–4, 63, 64n.2, 65–8, 74–5, 101
  of belief states 7, 33–4, 56–7, 223
  and inheriting the properties of an object 100–1
  and the modal view 74, 95
  of ownership 42–4
  and propositions 94
  of sortals 39–40
  and states of knowing 83–4
inference
  and actions 170–2, 177
  and activity 183
  and agency of belief 161, 170

240   INDEX

inference (*cont.*)
  Alvarez 171–2
  Bach, Kent 171–2, 174
  Boghossian 167–8
  Boyle 170–1
  Broome 188
  Broome, John 162, 167–8, 176nn.4, 5
  as capacities 30–1
  Carroll 161
  Chisholm 171–2, 182–3, 184n.15
  Chrisman, Matthew 169–70
  and concluding 163
  and deduction 164–6, 185–91
  and dispositions 170, 176n.5
  and doxastic options 183, 189
  and duration 164–5
  epistemic agency 182n.11, 183, 192
  and epistemology 167, 182n.11, 184n.16,
    187–8, 192
  ethics of belief 180
  evidentialism 184n.15
  Frege's astronomer case 187
  Govier 183
  Hampshire 168
  Hampshire, Stuart 169
  Heil 172, 181–2, 187–8
  Hieronymi 170–1, 178–9
  Hyman 171–4
  is a causing of believing 161–3
  is acting on oneself 168–71
  is not an achievement 165–6
  is not an onset of believing 164–8
  is not intentional 177–80
  is to believe by attending to reasons 161–3
  and knowledge 175–6
  and linguistics 166
  logical omniscience 222n.4
  Marcus, E. 188n.20
  and mental states 25–6, 165, 167, 178
  Nickel 183–5, 187, 189
  Owens 181–2
  para-mechanical idea of 167–8
  and reasons 4–5
  Reid 171–2
  restricted focus of 161
  Ryle 164–8, 175
  and self-knowledge 4–5
  Shah 187–8, 198–9
  Strawson, P. 171–2
  sustaining belief 162–3
  Thomson 165, 171–4
  and truth 161, 168, 189–90, 198
  unwilling 191–2
  voluntariness of 4–5, 180–6

  Von Wright, Georg 171–2
  White 178
  Williams 182
intentional realism 23–4

Jackson, Frank 99, 127–8

Kant, Immanuel 136
the KB Principle 133
Kenny, Anthony 28–9, 41, 45, 57, 108, 197
Kim, Jaegwon 99, 104–5
the KK Principle 133–4, 146–7
knowledge. *See also* practical knowledge;
  reflective knowledge; self-knowledge
  and actions 31–2
  and belief 43–4, 134, 136
  and believing 16, 31, 43–4
  and credal norms 202–7
  Fricker 43–4
  and inference 175–6
  and introspection 135
  and likelihood of possibilities 16–17
  manifesting 31–2
  objects of 2–3, 64, 83–5, 88
  of one's psychological state 137
  properties 199
  and reasons 16–18, 29, 32–4, 85
  and self-knowledge 133
  standard accounts of 144
  Turner 43–4
knowledge directives 202–3, 207–8, 207n.16,
  208–9, 213–14

Lewis, D.
  center the possibility 140
  commuter story 221, 225–6
  propositions 92
  on Sleeping Beauty 119–20
  story of two Gods 73, 154–5, 159
Libertarianism 20
limits of belief
  and credal illusions 1–2, 4, 74, 111, 116,
    121, 191
  objectivity of 111, 131–2, 159
  and objects of belief 3, 113
  sources of 4
  subjectivity of 4, 111, 131–2, 159

Marcus, Eric 27, 135, 146–7, 188n.20
Marcus, Ruth Barcan 64n.1, 92–3
Mates, Benson 73n.9
Mele, Al 27
mental realizations 45, 104
mental representations 7

INDEX 241

mental states
  agnosticism 80
  are not representations 82–3
  and the BB Principle 133, 136–7, 147, 152, 158
  belief vs believing 102
  believing as 1, 7, 22–3, 33–4, 42, 45, 47, 56–7,
    64n.1, 197
  as causes 27
  characterizations of 97
  concept of 20
  and fragmented believing 222
  hypostasizing 196
  and inference 25–6, 165, 167, 178
  and linguistic meaning 46
  the object of a 88–9
  as objects of speech acts 66
  and possibilities 85–6
  procuring content of 99
  tokens of 101–2
Meylan, Anne 214–15
modality 53–4, 89–90, 92–3
the modal view of objects of belief 64–5
  and action 83, 85
  agnosticism 80
  Anscombe 71–2, 130
  Armstrong 83n.19
  belief compared to perception 74
  beliefs are representational 65
  Carnap 92
  and certainty 75–9
  and credal illusions 116, 127–30
  credal necessities and 131, 140
  and determinism 77–80
  and dispositions 15–16, 76, 80
  ethics of belief 74–5, 112–13
  as false 69
  Frege 69–71, 73–4, 90
  Friedman 80
  history of 89–93
  and impossibility 70–4, 86–7
  individuation and the 74, 95
  Lewis 73, 92
  linguistics 71, 73n.9
  Marcus, R. 64n.1, 92–3
  Mates 73n.9
  and objects of knowledge 83–5
  omniscient God 73
  Perry's shopper 72
  probability 67–8, 75, 77–8, 80n.16
  and pure cases 68–75
  pure cases and 68–75
  Quine 92
  and rational inquiry 83–5
  reasons and knowledge 85

Russell 90–1
Ryle 92
speech acts 81
Stalnaker 92
and subjective limits 131, 138
subjectivity of 72, 111
Twain 86–7
Vendler 81
Wittgenstein 71–2
Moore, G. E. 91–2
moral psychology 26–7
Moran, R. 135
Mourelatos, A. 48

Nagel, Thomas 140
naturalism 8, 33–5
Nickel, Philip 183–5, 187, 189
Norby, Aaron 222n.2

objective limits. *See also* credal illusions
  Anscombe 130
  and beliefs about properties 117–19
  and credal illusions 4, 111–22, 128–30
  and denying objectivity 125–8
  Frege 111–12, 116
  Jackson 127–8
  and the modal view 111–14, 116, 127–8
  naïve conception of inquiry 125–7
  and plans and intentions 121
  and the propositional view 113, 116
  sources of 114–15
  Twin Earth cases 111–12, 124–5, 128
  and visual illusions 113, 115
objects of belief. *See also* the modal view
    of objects of belief
  analytic philosophy 64–5
  individuating belief properties 65–8
  and limits of belief 3, 113
  Marcus, R. 64n.1
  not as possibilities 68–9
  as possibilities 2–4, 64
  as potential reasons 2–3
  propositional view 65, 67
  as propositions 65–6
  as representations 4
  White 64n.2, 83n.19, 91n.27
  Wittgenstein 64n.1
objects of knowledge 64, 83–5, 88
omniscience 62, 73, 155, 222n.4
Owens, David 181–2
ownership
  as analogous to belief properties 42–4
  individuation of 42–4
  and transparency of belief 149–50

242 INDEX

Peels, Rik 214–15
Perry, John 67n.3, 154
 shopper case 72, 154–5
physicalism 97, 104
possibilities
 defined 7–8, 12–13, 37–8
 and agents 7–8
 Austin on 37–8
 belief properties as 7
 contrasted with facts 11–12
 and credal illusions 122–5
 and dispositions 30–1
 distinction between a witness and 120–1
 and fragmented believing 222–3
 future 119–22
 inference in light of a 174–7
 knowledge and likelihood of 16–17
 likelihood of 15–16
 and linguistics 12–13, 116, 190–1
 and mental states 85–6
 objects of belief as 64–8
 out-numbered by belief properties 68–9
 as a property 12–13
 and reasons 6, 12, 33
 shed light on an action 14–18
 that obtain 12, 16–18
 that remain open 12
 unbelievable 116–19
practical knowledge 154n.12, *See also* knowledge;
  reflective knowledge; self-knowledge
probability
 and linguistics 77–80
 and the modal view 67–8, 75, 77–8, 80n.16
probability spaces 67–8
properties. *See also* sortals
 monadic 53
 of ownership 43
 sortals compared to other 39–41
 and truth 117
 of truth and falsity 51–2
propositional view of objects of belief
 Austin 88–9, 94
 Austin, J. L. 87
 Hyman 89
 Moore 91–2
 Richard 94–5
 Russell 87–8, 92
 Soames 93–4
 Strawson 87–8
 Twain 86–7
 Vendler 81
the propositional view of objects of belief
 and aboutness 82–3
 and beliefs are true 93–4

each proposition determines a possibility 85–7
 and a fact is a true proposition 87–9
 and facts as a kind of proposition 87–8
 and impossibilities 73n.10
 and object of knowing is a fact 85–9
 and representation without propositions 93–5
 and speech acts 81
 and truth 64
propositions
 as act types 51
 linguistics 92
 nature of 37
 object as truth of a 89
 Soames 51–2
 and truth 88, 92, 222–3
 and truth conditions 37, 51, 61–2, 67, 93
Putnam, Hilary 46, 122, 124–5, 129n.8

Quine, W. 92, 102, 139–40

rational action
 and belief in a want 108n.9
 and believer's position 26–7
 and subjective limits 150, 155–9
rational agency 14, 135–6
rationalism 36
Rattan, Gurpreet 60–1
Ravenscroft, Ian 99, 104
realism, intentional 23–4
reasons
 for agents acting 8, 11, 13–16, 33
 are affected by belief 27
 and being in a position 2–3, 8, 29–30, 32, 143
 and belief properties 41–2, 47, 52
 beliefs effect on 18
 for believers acting on 1–2, 8, 11, 14
 and capacities 8, 110
 as causal explanation for action 21
 and dispositions 8, 110
 as facts 13–14
 and inference 4–5
 and knowledge 16–18, 29, 32–4, 85
 nature of 13–14
 and objects of belief 2–3
 and possibilities 6, 12, 33
 and subjective limits 4–5
reflective knowledge 148, *See also* knowledge;
  practical knowledge; self-knowledge
Reid, Thomas 20–2, 166
relations
 are reversible 57–8
 compared to monadic properties 53
 complement do not modify 59–60
 fixed polyadicity of 58–9

INDEX 243

representations. *See* objects of belief
Richard, Mark 50–1, 64n.1, 65, 94–5
Rödl, Sebastian 150–2
Rosen, Gideon 193
Russell, Bertrand 36
  on belief about individuals 116–17
  credal illusions 111–12, 116–19, 124
  propositional view of objects of belief 90–2
  propositions and facts 87–8
Ryle, Gilbert
  believing is a state 48
  The Concept of Mind, 36
  inference 164–8, 175
  on knowing how to infer 175
  para-mechanical idea of inference 167–8
  propositional hook 92
  thin ice belief 31–2, 223–4

Schwitzgebel, Eric 221, 224
self-knowledge. *See also* knowledge; practical
    knowledge; reflective knowledge
  acting on reasons 14
  and the BB Principle 133–5, 137, 139, 147
  believing involves 47
  and inference 4–5, 176
  and knowledge 133
  and subjective limits 133–5, 134n.2, 137, 139
semantic puzzle 127–8
semantics
  an act 104
  the BB Principle 138–9, 141
  belief properties 100–1, 106
  beliefs 97–9
  belief states 2, 7, 82–3
  belief tokens 101–2
  and believing 4, 6
  the center of conception 137–9
  and conditional belief 77
  the fusion view 55–6
  grasping a proposition 61–2
  internal realizers 46
  and mathematical reasoning 190–1
  objectivity 125, 127
  possibilities 37–8
  propositions 94
  representations 24
Setiya, Kieran 31n.15
Shah, Nishi 187–8, 198–9
Shoemaker, S. 47–8, 135
Soames, Scott 51–2, 93–4, 106
sortals 5–6
  belief properties are not 2, 41–3, 152
  compared to characterizing universals 40–1
  compared to other properties 39–41

compared to qualities 8, 22–4, 39–40
and credal credits 6
and goodness-fixing 5, 194–5, 200
and humor 41
individuation of 39–40
and linguistics 40
and norms of belief 193–4
representations as instantiations of 23–4
Strawson 40–1
and truth 197–8
in a spatial position 2
Stalnaker, R. 28–9, 64n.1, 92, 115n.2, 121–2,
  146–7
state causation. *See* causation
Stich, S. 100, 102
Strawson, P. 40–1, 87–8, 171–2
subjective limits. *See also* the BB Principle
  and actions 145, 156–8
  Anscombe 137
  being in a position 141–7
  Boyle 137, 147–9
  and the center of conception 137–41
  and content 150–3
  and credal necessities 4, 72, 111, 132–7
  and desire 156–8
  Evans, Gareth 147
  and force 150–3
  Greco 146–7
  Inter-Personal Explanation 157
  Inter-Personal Reasons 158
  Intra-Personal Explanation 157
  Intra-Personal Reasons 158
  Kant 136
  Lewis 140, 154–5, 159
  and limits of belief 131–2, 159
  Marcus, E. 135, 146–7
  and the modal view 131, 138, 140
  Moran 135
  Nagel 140
  objectivity and 111
  Perry, John 154
  Quine, W. 139–40
  and rational action 150, 155–9
  and reasons 4–5
  Rödl 150–2
  and self-knowledge 133–5, 134n.2, 137, 139
  Shoemaker 135
  Stalnaker 146–7
  and transparency 137, 147–50
  and uncertainty 153–5

Thomson, Judith Jarvis 165, 171–4, 202, 204
tokens and linguistics 102 *See also* belief tokens
transparency of belief

244 INDEX

transparency of belief (*cont.*)
    and the BB Principle 134–5, 137, 147–9
    and credal necessities 147–50, 159
    ownership and 149–50
    and subjective limits 137, 147–50
Turner, Dale 43–4

Velleman, David 221
Vendler, Zeno 81–2
verificationism 62

visual illusions 3, 74, 113, 115
Von Wright, Georg 171–2

White, Alan 64n.2, 83n.19, 91n.27,
    165–6, 178
Williams, Bernard 98, 107, 182
Williamson, Tim 31n.15
Wittgenstein, Ludwig 64n.1, 71–2, 129n.7

Yalcin, Seth 222n.4